T0301677

Geofinance between Political and Financial Geographies

Geofinance between Political and Financial Geographies

A Focus on the Semi-Periphery of the Global Financial System

Edited by

Silvia Grandi

Department of Statistical Sciences 'Paolo Fortunati', University of Bologna, Italy

Christian Sellar

Department of Public Policy Leadership, University of Mississippi, USA

Juvaria Jafri

Department of International Politics, City, University of London, UK

Edward Elgar
PUBLISHING

Cheltenham, UK • Northampton, MA, USA

Published by
Edward Elgar Publishing Limited
The Lypiatts
15 Lansdown Road
Cheltenham
Glos GL50 2JA
UK

Edward Elgar Publishing, Inc.
William Pratt House
9 Dewey Court
Northampton
Massachusetts 01060
USA

A catalogue record for this book
is available from the British Library

Library of Congress Control Number: 2019951605

This book is available electronically in the **Elgar**online
Economics subject collection
DOI 10.4337/9781789903850

ISBN 978 1 78990 384 3 (cased)
ISBN 978 1 78990 385 0 (eBook)

Typeset by Servis Filmsetting Ltd, Stockport, Cheshire

Printed and bound by CPI Group (UK) Ltd, Croydon, CR0 4YY

Contents

Contributors

Svetlana Ageeva, Institute of Economics and Industrial Engineering of the Siberian Branch of the Russian Academy of Sciences, Novosibirsk State University, Russia.

Gianfranco Battisti, University of Trieste, Italy.

Fabio Betioli Contel, University of São Paulo, Brazil.

Silvia Grandi, University of Bologna, Italy.

Juvaria Jafri, City, University of London, UK.

Guanie Lim, Nanyang Technological University, Singapore.

Anna Mishura, Institute of Economics and Industrial Engineering of the Siberian Branch of the Russian Academy of Sciences, Novosibirsk State University, Russia.

Thong Tien Nguyen, Ho Chi Minh University of Technology, Vietnam.

Marco Percoco, Bocconi University, Italy.

Umberto Rosati, University of Torino, Italy.

Christian Sellar, University of Mississippi, USA.

Elena Stavrova, South-West University 'Neofit Rilski' – Blagoevgrad, Bulgaria.

Engin Yılmaz, Ministry of Finance of Turkey, Turkey.

Foreword

Is not financial geography an oxymoron? Why should geographers, naturally interested in travel, outdoors, breathing fresh air while doing fieldwork, be interested in money, taxes, assets and liabilities? If you were interested in these things, would not you become an economist or at least an accountant rather than a geographer? Would you not do much better financially if you did so?

Pause for a moment and think about the market for foreign exchange trading. The first striking feature of this market is the scale of its activity. Currencies worth over US$5 trillion are traded daily, compared to foreign trade in all goods and services of US$7 trillion annually. This illustrates how financialized the world economy is. The US dollar is on one side of over 80 percent of all foreign exchange trades, and this percentage has not changed significantly for decades. The euro has never challenged the hegemony of the US dollar. The Chinese currency is rising but still beyond the top five. Even a simple collection of basic facts such as these can be a starting point for a discussion on political economy and geopolitics. However, the broader point it illustrates is that geography is fundamental to understanding finance, and vice versa. Finance is one of the most globalized and networked of human activities. Financial centres as nodes in these networks epitomize modern capitalism. Just as pyramids symbolize ancient Egypt and the late Middle Ages are associated with Gothic cathedrals, skyscrapers filled with financial and related professionals will for posterity symbolize twentieth-century capitalism.

As Gordon L. Clark, one of the pioneers of financial geography, put it, money flows like mercury. It penetrates every nook and cranny of the global economy, changing social and political relations. Geoffrey Ingham, a sociologist, stated that together with writing and number, money is one of our essential social technologies. Over 100 years ago, Max Weber characterized money as a weapon in the struggle for economic existence.

While its significance should be obvious, finance is still poorly understood in economics and social sciences. Mainstream economists live in Neverland, where space does not matter to finance and finance matters little to economic development. The view of finance in economics became as detached from the social reality of finance as some financial practices, for example, tens of trillions of US dollars' worth of derivatives traded mainly among banks, became detached from society. Social scientists, in turn, neglected money and finance, assuming it was taken care of by economists.

This failure of scientists to understand finance, highlighted by the global financial crisis, represents an opportunity. With the subprime crisis, the eurozone crisis, Brexit, as well as new financial technology threatening to transform finance, the map of the financial world is in a state of turmoil, with major implications for development. Geography is well positioned to take advantage of this opportunity, because of its open mixed-methods approach. Studying the significance of location, place, space, territory and scale in finance is crucial for advancing knowledge and public policy. It could also be a way to rally social sciences around the questions of money and finance, and perhaps even a chance to contribute to a much needed reintegration of social sciences.

Financial geography has started a long process of addressing this gap. Broadly, it can be defined as the study of the spatiality of money and finance and its implications for the economy, society and nature. To do financial geography you have to be numerically literate, but you do not have to focus on quantitative research – it can be qualitative as well. Financial geography transcends the division of geography into its economic, political, social and cultural branches. It involves environmental geography too, as financial markets price commodities, and the natural environment currently and into the future, through insurance contracts, securities and derivatives.

My interest in financial geography started in the mid-1990s. Most of the references I could find in libraries, as this was before Google Scholar, focused on the UK and the USA. Later in my career, I discovered a much broader body of relevant scholarship by people such as Gordon Clark, Ron Martin, Nigel Thrift and Andrew Leyshon, as well as theoretical works of most relevance, with David Harvey's *The Limits to Capital* in the lead. While conceptually rich, empirically, most of the work on financial geography still focused on North America and a few leading economies of Western Europe, with the major focus on the UK and Germany.

Much has changed in the past 20 years, during which time financial geography has established itself as a vibrant interdisciplinary field of research. Major contributions have come from scholars using heterodox economic approaches, a cultural economy lens and a financialization perspective, among others. The geographical scope of scholarship on financial geography has expanded too, with a major wave of research on China in particular, but the geographical coverage remains limited. It is still a struggle to find works, particularly in the English language, that focus on

Latin America, southern or Eastern Europe, western and southern Asia or Africa.

For this reason, this book represents a major contribution to financial geography. Silvia Grandi, Christian Sellar and Juvaria Jafri have assembled a team of contributors to investigate financial spaces that have hitherto been neglected in English-language scholarship. We find chapters here focusing on Italy, Russia, Central and Eastern Europe, Bulgaria, Vietnam, Turkey and Pakistan. However, beyond its empirical diversity and richness, the book also offers important conceptual ideas. Building on Wallerstein's world-systems theory, the book coins the phrase 'semi-peripheral financial areas' to refer to 'established industrial or emerging economies outside the financial centers of North America, north-western Europe and East Asia where financial industries are established, but do not have the same level of global influence as the core' (see the Introduction to this volume, p. 3).

The book also presents a promising new conceptual framework linking political and financial geography, named geofinance or geobanking. The latter is understood broadly as 'the various public and private aspects of banking that shape territorial politics and vice versa' (see the Introduction to this volume, p. 20). More specifically, geofinance/banking is conceptualized at three levels as '(1) the policies of the territorial states in the financial semi-periphery, (2) the interactions between these policies and globalizing processes originating in the financial core and (3) the resulting impact on financial flows and practices affecting specific national and local economies in the semi-periphery' (see the Introduction to this volume, pp. 21–2). This focus on the relationship between financial geography and political geography, including geopolitics, is very important and timely. While the past two decades brought rich research on the economic, cultural and social aspects of financial geography, arguably, research on the political aspects has been neglected, and so has the interaction of financial geographers with political scientists and political economists. This is where the concept of geofinance/banking, combined with that of semi-periphery, can help provide a much needed boost to research.

There is a lot of work to be done to bring finance back to planet Earth, both in terms of financial practices and policies, and in terms of research. A few years ago, with colleagues around the world, we set up the Global Network on Financial Geography (FinGeo; www.fingeo.net) as an open and interdisciplinary network of academics, practitioners and experts interested in research on the spatiality of money and finance, and its implications for the economy, society and nature. In March 2019 we had nearly 600 members in more than 60 countries. Indeed, I first met Silvia Grandi and found out about her book idea at events organized by FinGeo. It is my honour, as the inaugural chair of FinGeo, to invite everyone to join our network, and my pleasure to recommend this book to readers.

Dariusz Wójcik
Professor of Economic Geography
School of Geography and the Environment
Fellow of St Peter's College
Oxford University, UK
Chair of the Global Network on Financial Geography – FinGeo

Introduction: theorizing semi-peripheral geographies of finance and banking

Christian Sellar, Silvia Grandi and Juvaria Jafri

1. BEYOND CORE-CENTERED FINANCIAL GEOGRAPHIES

This edited collection explores the boundaries between political and financial geographies: it interrogates linkages between the changing spatialities and policies of the state, the evolution of a globalizing financial system, and the consequences of this for people and firms. Empirically, it focuses on the semi-periphery of the financial system to generate new perspectives on the entanglement between (geo)politics and finance: these complement and overlap with the core-centered analyses of what has come to be an Anglo-American geography of finance. Conceptually, it engages with insights from a variety of disciplines in order to explore the connections between geopolitical and geo-economic discourses, public finance and foreign policy, the practices and localization of financial institutions, and the evolution of strategies for globalizing firms. Such topics are becoming increasingly relevant, as evidenced in a speech by the UK Deputy Governor for Prudential Regulation in which the term 'geofinance' is presented as a dynamic to acknowledge the 'impact of geography on the shape of banks, insurers and financial regulation ... With the revolution in regulation following the financial crisis coming to its end, and with changes to the geopolitical landscape looming large'. He observed that geofinance will be 'the defining challenge of the next few years' (Woods 2017).

The chapters in this book explore trends, data, policies and geographies in Bulgaria, Brazil, Italy, Pakistan, Russia, Turkey and Vietnam. In addition, they offer cross-country analyses for Central and Eastern Europe, and examine the evolutionary patterns of international financial institutions and other supranational financial players. All this has resulted in a complex web of relationships between governments and actors in finance which has, in turn, had an impact on firms as well as households (Figure I.1). Taken together, these are under-represented locations in the geography of finance: the focus on these underpins the originality of this

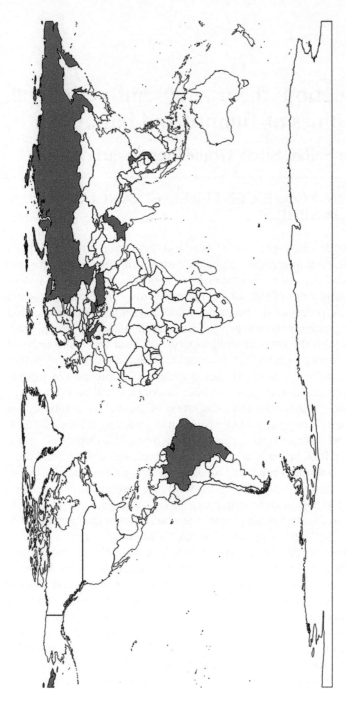

Source: Figure by Silvia Grandi.

Figure I.1 Research areas

book. Recalling Wallerstein's original formulation of world-systems theory (Wallerstein 1974), but also older formulations such as Walter Christaller's central place theory (Christaller 1966; see also Lösch 1954), the spaces covered in this book are collectively defined as semi-peripheral financial areas. Wallerstein's (1974, p. 102) analysis of capitalism in early modern Europe described the semi-periphery as areas with relatively limited or declining access to international and high-quality banking services that engaged in the production of high-quality goods but nevertheless were subjugated to international trade or finance. More recently, Arrighi (2010) extended his reasoning to include finance more explicitly. Thus, building on their work, here, the notion of semi-peripheral financial areas refers to established industrial or emerging economies outside the financial centers of North America, north-western Europe and East Asia, where financial industries are established but do not have the same level of global influence as the core. Our view is that the latter point distinguishes the cases discussed in this book from more commonly used notions such as fringes, edges or margins, and in particular from research that takes as its central concern the lack of established traditional financial sectors, and sometimes reverse innovation and new forms of finance (Govindarajan and Trimble 2012; Klagge and Zademach 2018; Yunus 2009). Taken together, the chapters in this book portray economies with well rooted 'bricks and mortar' financial institutions, and a clearly discernible – whether explicit or implicit – role of the state in creating financial flows and supporting the financing of firm and household activity.

2. SPEAKING FROM THE SEMI-PERIPHERY

This book's engagement with the semi-periphery is rooted in our reflexive positions as editors: this frames our own engagement with the authors, and with the larger field of financial geography. We are two women, one man; two immigrants, one working in her own country of origin; two working within the boundaries of Anglo-American academia, and one outside. Ethically, we felt a duty to facilitate the inclusion of a wider range of scholars in the mainstream debates of the discipline. Conceptually, three issues attracted our attention. First, and unsurprisingly, a survey of financial geography we did in early 2018 (Clark and Wójcik 2007; Dixon and Monk 2014; Elson 2011; Grote et al. 2017; Wójcik et al. 2017), including working papers published by the Global Network on Financial Geography (FinGeo 2019) revealed analyses firmly placed within economic geography. Since then, a few papers have begun investigating the geopolitical dimensions of banking and finance (Aalbers 2018; Bassens and Van Meeteren 2018; Karwowski and Centurion-Vicencio 2018), but there is still some inattention to the ways in which state geo-economic strategies may shape the financial sector, and vice versa. Second, while our Italian colleagues were keen to study the role of banking and finance in shaping the internationalization of small and medium-sized enterprises, Anglo-American geography seemed less interested in exploring the links between manufacturing value chains and international finance. Third, and surprisingly, the majority of papers on financial geographies we read by the beginning of our collaboration in summer 2017 had a distinctive spatial bias. Methodologically, they were based either on data about large global players such as sovereign wealth funds or transnational consulting and accounting firms (Dixon and Monk 2014; Dörry 2018), or on empirical research collected in or around the core of the global financial system in the UK (Pažitka and Wójcik 2017) and the US (Wójcik and Cojoianu 2017), as well as the emerging financial centers of China (Pan et al. 2018). A smaller number of researchers focused on the fringes of the financial system (Klagge and Zademach 2018; Roy 2010), but intermediate areas, with established but non-dominant financial institutions, seemed to be missing. This bias seemed to be specific to geography, because several works in heterodox finance had a focus on the semi-periphery (Braun et al. 2018). We thus observed an empirical research deficit in geography that obscured several perspectives, including those on economies outside the financial core, as well as those of players that are not the best-known global investment, insurance and consulting firms.

Building on these earlier intuitions, our call for chapters had two objectives. The first was conceptual: we wanted to present a book about globalizing finance and banks that spoke directly to debates in geopolitics and political geography. We particularly wanted to insert banks and finance within larger geostrategic processes affecting the spatiality of the nation state. For this, we sought to show the links between the political geographies of the state and more conventional economic geography themes, placing finance in the context of politics and firms and household behavior. The second goal was to broaden the empirical reach of financial geographies by disseminating our call to draw in scholars writing about finance outside the financial centers of the US, the UK, Western Europe and East Asia. Our own situational perspective, especially given our connections with Italy, where there is a strong tradition of commercial diplomacy via state-owned financial instruments (Vergara Caffarelli and Veronese 2018), framed the two hypotheses connecting the two goals. These hypotheses are (1) there is a variety of relationships between state-level geo-economic and development strategies, the institutions and goals of the financial sector, and the credit available to firms and households, and (2) such relations are more readily visible outside the US and the UK, where long-standing classical liberal and neoliberal traditions tend to limit government involvement in bank lending decisions.

3. CONTRIBUTOR-DRIVEN THEORIZATION

To accomplish the above goals, we cast the call for papers as widely as possible, stating that foci of the book were the 'various public and private aspects of banking that shape geopolitical trends and vice versa' with the goal of 'exploring the links between state geo-economic strategies, financial institutions and firm internationalization'. As a result, we collected a variety of papers (hereafter chapters) discussing under-represented geographies of finance, as shown in Figure I.1, that create what we named semi-peripheral financial areas: this is a belt between core financial countries and emerging and developing countries where, in general, the struggle between state–bank relationships is unresolved, innovation lags financial processes and banking policies are not always centered on firm and household needs.

The authors of these chapters represent a wide array of disciplines, career stages, and training, only some of which is rooted in Anglo-American academia. To help facilitate authors trained outside this tradition, Juvaria Jafri joined the editorial team to edit submissions. This entailed a discussion within the expanded editorial team about how to incorporate a wide array of criteria of what constitutes good scholarship in ways that could be meaningful to a wider international audience. Indeed, geographers have long questioned the extent to which the knowledge they produce is truly international (Gutierrez and Lopez-Nieva 2001; Kitchin 2003; Rodríguez-Pose 2004, 2006). The first, and obvious, critique has been that the international geographical journals are British and American, and foreign scholars rarely get published unless they hold PhDs from universities in the US or UK (Aalbers 2004; Aalbers and Rossi 2007). Theoretical pieces that build upon non-Anglo-American scholarly traditions are rarely accepted (Minca 2000). Responding to this critique, several journal special issues have focused on the need to open up international human geography to the contributions of non-English speaking scholars and traditions (Environment and Planning 2003; Berg 2004; European Urban and Regional Studies 2004).

The critical issue that runs across such scholarship is the expectation that theory is produced by scholars working in a narrow band of elite – Anglo-American – universities, while the rest of us can at best provide empirical evidence. On the one hand, we are keenly aware that theory that is appreciated by the wider scholarly community is produced according to highly specific codes and is usually restricted to a handful of universities. On the other hand, such codes can potentially obscure variant interpretations of data and, more generally, impede scholarship from those trained outside the core. So, in order to be as inclusive as possible, we sought to strike a balance between contributions written by scholars and practitioners, as well as those from scholars trained and working within Anglo-American academia versus those trained in the countries under scrutiny. This variety in academic standards and styles allowed for the collection of multiple disciplinary perspectives, including geography, business, regional development, political science and economics.

After collecting the chapters, we engaged in contributor-driven theorization: we let the authors interpret our call and produce chapters on their own terms, and we limited our editing to ensuring that the chapters are clearly written and understandable to an international audience. After collecting the chapters, we identified recurrent themes: first, a macro-level perspective on the global institutions that drive banking and finance; second, an attention to how state policies affects banks; and third, several discussions of how banks' and other financial institutions' choices reflect in lending practices. Finally, we tied these foci together in a theoretically meaningful argument. To do this, first we linked political geography – especially works on the changing spatialities of the state – with finance. Second, we emphasized the role of banks as a site for bridging state policies with the larger world of finance. As a result, we developed the notion of geofinance/banking. This concept signals that banks and other lending institutions play a key and under-explored role in connecting policies of the state in the semi-periphery with globalizing trends originating in the financial core: these are articulated through flows of financial resources and their distribution in specific sub-national and national settings.

4.   ORGANIZATION OF THE BOOK

The remainder of the book commences with a chapter that introduces the notion of geofinance/banking. Subsequent chapters are grouped in three parts, roughly corresponding to three scalar levels: the global and supranational, the national and the micro levels. The first part carries those contributions that engage with the spatial structures of banking. The second part explores the policy–politics–banks–firms nexus with finance in the semi-peripheries. The third and final part highlights the micro-level dimension of people and firm responses.

Chapter 1 is by the editorial team and links political geography with banking and finance through geofinance/banking. In so doing, we understand political geography as an umbrella term covering geopolitics as well as a wide array of perspectives on the spatialization of politics. We build on Sami Moisio's *Geopolitics of the Knowledge-Based Economy* (2018) as well as on Jones's (2016) work on new political geography. Moisio develops Çalışkan and Callon's (2009) notion of economization, understood as 'the material processes of knowledge-intensive capitalism ... and the processes whereby this form of capitalism is constructed discursively' (Moisio 2018, p. 1). His key claim is that economization includes a key geopolitical dimension, constituted by both the territorial power of states and the imagery of hubs, networks and flows that permeates the late capitalist economy. Economization connects firms and political communities (Moisio 2018, p. 16) and accounts for the reshuffling of territoriality (Moisio 2018, p. 19). Extending this argument to banking and finance, we argue that finance and its geographies constitute an under-explored but crucial factor linking the evolving – bounded and relational – territorialities of the nation-state to firms and citizens. To operationalize geofinance/banking, we start from Jones's (2016, p. 2) conceptualization of political geography as a 'double triangle', the first triangle including power, politics and policy, and a second consisting of space, place and territory. To this we add three additional terms: financial flows (the flows and management of money and other financial tools), institutions (banks, international financial institutions and other actors) and client firms and households. We see the chapters in our edited collection as engaging with, albeit not exhaustively, the permutations of these nine concepts (Table I.1).

After the chapter on geofinance/banking, Part I starts with Silvia Grandi's analysis of the geographical patterns of the international financial institutions (IFIs) that tend to be marginalized in the mainstream finance literature, particularly in the context of the semi-peripheries (Chapter 2). These institutions have shaped global finance and the outlook and geography of the world banking system: they are thus key drivers of geobanking/finance. The chapter shows patterns in the distribution of headquarters versus areas of investments, as well as the power relationships between boards and the rest of each organization. The chapter also discusses the uneven access to financial institutions, making the case that in the semi-periphery, private finance is oftern substituted for or supplemented by government funds obtained via IFIs. Chapter 2 thus shows the complexity of global financial institutions where power, policies, politics and finance can significantly shape places.

Also in Part I, Gianfranco Battisti explores the spatial and organizational boundaries of the financial system by discussing the articulation

Table 1.1 *Relational elements investigated in each chapter referred to the conceptualization diamond among new political geography entities and those of geofinance/banking*

Chapter	Authors	Politics	Policy	Power	Space	Place	Territory	Finance flows	Firms and households	Banking institutions
2	Grandi	x	x	x	x	x		x		x
3	Battisti	x	x		x			x		x
4	Rosati			x			x	x		
5	Contel	x			x	x	x	x	x	x
6	Sellar	x		x			x	x	x	x
7	Ageeva and Mishura		x	x	x		x	x	x	x
8	Stavrova	x	x					x		x
9	Lim and Nguyen	x	x					x		
10	Yilmaz	x		x				x	x	x
11	Percoco	x			x	x	x	x	x	x
12	Jafri		x		x	x	x	x	x	

8

between shadow banking and the formal financial system (Chapter 3). In so doing, this chapter highlights the highly fragmented nature of shadow banking, noting that it does not constitute a system parallel to official banking and financial institutions; instead, shadow banks are a long-standing phenomenon traced back to the seventeenth century that is co-dependent and intertwined with its more regulated, official counterpart. The chapter explores the evolution of this entanglement around the global financial crisis of 2008. While regulators seemed taken by surprise by the importance of the sector and by the inadequacy of existing regulations to curb the crisis outside the boundary of official banking, insiders were aware of the relationships between banking and shadow banking. In particular, Battisti traces the growth of shadow banking in the years preceding the crisis in the decisions taken by official banking institutions to refocus their business, opening up market spaces to shadow – and thus less regulated – institutions. Shadow banking exists in a collaborative, but at the same time competitive, relationship with official finance and banking.

Umberto Rosati explores the financial centre perspective in classical models of the urban concentration of banks, stock markets, insurance and financial companies (Chapter 4) where two different economic forces – centrifugal and centripetal – operate within the financial space to define the spatial structure of the financial economy. In particular, Rosati's analysis notes that offshoring, seen here as a located in the semi-periphery, also plays a core role in shaping spaces, territories and local–global–local finance. Thus, offshore banking creates peculiar local systems where offshore places are located as well as clusters where this form of finance is spread.

A further form of spatiality is analyzed by Fabio Betioli Contel (Chapter 5) which relates to the urban effects of the Brazilian financial system. This is achieved through the identification of the main cities that behave similarly to financial centers. The study of financial centers is through frames that are historical and theoretical. This Brazilian case hence reveals the primacy of the city of São Paulo and the dispute over 'lower' functions by the cities of Brasilia and Rio de Janeiro in the national urban network creating national centers and sub national financial semi-peripheries.

Part II of the book explores the state–policy–politics–bank-firm nexus in the finance semi-peripheries and opens with the bank–business services relationship. Conceived thus, this is another form of the spatial structure of banking as well as a pathway for engagement with the state–bank–firm nexus in the finance semi-peripheries. Christian Sellar addresses this topic in a study of Italian banks and business services as well as their relationships to small and medium-sized enterprise (SME) outsourcing in Central and Eastern Europe (Chapter 6). The relationship between the internationalization of banks, services and SMEs as banks and services enables resource mobilization in the form of knowledge pipelines between Italian firms and Central and Eastern European regional economies.

The policy–bank–firm relationship, especially for SMEs, is also addressed by Svetlana Ageeva and Anna Mishura (Chapter 7) who analyze the role of the Russian banking system in the allocation of financial resources across regions where, over the past two decades, the number of Russian banks has declined. The geobanking phenomenon here is a repolarization to the capital and an increasingly Moscow-centered and state-orientated banking system. This has been to the detriment of privately owned smaller and regional banks, resulting in precarious access to credit for peripheral SMEs. Large network banks, headquartered mainly in Moscow, provide regular flows of financial resources concentrated in the capital for the lending needs of other regions. However, according to the Ageeva and Mishua study, the 'flight to home' and 'flight to quality' effects during the crisis period after 2014 show that, despite a significant state-based policy intervention, lending to SMEs and new enterprises remains very vulnerable, and is still largely dependent on government support programs and on central bank requirements for SME-orientated banks.

Elena Stavrova presents a historical account of the development of the banking system in Bulgaria where the economy transitioned from being command administered to market based. She thus analyzes the transformational patterns of national policy, foreign investment and the involvement of international financial institutions given the relatively sudden privatization of banks (Chapter 8). This 30-year process entailed a complex mix of policies that led to cycles of stability, but also crises, inflation and the proliferation, fragmentation and concentration of a banking system which includes state-controlled and foreign banks. Stavrova's study is thus one of geobanking development in the former satellite countries of the Soviet Union and offers an archetypal perspective on the complexity of transitions to a private system.

The role of the state is also a focal point for Guanie Lim and Thong Tien Nguyen who study the *doi moi* (renovation) reforms in Vietnam in the late 1980s. Through this, they explore the power–policy–banking–firm nexus in an Asian transition economy and a fast-moving semi-periphery financial area (Chapter 9). The membership of the Association of Southeast Asian Nations (ASEAN) and the accession in 2007 to the World Trade Organization (WTO) have unlocked new export markets for Vietnamese firms and integrated them, albeit unevenly, in global value chains. However, this story is more nuanced than that of a push towards neoliberalism, and the authors argue that a closer examination of the Vietnamese banking industry reveals that state-owned firms and banks are still subject to substantial direct or indirect political control. This moderates the effects of foreign capital on socio-economic structures and preserves power and capital structures in the banking system.

The contributions gathered in Part III share a concern for the micro-level dimension, the actions of financial institutions. Lending practices are a common thread in all three chapters of this part, and they offer a context for many of the opportunities and risks that shape places and territory. Part III opens with the chapter by Engin Yılmaz investigating the practice adopted by Turkish banks of cross-currency swap as driving an unwieldy expansion of credit (Chapter 10). The growth of the Turkish economy and the enlargement of household wealth underlie a political consensus that is debt driven and the basis for economic vulnerability given potential financial crisis. The liaison between politics–policy–banking and household growth in Turkey highlights the complex and subtle risks associated with loan creation from a cross-currency swap mechanism. It is a commentary on how the overuse of derivatives reflects an unsustainable system in which the expansion of local loans has surpassed the local deposit base of Turkish banks, and where non-core and foreign currency liabilities (dollarization) plug this gap in the banking system.

Marco Percoco adds to the discourse on financial crises with a spatial, Schumpeterian and Marshallian perspective on the Italian cases of crises that affected four major local commercial banks in Italy (Chapter 11). Commonalities shared by these banks are that they have a sub-regional spatial concentration of branches, and they were reliant on the local economy to lend to local firms which are often SMEs active in export-orientated industrial clusters. Percoco argues that the reasons for these four banks facing crises should not be sought simply in the context of the financial investment made, but also elsewhere. One of these reasons is the exposure to international trade shocks faced by sectors directly tied to local industrial clusters and thus to firms. The second reason which Percoco draws attention to is particularly interesting as it highlights the importance for research in geobanking, and on the role, composition and strategies of corporate governance bodies, banks and the local ties of their personnel. Percoco argues that local social networks can limit information costs in credit score evaluation and thus address the problem of asymmetric information. Nevertheless, there is a 'dark side' where social pressures from local powers push biased credit choices and financial imbalances, and eventually result in the need for bail-outs. The effects are thus felt not only by the banks themselves, but also by firms, local households and national policies.

The final chapter pertains to the alternative banking approaches of microfinance and digital financial services; thus addressing financial activities of individuals and households who occupy the grey area between formality and informality (Chapter 12). By engaging with the notion of shadow banking and relating it to financial citizenship – described as the right and ability of individuals and households to participate fully in the economy and to accumulate wealth – Juvaria Jafri discusses issues of geobanking evolution and financial inclusion and exclusion in Pakistan. The configuration of financial inclusion and exclusion as opposite and mutually exclusive concepts is thus interrogated, and this reveals a fundamental contradiction of inclusive finance: the tendency to promote economic dualism by bifurcating the financial sector. Bifurcation creates an inferior form of inclusion and access to finance, but is nevertheless a crucial development policy tool in the Global South, drawing countries to the frontiers of semi-periphery finance areas. The proposition of connecting with global circuits of financial capital has underpinned the success of inclusive finance programs. The Pakistan case shows how inclusive finance has become increasingly commercial and digitally orientated, while being heavily regulated. These features make it particularly attractive for global capital which is often in the form of development assistance or private funds. The concept of shadow financial citizenship is a tool to critique the inclusive finance paradigm in the light of the financialization of development, which departs from traditional and formal mainstream banking practices to create an uneven, bifurcated form of development.

REFERENCES

Aalbers, M.B. (2004), 'Creative destruction through the Anglo-American hegemony: a non-Anglo-American view on publications, referees and language', *Area*, **36** (3) 319–22.

Aalbers, M.B. (2018), 'Financial geography I: geographies of tax', *Progress in Human Geography*, **42** (6), 916–27.

Aalbers, M.B. and Rossi, U. (2007), 'A coming community: young geographers coping with multi-tier spaces of academic publishing across Europe', *Social & Cultural Geography*, **8** (2), 283–302.

Arrighi, G. (2010), *The Long Twentieth Century. Money, Power and the Origins of our Times*, London and New York: Verso.

Bassens, D. and Van Meeteren, M. (2018), 'Geographies of finance in a globalizing world', in R.C. Kloosterman, V. Mamadouh and P. Terhorst (eds), *Handbook on the Geographies of Globalization*, Cheltenham, UK and Northampton, MA, USA: Edward Elgar, pp. 248–57.

Berg, L. (2004), 'The spaces of critical geography', *Geoforum*, **35** (special issue), 523–58.

Braun, B., Gabor, D. and Hübner, M. (2018), 'Governing through financial markets: towards a critical political economy of Capital Markets Union', *Competition & Change*, **22** (2), 101–16.

Çalışkan, K. and Callon, M. (2009), 'Economization, part 1: shifting attention from the economy towards processes of economization', *Economy and Society*, **38** (3), 369–98.

Christaller, W. (1966), *Central Places in Southern Germany*, Englewood Cliffs, NJ: Prentice Hall.

Clark, G.L. and Wójcik, D. (2007), *The Geography of Finance: Corporate Governance in the Global Marketplace*, Oxford: Oxford University Press.

Dixon, A.D. and Monk, A. (2014), 'Frontier finance', *Annals of the Association of American Geographers*, **104** (4), 852–68.

Dörry, S. (2018), 'Creating institutional power in financialised economies: the firm–profession nexus of advanced business services', *FinGeo Working Paper No. 12*, March, Global Network on Financial Geography, Oxford University.

Elson, A. (2011), *Governing Global Finance: The Evolution and Reform of the International Financial Architecture*, New York: Palgrave Macmillan.

Environment and Planning (2003), 'Guest editorials', *Environment and Planning D: Society and Space*, **21** (special issue), 131–68.

European Urban and Regional Studies (2004), 'Euro commentaries themed section', *European Urban and Regional Studies*, **11** (special issue), 335–81.

Global Network on Financial Geography (FinGeo) (2019), Working papers, Global Network on Financial Geography, Oxford University, accessed 9 February 2019 at http://www.fingeo.net/fingeo-working-paper-series/.

Govindarajan, V. and Trimble, C. (2012), *Reverse Innovation: Create Far from Home, Win Everywhere*, Brighton, MA: Harvard Business Press.

Grote, M., Zook, H.M. and Heidorn, T. (2017), 'Geographical limits to arbitrage in the global oil market', *FinGeo Working Paper No. 7*, August, Global Network on Financial Geography, Oxford University.

Gutierrez, J. and Lopez-Nieva, P. (2001), 'Are international journals of human geography really international?', *Progress in Human Geography*, **25** (1), 53–69.

Jones, M. (2016), 'Polymorphic political geographies', *Territory, Politics, Governance*, **4** (1), 1–7.

Karwowski, E. and Centurion-Vicencio, M. (2018), 'Financialising the state: recent developments in fiscal and monetary policy', *FinGeo Working Paper No. 11*, February, Global Network on Financial Geography, Oxford University.

Kitchin, R. (2003), 'Cuestionando y desetabilizando la hegemonia angloamericana y del ingles en geografia' ('Questioning and de-stabilizing the Anglo-American hegemony of English language in geography'), *Documents d'Analisi Geografica*, **42**, 17–36.

Klagge, B. and Zademach, H.-M. (2018), 'International capital flows, stock markets, and uneven development: the case of sub-Saharan Africa and the Sustainable Stock Exchanges Initiative (SSEI)', *Zeitschrift Für Wirtschaftsgeographie*, **62** (2), 92–107.

Lösch, A. (1954), *The Economics of Location*, New Haven, CT and London: Yale University Press.

Minca, C. (2000), 'Venetian geographical praxis', *Environment and Planning D: Society and Space*, **18** (3), 285–9.

Moisio, S. (2018), *Geopolitics of the Knowledge-Based Economy*, London: Routledge.

Pan, F., Hall, S. and Zhang, H. (2018), 'The geographies of financial activities within an emerging international financial center: the case of Beijing', *FinGeo Working Paper No. 10*, January, Global Network on Financial Geography, Oxford University.

Pažitka, V. and Wójcik, D. (2017), 'Cluster dynamics of financial centres in the United Kingdom: do connected firms grow faster?', *FinGeo Working Paper No. 4*, July, Global Network on Financial Geography, Oxford University.

Rodríguez-Pose, A. (2004), 'On English as a vehicle to preserve geographical diversity', *Progress in Human Geography*, **28** (1), 1–4.

Rodríguez-Pose, A. (2006), 'Commentary: is there an "Anglo-American" domination in human geography? And, is it bad?', *Environment & Planning A*, **38** (4), 603–10.

Roy, A. (2010), *Poverty Capital: Microfinance and the Making of Development*, London: Routledge.

Vergara Caffarelli, F. and Veronese, G. (2018), 'Costs of Italian economic diplomacy: a comparative perspective', in P. Van Bergeijk and S. Moons (eds), *Research Handbook on Economic Diplomacy Bilateral Relations in a Context of Geopolitical Change*, Cheltenham, UK and Northampton, MA, USA: Edgar Elgar, pp. 204–19.

Wallerstein, I. (1974), *The Modern World-System: Capitalist Agriculture and the Origins of the European World-Economy in the Sixteenth Century*, New York: Academic Press.

Wójcik, D. and Cojoianu, T. (2017), 'Unfinished business: change in the US securities industry since 2008', *FinGeo Working Paper No. 9*, October, Global Network on Financial Geography, Oxford University.

Wójcik, D., Knight, E., O'Neill, P. and Pažitka, V. (2017), 'Investment banking since 2008: geography of shrinkage and shift', *FinGeo Working Paper No. 3*, March, Global Network on Financial Geography, Oxford University.

Woods, S. (2017), 'Geofinance – speech by Sam Woods. Given at the Mansion House City Banquet, London', Bank of England, London, 4 October, accessed 16 July 2019 at https://www.bankofengland.co.uk/speech/2017/geofinance-speech-by-sam-woods.

Yunus, M. (2009), *Creating a World without Poverty: Social Business and the Future of Capitalism*, New York: Public Affairs.

1. Geofinance/banking between political and financial geographies

Christian Sellar, Silvia Grandi and Juvaria Jafri

1. FINANCIAL GEOGRAPHIES

This chapter proposes the notion of geofinance/banking to engage in and advance debates in both financial and political geography. Therefore, this section of the chapter summarizes key concepts in financial geography; the second section makes the case for looking at finance from a political geographical standpoint; the third expands on the notion of geofinance/banking; and the fourth and fifth sections discuss broader implications of this as a model to understand finance in the semi-peripheries.

A rapidly developing field, financial geography is establishing itself as a multi-scalar and multidisciplinary area of study, with at least three recognizable foci (FinGeo 2018), which emerge habitually – but not exclusively – from the core of the financial system: (1) a sectoral focus which encompasses corporate finance, financial markets and intermediaries, personal finance, and government and regulation; (2) a cross-sectoral focus which emphasizes multidisciplinary research, such as on real estate, the geographies of financial flows, financial centers and networks, and financial technology (fintech); and (3) a development focus, which interrogates financial equality and its relationship with social justice, crises and responsible investment.

Sectoral studies, which are given to geographical contexts, reveal the crucial role of advanced business services – particularly core-based transnational consulting and accounting firms – in constituting and sustaining the legitimacy of a financialized economy (Dörry 2018). Thus, a missing critical mass of advanced financial services is a marker of a semi-peripheral financial area. Moreover, a sectoral focus highlights how conflict between established actors and emerging frontier financial systems, which are connected to the major financial centers, reshapes both the spatialities and the organization of the industry (Dixon and Monk 2014; Grandi 2018; Grandi and Parenti 2019; Parenti and Rosati 2018). Even though the basic power structure of finance, centered on New York and London, remains overwhelmingly intact (Cassis and Wójcik 2018; Wójcik 2013), such conflicts and re-organization are increasingly relevant, as the financialized economy swells at the expense of national models of stakeholder capitalism (Clark and Wójcik 2007).

The cross-sectoral focus captures, for instance, the notion that housing is 'a central carrier of practices of financialization' and that it 'bridges the balance sheet of households (debt and equity) with financial institutions' (Fernandez 2017, p. 1; see also Byrne and Norris 2017). Another example of a cross-sectoral focus is how discussions of fintech highlight how the 'organizational models coming out of Silicon Valley', such as 'Big Data' mining, digital money, distributed ledger technology, robo-advice and other forms of integration of information technology and finance, are being adopted by traditional financial firms, notwithstanding their size, legacies and sunken costs (Bassens et al. 2017).

Discussions on development include patterns of growth for financial service firms in the UK after the global financial crisis of 2007–09 and the ongoing process of leaving the European Union, showing that firms networked with other financial hubs grow faster, generating negative spillovers and divergent growth patterns within the local financial cluster (Pažitka and Wójcik 2017). On the other side of the Atlantic, the changing geography of US investment banking after the financial crisis is discussed; this highlights a shrinking industry, its spatial dispersion through offshoring and nearshoring, and the persistence of gender imbalances in the workforce (Wójcik and Cojoianu 2017). These findings are confirmed at the global level, where an overall contraction and dispersion of investment banking is detected (Wójcik et al. 2017). Development-focused works on finance also include the exploration of new trends, such as the evolution of philanthropy from grant-making towards a profit-orientated investment process (Stolz and Lai 2018), the role of stock exchanges in Africa (Klagge and Zademach 2018) and the absorption of microfinance in global circuits of capital (Mader 2018; Roy 2010)

The scope of this work is also revealed in recent analyses of governments and regulations which underline connections with the semi-periphery or emerging new centers. Sokol (2017) highlights the relationship between financialization and uneven development by discussing the financial links between core and peripheral areas in Europe. Karwowski and Centurion-Vicencio's (2018) work on the changing relations between states and financial markets is in part financed by a Brazilian federal agency. Alessandrini et al. (2008, 2009) show the impact of regulation – and technological change – on the spatial distribution of finance, characterized by the twin processes of institutional consolidation and geographical diffusion of banking services. Policy-focused research conducted in China shows that agglomeration economies and urban planning are crucial in the emergence of Beijing's financial center (Pan et al. 2018).

2.   TOWARDS SEMI-PERIPHERY FOCUSED FINANCIAL GEOGRAPHIES: A POLITICAL INTERPRETATION

Building on the intuition that the state has a special role in the financial geographies of the semi-periphery, we focus on political geographical approaches for two main reasons. First and foremost, despite increasing attention to theoretical perspectives on the dynamics of state and firm production networks (Gereffi 2014; Neilson et al. 2014; Pickles et al. 2016), most scholarship resists engagement with the claims made by political geographers about structural changes in state power, organization and territoriality. Therefore, while there are rich analyses showing how regulators shape value chains and production networks, there is only limited focus on how changes in economic actors reshape various organizations within the state. Incidentally, until very recently political geography has been prone to a bias; even though several studies under the rubric of geo-economics acknowledge the role of markets in larger political decisions (Cowen and Smith 2009), they remain vague on how firm-level and consumer-level decisions affect the political sphere. Such biases are partly due to subject-matter differentiation: the focus of economic geography is on firms as pivotal actors in the modern economy, whereas political geography prioritizes organizations involved in politics (Müller 2015, p. 305). Subject-matter differentiation thus obscures analyses on the political role of economic actors in shaping and reshaping the political geographies of the nation state (Agnew 2010; Jessop 2001). By investigating the shared influences on broadly conceived (geo)political processes and the financial system (Grandi and Parenti 2019), we seek to uncover the geospatial and organizational features that have fallen through the disciplinary crevices between political and economic geography (Sellar et al. 2018).

The second reason to explore the links between political and financial geographies is because the role of the financial sector as an intermediary – with transformative potential – is only diminutively understood. Thus far, economic geography research on intermediaries has focused on location consultants and investment promotion agencies (Phelps and Wood 2006, 2018); in this book we present cases in which financial institutions play an important role in shaping firms' location alongside consultants (Chapter 6), while themselves being shaped by the politics of regulation and decision making (Chapters 2, 7, 8, 9 and 10). This intermediary role relates to the reflexivity of the financial system, which responds to its own internal logic of profit as well as to external pressures from regulators, firms and systemic crises (Chapters 8, 9, 10 and 11 in this book).

There is currently an emergent thread of research on the nexus between governments, banks and the locational choices of firms. Many Italian scholars are aware of the governmental mechanisms of coordination, starting from strategic directions issued by the government, to their implementation from various ministries, and the work of public agencies in disbursing financial support and guarantees to banks and firms for export and internationalization (Vergara Caffarelli and Veronese 2018, p. 213). Within this system, banks remain independent private actors but the availability of government funds impels bank lending for internationalization projects, which are a government priority. This is a very different model from, for example, the tight state control of finance exercised by China and the various degrees of political control of finance in East Asian developmental states (Harvey 2007; Ufen 2015). Differences notwithstanding, these findings suggest caution in extending assumptions valid in and around the financial cores to the semi-periphery. In particular, many of the processes described by core-driven financial geographers pertain to a privately owned financial sector which allocates and reallocates resources – sometimes from state control at the expense of democratic processes – given a profit-seeking logic. The alternative we propose is a semi-peripheral view in which non-financial actors – namely, but not exclusively, the state – affect the resources and the opportunities available to finance and, by extension, firms. This perspective sees the profit-driven process of allocating financial resources to firms and consumers less as the result of a simple calculation on return of investment. Instead, it comes across as a negotiation between various interests: that is, a political process. Herein is the rationale to interpret finance with a political-geographical lens.

3. GEOFINANCE/BANKING AS A CONCEPTUAL FRAMEWORK LINKING POLITICAL GEOGRAPHY AND FINANCE

As a field, political geography has developed a multiplicity of approaches since its emergence in the nineteenth century (Jones 2016). Mid-twentieth-century positivist approaches viewed it as the study of politically bounded territorial units (Alexander 1963), and later embraced all political processes. This type of approach is distinct from political science because of the application of quantitative spatial analysis (Burnett et al. 1981). Later, structuralist and post-structuralist approaches focused on key concepts such as territory and the state (Cox 2002, 2003). More recently, a new political geography (Jones 2016) has opened up the field to interdisciplinary contributions, merging the political and the geographical. The former may be conceptualized as a 'triangle' including power, politics and policy, and the latter conceptualized as a 'triangle' of space, place and territory (Jones 2016, p. 2). Political geography research thus involves some, but not necessarily all, permutations of these six concepts.

Within these permutations, we are particularly interested in the relationships between policy, politics and territory. These relationships – a fixture in the discussion over the nature of the state – are treated by geographers either as static territorial frames, or as dynamic, multi-scalar and networked social processes (Jessop 2007; Moisio 2018; Moisio and Paasi 2013b). Works on state theory include the strategic relational understanding of the state (Jessop 2001). These emphasize the reciprocal influence exerted across capitalist state institutions and social action; certain institutional structures 'may privilege some actors, some identities, some strategies' that actors need to deploy to achieve their goals (Jessop 2001, p. 1220). In turn, the strategic actions of these actors shape how institutions evolve. There is thus a dialectic tension between the territorial and networked views of the state, showing that state power is the result of the interaction between territorially framed institutions and the social forces operating within and around these institutions. In the editorial of a special issue for the journal *Geopolitics*, Moisio and Paasi (2013a) suggest a rethink of the contrast between territorial and relational government practices. That is, states use both traditional territorial jurisdictions and relational networks in different contexts to further their resources and their reach. The fourth issue of 2010 in the same journal presents a round-table discussion of John Agnew's concept of the territorial trap (Reid-Henry 2010). This concept draws attention to the assumptions of conventional territoriality, in which state organizations and societies are neatly contained within national boundaries. The special issue advances the concept by exploring the history of the territorial state, considering forms of power other than sovereignty and rethinking the relationships among power, space and political systems (Elden 2010). Jonas (2012) builds on this to suggest that it is possible to transcend the distinction between territorial and relational by drawing on the constantly reassembled, bounded and unbounded factors that shape territory and territorial politics.

Most recently, cross-disciplinary literature discusses the role of economic actors – including, but not limited to, firms and their value chains – in the assembly and reassembly of territories and politics. Sellar's (2019; Sellar et al. 2018) argument that transnational firms and expatriate entrepreneurs act as political actors and contribute to the network-like transformation of state bureaucracies is relevant here. Building on Çalışkan and Callon

(2009), Moisio (2018, p. 1) presents the notion of economization, under-stood as 'the material processes of knowledge-intensive capitalism . . . and the processes whereby this form of capitalism is constructed discursively'. Moisio's key claim is that economization includes a key geopolitical dimension, constituted by both the territorial power of states and the imagery of hubs, networks and flows that permeates the late capitalist economy. Economization is able to connect firms and political communities (Moisio 2018, p. 16) and account for the reshuffling of territoriality (Moisio 2018, p. 19). Developing Moisio's point, we argue that finance and its geographies are an underexplored and crucial factor linking the evolving (bounded and relational) territorialities of the nation state with firms and citizens.

To bring together political and financial geographies is to emphasize that states and regulations are crucial in shaping the financial sector (Karwowski and Centurion-Vicencio 2018; Pan et al. 2018). In addition, the sector itself teems with a variety of organizations operating at multiple scales (Dörry 2018; Stolz and Lai 2018). Moreover, these organizations are rapidly evolving as they respond to the spatiality of finance and the state (Wójcik and Cojoianu 2017; Wójcik et al. 2017; Bassens et al. 2017). Building on these findings, we propose the notion of geofinance/banking as a way to tie together the contributions in this book while also highlight-ing the political-geographical role of finance; the various public and private aspects of banking that shape territorial politics, and vice versa. Figure 1.1 is a visual representation of the concept of geofinance/banking.

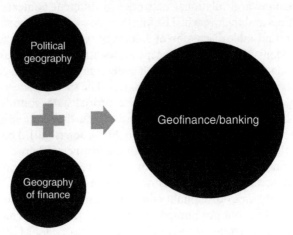

Source: Figure by Silvia Grandi, 2018.

Figure 1.1   Geofinance/banking

In our view, geofinance/banking refers to a complex and multi-scalar system which includes physical infrastructure and social interactions, in person as well as through digital media. Actors in the system represent a wide range of agents. These include: international financial institutions (IFIs) such as the World Bank and the European Investment Bank; large financial players including pension funds, sovereign wealth funds and stock exchanges; state-owned banks and insurers; private insurance companies and other financial service providers; and international commercial banks, offshore banks and smaller-scale financial institutions operating at the local level, including local and cooperative banks. More recently, new actors have emerged and complement these institutions and their practices: these include fintech, Islamic finance, frontier finance, crowd funding and microfinance. The term banking synthesizes the main actors, processes and fluxes of the geographies of finance. Geofinance/banking thus shapes, and is shaped by, global forces exerted simultaneously at the international, national and local scales. Particularly at the national and sub-national levels, material and immaterial landscapes of state-owned organizations, as well as private firms, which encompass large multinational corporations (MNCs) and small and medium-sized enterprises (SMEs) are shaped by, and are shaping, geofinance/banking.

Our conceptualization, which builds on Jones (2016), is thus: financial political geography focuses on the relationships among two or more of nine entities, which are either political (power, politics and policy), geographical (space, place and territory) or financial (flows, firms and institutions). While power, politics and policy with space, place and territory represent political geography, geofinance/banking adds a further triangle consisting of financial flows – labelled flows in Figure 1.2 for the sake of simplicity and which refer to the flows and management of money and other financial tools – and institutions (banks, IFIs and other actors) and client (firms and consumers). The polygon in Figure 1.2 resulting from the merger of the three triangles shows the possible influences between political and economic geographies, as mediated by finance.

The relationships shown in Figure 1.2 rest upon the semi-periphery centered assumptions discussed above; that the state influences domestic finance, which in turn shapes resources available to firms and people, while at the same time importing and adapting models from the core. We understand these relationships as a set of mutually interdependent processes of adaptation, synergies and incentives as well as threats. Thus, the permutations of geofinance/banking represent the possible links between (1) the policies of territorial states in the financial semi-periphery, (2) the interactions between these policies and globalizing processes originating in the financial core, and (3) the resulting impact on financial flows

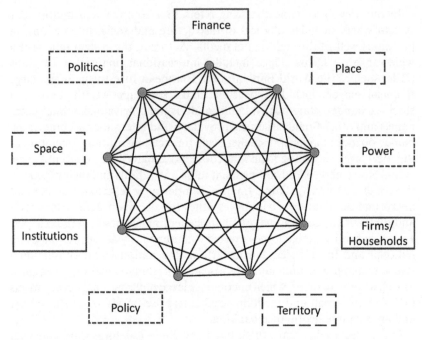

Source: Figure by Silvia Grandi, 2018.

*Figure 1.2   The relational conceptualization among new political
                geography entities and those of geofinance/banking*

and practices affecting specific national and local economies in the
semi-periphery.

Findings from each chapter flesh out our initial hypothesis of a relationship between constantly reassembled territorial politics and policies,
finance, firms and people. The authors depict a rapidly evolving regulatory system, which simultaneously reacts to and constitutes a globalizing
political economy. Contributions by Silvia Grandi, Gianfranco Battisti
and Umberto Rosati (Chapters 2–4) set the stage by observing how a
global system of financial governance, whose complex boundaries encompass both official finance and shadow banking, arises from the need to
regulate the economy beyond the spatialities of the nation state; thus, the
governance of finance is consistent with relational governmental practices.
Contributions by Elena Stavrova and by Guanie Lim and Thong Tien
Nguyen (Chapters 8 and 9) show how global pressures to implement neoliberal reforms are mediated and domesticated by national regulation of
the financial system in Bulgaria and Vietnam, respectively. The influence

of national governments is also addressed in Chapter 7 by Ageeva and Mishura, which examines the financial sector in Russia and its predilection for state-owned and Moscow-based banks, at the expense of independent regional financial institutions. Yılmaz and Percoco (Chapters 10 and 11) offer a different take when they show how national and sub-national banking systems have responded to the challenges presented by financial crises with the acquiescence of national regulators. In turn, banks and other actors in the financial sector shape the opportunities available to firms and the public, creating support networks for internationalizing firms (Sellar, in Chapter 6), as well as patterns of inclusion/exclusion defining financial citizenship (Jafri, in Chapter 12).

4.   THE QUESTION OF INNOVATION

Responding to the call for chapters on geofinance/banking, contributors chose to highlight some issues more than others. The most glaring absence is that none of the authors is especially concerned with technology or innovation. This might be surprising, given how much emphasis contemporary financial geography places on innovation, both relating to technology and organization (Bassens et al. 2017; Clark and Wójcik 2007; Stolz and Lai 2018). More broadly, much of economic geography's drive to understand regional economies, clusters and networks of the past 30 years has been driven by an interest in innovation (Breschi and Lenzi 2014; Cooke et al. 2004; Fromhold-Eisebith and Eisebith 2005; Saxenian 1994; Storper 1997). Even from a geopolitics standpoint, the main driver behind Moisio's discussion of economization is to enhance analyses of the knowledge-based economy; itself an ambiguous term that pertains to, among other things, high-technology, innovation-driven capitalism (Moisio 2018). Several contributors do comment on the transfer of innovation and fintech from the core financial regions. Other than the personal research interests of the contributors, limited engagement here is consistent with the classical work of Wallerstein (1974) in which innovation – in the form of capitalism and industrialism – allowed the core regions to emerge in the first place, and in which the semi-periphery either declines or seeks to join this core through the adoption of innovations generated by the main global financial centers.

While the old model of transmission of innovation from the core is now challenged by the emergence of reverse innovation technologies with potentially no boundaries (Govindarajan and Trimble 2012), there is still space for the transfer and adaptation of core-driven models. For example, in this collection Chapter 8 by Elena Stavrova configures the historical evolution of Bulgarian banking as a 'path to normality' from state socialism to a European model driven by transfers of technology and practices by foreign investors. Fabio Betioli Contel makes comparable arguments about Brazil in Chapter 5, and Svetlana Ageeva and Anna Mishura take a similar approach for Russia in Chapter 7. Thus, rather than an omission, the lack of focus on innovation by our contributors suggests a need for more nuance on the relative importance of innovation in non-core based research.

It is not that Bulgaria – or Italy, or Turkey and the other cases represented here – are incapable of financial innovation; quite the opposite. Indeed, Wallerstein (1976) noticed that the attempts by the semi-peripheries to join the core may lead to revolutions and daring experimentations. Most recently, in the field of finance, formerly semi-peripheral areas in East Asia have driven innovation in fintech (Lai 2018). Rather than denying the importance of innovation, our cases note that innovation is one among many options available to actors in the semi-periphery. For example, in the particular cases discussed in the following chapters, local interests have steered public and academic discourse to an emphasis on imported models, rather than highlighting home-grown innovation.[1] In turn, those models are transformed and adapted in practice, even when not in rhetoric, as shown in by Lim and Nguyen in Chapter 9 on banking reforms in Vietnam, where strictly neoliberal economic reforms were stalled and tweaked during implementation.

5.   REFLECTIONS ON THE BROADER ROLE OF FINANCIAL SEMI-PERIPHERIES

Problematizing the role of innovation leads to bigger questions about the role of the semi-periphery in the global financial system. On the one hand, the empirical material discussed in the following chapters does not lend itself to large-scale generalizations about the influence of the semi-periphery on the core and the periphery. On the other hand, our own conceptual tool of geofinance/banking is designed to investigate multi-scalar trends owing to the entanglement between finance and the state, rather than a macro-level picture of semi-peripheries as buffer and the expansion zone for peripheralizing and core-forming processes (Arrighi and Drangel 1986). In summary, this work seeks to be a starting point for a discussion about two gaps in financial geography by (1) introducing the perspective of the semi-peripheries and (2) calling for a closer attention to the politics and geopolitics of finance. While much more has been written on politics and finance – for example, Hardie (2012) on the constraints of government borrowing in emerging markets, or Krijnen et al. (2017) for analyses of finance in the world-city tradition – we as editors resist over-theorizing by keeping the conceptual contribution focused on geography.

While the theoretical contribution of the whole book is targeted and specific, the empirical content is wide ranging: the chapters connect with a variety of disciplines and engage with two trends on the broader role of the semi-periphery of global finance. First, some chapters point to vulnerabilities and dependence on the core; for example, bank lending practices in Turkey, the vulnerability of Italian regional banks to crises and the reactive nature of banking policies in Bulgaria. Second, there are clear signs of pushbacks in which the orchestration of finance by the state mediates the pressures from the core: this is seen in Chapters 7 and 9 on Russia and Vietnam, respectively. The book seeks to view the semi-periphery as a place of experimentation for the politics of finance – albeit perhaps less daring in financial innovation than the periphery owing to the path dependency of already established 'brick and mortar' banking – but also presenting a variety of entanglements between states and markets that are not immediately apparent.

The three parts and the chapters of this book together highlight the need for focused research on the middle ground between financial cores and places at the margins of finance: we refer to these as semi-peripheral financial areas. Our approach thus complements perspectives on core financial centers and articulates the presence of a geofinance/banking landscape which encompasses meso-level as well as micro-level structures. Moreover, by juxtaposing the fixtures of political science – politics, policy and power – with those from political geography fixtures – such as space, place and territory – and then enriching them with fixtures from finance – such as flows, banking institutions and firms/households – we arrive at a conceptual and analytical framework for geofinance/banking.

NOTE

1. Another Bulgarian example of manipulating Western discourses on innovation is reported by Sellar et al. (2011), showing how European Union innovation policies conceived in Brussels with the explicit aim of competing with Silicon Valley over cutting-edge innovation were reinterpreted in Bulgaria as a tool to acquire resources to revitalize old industrial centers.

REFERENCES

Agnew, J. (2010), 'Still trapped in territory?', *Geopolitics*, **15** (4), 779–84.
Alessandrini, P., Presbitero, A.F. and Zazzaro, A. (2008), 'Banks, distances and firms' financing constraints', *Review of Finance*, **13** (2), 261–307.

Alessandrini, P., Presbitero, A.F. and Zazzaro, A. (2009), 'Geographical organization of banking systems and innovation diffusion', in P. Alessandrini, P. Fratianni and A. Zazzaro (eds), *The Changing Geography of Banking and Finance*, New York: Springer, pp. 75–108.

Alexander, L.M. (1963), *World Political Patterns*, Chicago, IL: Rand McNally.

Arrighi, G. and Drangel, J. (1986), 'The stratification of the world-economy: an exploration of the semiperipheral zone', *Review (Fernand Braudel Center)*, **10** (1), 9–74.

Bassens, D., Hendrikse, R. and Van Meeteren, M. (2017), 'The Appleization of finance – reflections on the Fintech (R)evolution', *FinGeo Working Paper No. 2*, March, Global Network on Financial Geography, Oxford University.

Breschi, S. and Lenzi, C. (2014), 'The role of external linkages and gatekeepers for the renewal and expansion of US cities, knowledge base, 1990–2004', *Regional Studies*, **49** (5), 782–97.

Burnett, A.D., Taylor, P.J. and Taylor, P.J. (1981), *Political Studies from Spatial Perspectives: Anglo-American Essays on Political Geography*, New York: John Wiley & Sons.

Byrne, M. and Norris, M. (2017), 'Financial circuits: cyclicality, leakiness and social housing finance in Ireland and Denmark', *FinGeo Working Paper No. 5*, July, Global Network on Financial Geography, Oxford University.

Çalışkan, K. and Callon, M. (2009), 'Economization, part 1: shifting attention from the economy towards processes of economization', *Economy and Society*, **38** (3), 369–98.

Cassis, Y. and Wójcik, D. (2018), *International Financial Centres after the Global Financial Crisis and Brexit*, Oxford: Oxford University Press.

Clark, G.L. and Wójcik, D. (2007), *The Geography of Finance: Corporate Governance in the Global Marketplace*, Oxford: Oxford University Press.

Cooke, P.N., Heidenreich, M. and Braczyk, H.-J. (2004), *Regional Innovation Systems: The Role of Governance in a Globalized World*, Hove: Psychology Press.

Cowen, D. and Smith, N. (2009), 'After geopolitics? From the geopolitical social to geoeconomics', *Antipode*, **41** (1), 22–48.

Cox, K.R. (2002), *Political Geography: Territory, State and Society*, Cambridge, MA: Blackwell.

Cox, K.R. (2003), 'Political geography and the territorial', *Political Geography*, **22** (6), 607–10.

Dixon, A.D. and Monk, A. (2014), 'Frontier finance', *Annals of the Association of American Geographers*, **104** (4), 852–68.

Dörry, S. (2018), 'Creating institutional power in financialised economies: the firm-profession nexus of advanced business services', *FinGeo Working Paper No. 12*, March, Global Network on Financial Geography, Oxford University.

Elden, S. (2010), 'Thinking territory historically', *Geopolitics*, **15** (4), 757–61.

Fernandez, R. (2017), 'Stylized facts from housing and finance: how do they relate across space and time?', *FinGeo Working Paper No. 1*, March, Global Network on Financial Geography, Oxford University.

FinGeo (2018), 'Research themes', accessed 16 July 219 at http://www.fingeo.net/research-themes/.

Fromhold-Eisebith, M. and Eisebith, G. (2005), 'How to institutionalize innovative clusters? Comparing explicit top-down and implicit bottom-up approaches', *Research Policy*, **34** (8), 1250–68.

Gereffi, G. (2014), 'Global value chains in a post-Washington consensus world', *Review of International Political Economy*, **21** (1), 9–37.

Govindarajan, V. and Trimble, C. (2012), *Reverse Innovation: Create far from Home, Win Everywhere*, Brighton, MA: Harvard Business Press.

Grandi, S. (2018), *Viaggio tra le concezioni dello sviluppo. Teorie ed evoluzioni* (*A Journey among Different Understandings of Development. Theories and Evolution*), Bologna: La Mandragora.

Grandi, S. and Parenti, F.M. (2019), 'Geography matters in finance? Frontiers, polarizations, alternatives and geopolitical elements for financial analysis', in S. Boubaker and D.K. Khuong Nguyen (eds), *Handbook of Global Financial Markets: Transformations, Dependence, and Risk Spillovers*, Singapore: World Scientific, pp. 767–88.

Hardie, I. (2012), *Financialization and Government Borrowing Capacity in Emerging Markets*, Basingstoke: Palgrave Macmillan.

Harvey, D. (2007), *A Brief History of Neoliberalism*, Oxford and New York: Oxford University Press.

Jessop, B. (2001), 'Institutional re(turns) and the strategic–relational approach', *Environment and Planning A*, **33** (7), 1213–36.

Jessop, B. (2007), *State Power*, Cambridge: Polity.

Jonas, A.E.G. (2012), 'Region and place: regionalism in question', *Progress in Human Geography*, **36** (2), 263–72.

Jones, M. (2016), 'Polymorphic political geographies', *Territory, Politics, Governance*, **4** (1), 1–7.

Karwowski, E. and Centurion-Vicencio, M. (2018), 'Financialising the state: recent developments in fiscal and monetary policy,' *FinGeo Working Paper No. 11*, February, Global Network on Financial Geography, Oxford University.

Klagge, B. and Zademach, H.-M. (2018), 'International capital flows, stock markets, and uneven development: the case of sub-Saharan Africa and the Sustainable Stock Exchanges Initiative (SSEI)', *Zeitschrift Für Wirtschaftsgeographie*, **62** (2), 92–107.

Krijnen, M., Bassens, D. and Van Meeteren, M. (2017), 'Manning circuits of value: Lebanese professionals and expatriate world-city formation in Beirut', *Environment and Planning A*, **49** (12), 2878–96.

Lai, K.P.Y. (2018), 'Singapore: connecting Asian markets with global finance', in Y. Cassis and D. Wójcik (eds), *International Financial Centres after the Global Financial Crisis and Brexit*, Oxford: Oxford University Press, pp. 154–81.

Mader, P. (2018), 'Contesting financial inclusion', *Development and Change*, **49** (2), 461–83.

Moisio, S. (2018), *Geopolitics of the Knowledge-Based Economy*, London: Routledge.

Moisio, S. and Paasi, A. (2013a), 'Beyond state-centricity: geopolitics of changing state spaces', *Geopolitics*, **18** (2), 255–66.

Moisio, S. and Paasi, A. (2013b), 'From geopolitical to geoeconomic? The changing political rationalities of state space', *Geopolitics*, **18** (2), 267–83.

Müller, M. (2015), 'Geography of organization', in J. Wright (ed.), *International Encyclopedia of the Social & Behavioral Sciences*, 2nd edn, Amsterdam: Elsevier, pp. 301–6.

Neilson, J., Pritchard, B. and Wai-chung Yeung, H. (2014), 'Global value chains and global production networks in the changing international political economy: an introduction', *Review of International Political Economy*, **21** (1), 1–8.

Pan, F., Hall, S. and Zhang, H. (2018), 'The geographies of financial activities within an emerging international financial center: the case of Beijing', *FinGeo Working Paper No. 10*, January, Global Network on Financial Geography, Oxford University.

Parenti, F. and Rosati, U. (2018), *Geofinance and Geopolitics*, Milan: Egea.

Pažitka, V. and Wójcik, D. (2017), 'Cluster dynamics of financial centres in the United Kingdom: do connected firms grow faster?', *FinGeo Working Paper No. 4*, July, Global Network on Financial Geography, Oxford University.

Phelps, N. and Wood, A. (2006), 'Lost in translation? Local interests, global actors and inward investment regimes', *Journal of Economic Geography*, **6** (4), 493–515.

Phelps, N. and Wood, A. (2018), 'The business of location: site selection consultants and the mobilisation of knowledge in the location decision', *Journal of Economic Geography*, **18** (5), 1023–44.

Pickles, J., Smith, A., Begg, R., Bucek, M., Roukova, P. and Rudolf, P. (2016), *Articulations of Capital: Global Production Networks and Regional Transformations*, New York: John Wiley & Sons.

Reid-Henry, S. (2010), 'The territorial trap fifteen years on', *Geopolitics*, **15** (4), 752–56.

Roy, A. (2010), *Poverty Capital: Microfinance and the Making of Development*, New York: Routledge.

Saxenian, A. (1994), *Regional Advantage: Culture and Competition in Silicon Valley and Route 128*, Cambridge, MA: Harvard University Press.

Sellar, C. (2019), 'Transnationalizing bureaucracies through investment promotion: the case of Informest', *Environment and Planning C: Politics and Space*, **37** (3), 461–79.

Sellar, C., Emilova, M., Petkova-Tancheva, C.D. and McNeil, K. (2011), 'Cluster policies in Bulgaria: European integration, postsocialist dynamics and local level initiatives', *International Journal of Urban and Regional Research*, **35** (2), 358–78.

Sellar, C., Lan, T. and Poli, U. (2018), 'The geoeconomics/politics of Italy's investment promotion community', *Geopolitics*, **23** (3), 690–717.

Sokol, M. (2017), 'Financialisation, financial chains and uneven geographical development: towards a research agenda', *Research in International Business and Finance*, **39**, 678–85.

Stolz, D. and Lai, K.P.Y. (2018), 'Philanthro-capitalism, social enterprises and global development', *FinGeo Working Paper No. 13*, March, Global Network on Financial Geography, Oxford University.

Storper, M. (1997), *The Regional World: Territorial Development in a Global Economy*, New York: Guilford Press.

Ufen, A. (2015), 'Laissez-faire versus strict control of political finance: hegemonic parties and developmental states in Malaysia and Singapore', *Critical Asian Studies*, **47** (4), 564–86.

Vergara Caffarelli, F. and Veronese, G. (2018), 'Costs of Italian economic diplomacy: a comparative perspective', in P. Van Bergeijk and S. Moons (eds), *Research Handbook on Economic Diplomacy Bilateral Relations in a Context of Geopolitical Change*, Cheltenham, UK and Northampton, MA, USA: Edgar Elgar, pp. 204–19.

Wallerstein, I. (1974), *The Modern World-System: Capitalist Agriculture and the Origins of the European World-Economy in the Sixteenth Century*, New York: Academic Press.

Wallerstein, I. (1976), 'Semi-peripheral countries and the contemporary world crisis', *Theory and Society*, **3** (4), 461–83.

Wójcik, D. (2013), 'The dark side of NY–LON: financial centres and the global financial crisis', *Urban Studies*, **50** (13), pp. 2736–52.

Wójcik, D. and Cojoianu, T. (2017), 'Unfinished business: change in the US securities industry since 2008', *FinGeo Working Paper No. 9*, October, Global Network on Financial Geography, Oxford University.

Wójcik, D., Knight, E., O'Neill, P. and Pažitka, V. (2017), 'Investment banking since 2008: geography of shrinkage and shift', *FinGeo Working Paper No. 3*, Global Network on Financial Geography, Oxford University.

PART I

Spatial Structures of Finance and Banking

2. The geography of International Financial Institutions: what can this tell us?

Silvia Grandi

1. INTRODUCTION

Although the size of their assets and capital flows are smaller than those of many large commercial banks, IFIs play a major role in social and economic development programs led by the state in advanced as well as emerging, transition and developing economies. In doing so they seek to catalyze other financing sources – including from the private sector, and domestic public sector revenues – to scale up resources for sustainable development (Engen and Prizzon 2018). The evolution of IFIs thus offers crucial insights on the global aspect of public finance, particularly the relationships between finance, geopolitics and macroeconomic perspectives on the geobanking and geofinance phenomena.

While a consensus on a single definition of IFIs is absent in the official and academic literature, the IFI structures discussed in this chapter are those associated with an intergovernmental cooperation model; therefore they must be established in at least two countries and be subject to international law, as is typified by a number of multilateral international organizations. Their operation entails the use of financial instruments including grants, loans, concessional loans, guarantees, lines of credit, equity, and advisory services related to policy making, funding instruments, outlooks and other studies, research, program and project development, the implementation of technical assistance, and monitoring and evaluation initiatives. These are captured in the following typologies:

1. Multilateral development banks (MDBs) are institutions that provide financing and professional advisory services for developmental purposes where actors tend to be divided in either donor countries or borrower countries.

2. Multilateral financial institutions (MFIs) are those financial institutions that have more limited memberships and often focus on financing specific types of projects or sectors.
3. Other international financial institutions (OIFIs) focus on international governance, particularly to control international, multilateral or bilateral financial flows.

Moreover, based on the Engen and Prizzon (2018) classification, global IFIs are those considered to have a wide geographical reach across several regions of the world. Examples include the World Bank Group's institutions: the International Monetary Fund (IMF) and the International Fund for Agricultural Development (IFAD). Regional IFIs' operations tend to be confined to a specific global region, albeit with some spillover to neighboring countries. This type of constraint applies to IFIs with a specific geographical focus, such as Africa, an example being the African Development Bank (AfDB), or a non-geographical focus, such as the Islamic Development Bank (IsDB), whose membership is linked to the Organisation of Islamic Cooperation (OIC). Finally, sub-regional IFIs focus on a subset of countries within a region; for example, the East African Development Bank (EADB) or the Caribbean Development Bank (CDB).

Given this framework, analyses of the geographical patterns of IFIs are on the margins of scholarship on finance. Traditional geographical factors including localization, polarization and distances to financial services, geopolitical institutions, as well as relational and managerial aspects of finance such as the composition of governing boards and the governance of the institutions, are all strategic factors that shape global finance and, by extension, macroeconomic structures. Some modelling is reported in Elson (2011), Wójcik (2013), Dixon and Monks (2014), Dixon (2017) and Parenti and Grandi (2016): this chapter draws on those analyses to examine spatial patterns in the distribution of headquarters, memberships and the investment activities of MDBs.

Such an interrogation relies on the mapping of transformations in the global financial architecture and is based on four questions:

1. What is the institutional global financial architecture?
2. What is the nature of the relationship between geopolitics and the IFI system?
3. What are the recent phenomena that may shape the IFI landscape?
4. What is the sort of spatial model that underlies the relationships among headquarter location, flows of capitals and IFI geographical reach?

Based on the above, the chapter offers an analysis which draws on the geo-elaboration of databases, policy reports and scientific literature. Additional insights are gleaned from the review of media reports, including a leading specialist trade magazine in finance and economics.

This chapter thus reveals the complex geography of IFIs, particularly in the light of the general theoretical frameworks conceptualized by the Elson model (2011) and those by Jones (2016). Building on these to incorporate IFIs and finance into the analysis, this chapter shows how power, policies, politics and finance shape places, spaces and territories, and vice versa. Disparities in the geographical distributions and flows of capitals seem to move in accordance with Wallerstein's world-systems theory (Wallerstein 1974): from the Global North to the Global South, underpinning the emergence of complex multicentered world systems, where Islamic and BRIC countries (Brazil, Russia, India and China), especially in Asia, tend to reshape geofinance and the geopolitics of IFIs.

2.   THE GLOBAL IFI ARCHITECTURE AND ITS GEOGRAPHICAL EVOLUTION

According to Elson's (2011) model, as reported in Figure 2.1, the geography of the global financial institutions is based on a reticular architecture. This network-like configuration describes a system where hubs (or nodes) are IFIs financial institutions, and edges can be grouped into two main types:

- relational (people-based), that is, occurring through direct contact or using information and telecommunication technologies; and
- spatial, when related to physical elements of the real economy (for example, transport systems, and business and productive areas) (Grandi and Parenti 2019).

In describing the global financial system, other authors focus on the analysis of financial centers (Gehrig 1998; Wójcik 2013; Yeandle 2015); Grote (2009) studies the role of face-to-face contacts and the virtualization of financial spaces; Dixon and Monk (2014) highlight frontier finance and sovereign wealth funds (Dixon 2017); and Dörry (2018) examines institutional power in the financial system. This reflects a tendency to focus on the global financial system, with limited attention paid to the geography of the IFIs. Engen and Prizzon (2018), building on an Overseas Development Institute (ODI) report (Humphrey et al. 2015), provide an interesting analysis of the MDBs, whereas Parenti and Grandi (2016) and Grandi and

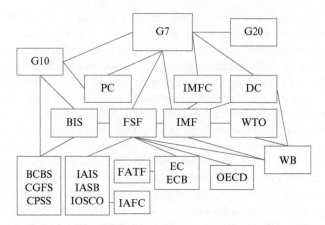

Note: BIS = Bank for International Settlements; BCBS = Basel Committee for Bank
Supervision; CGFS = Committee on the Global Financial System; CPSS = Committee
on Payment and Settlement Systems; DC = Development Committee; EC = European
Commission; ECB = European Central Bank; FATF = Financial Action Task Force; FSF
= Financial Stability Forum; G7 = Canada, France, Germany, Italy, Japan, the UK and
the US; G10 = G7 countries plus Belgium, the Netherlands, Sweden and Switzerland;
G20 = G7 countries plus Argentina, Australia, Brazil, China, the European Union, India,
Indonesia, Mexico, Russia, Saudi Arabia, South Africa, the Republic of Korea and
Turkey; IAIS = International Association of Insurance Supervisors; IASB = International
Accounting Standards Board; IFAC = International Federation of Accountants; IMF =
International Monetary Fund; IMFC = International Monetary and Financial Committee;
IOSCO = International Organization of Securities Commissions; OECD = Organisation for
Economic Co-operation and Development; PC = Paris Club; WB = World Bank; WTO =
World Trade Organization.

Source: Elson (2011), with author's revisions.

Figure 2.1   Architecture of the IFIs system according the Elson model

Parenti (2019) reviews the role of geopolitics and geofinance in the global
financial architecture in the aftermath of the 2007–09 financial crises. In
what follows, IFIs are evaluated in terms of a geo-historical perspective
that highlights the policies and political forces that shape decisions on the
spatial dimension of IFIs.

2.1   A Geohistorical Evolution of IFIs

International financial institutions have their roots in the early years of the
twentieth century when modern multilateralism found its first main expres-
sion in the League of Nations; the inception of geobanking is traced to the
founding of the Bank of the International Settlement (BIS) in 1930. The
latter may be considered the first archetype of an international financial

institution characterized by an intergovernmental cooperation model focused on financial activities and macroeconomic advisory services. The choice of Switzerland as the headquarters reflects the compromise between BIS founding countries, namely, Belgium, France, Germany, Italy, Japan, the UK and the US. Since consensus could not be reached on locating the BIS in London, Brussels or Amsterdam, the choice fell on Switzerland which was seen as a neutral state. According to the BIS historical archives (BIS 2005), the choice to localize the headquarters of the BIS in Basel was based on several reasons:

1. Centrality (Switzerland was in a central position in Europe).
2. Distribution (Geneva had already hosted the League of Nations).
3. City size (Lausanne was considered too small).
4. Geopolitical influence (Zurich was 'too German').
5. Connectivity (Basel at that time could count on excellent railway connections in all directions).

The role of the US rose significantly as Washington, DC, emerged as a key location for the Bretton Woods organizations. After World War II, the headquarters of the International Monetary Fund (IMF) and of the World Bank Group – including the International Bank for Reconstruction and Development (IBRD), the International Finance Corporation (IFC), the International Development Association (IDA), the International Centre for Settlement of Investment Disputes (ICSID) and the Multilateral Investment Guarantee Agency – were localized in Washington, DC. Moreover, in 1959, the InterAmerican Development Bank (IADB) chose the same location for its headquarters, as did as other organizations benefitting from the 'Marshallian effects' of labor (Marshall 1920, 1947) and of policy knowledge spillovers and circulation of ideas of urban centers (Boekema et al. 2001; Dixon and Monks 2014; Saxenian 1994).

Drawing on the experience of the IBRD in 1944 on the back of the Bretton Woods agreements, and recalling the general evolution of MDBs, Engen and Prizzon (2018) identify four main phases. The first corresponds to the establishment of the Bretton Woods-related IFIs and the Marshall Plan management fund and the organization – initially the Organisation for European Economic Cooperation – which became the Organisation for Economic Co-operation and Development (OECD). The second phase occurred in the late 1950s and early 1960s and is connected to the establishment of the RDBs: the IADB, the AfDB and the Asian Development Bank (AsDB). In part, this phase was a response to disappointment among developing countries at the lack of attention they received from the World Bank and, in part, because the US and other Western countries realized that IFIs were useful instruments in Cold War disputes. The third phase is associated with the establishment of sub-regional IFIs in the late 1960s and 1970s, mostly in Latin America and Africa, corresponding with the decolonization processes, the rise of the African regionalism and international cooperation for development strategies. The 1970s also saw the establishment of Arab banks from oil-producing Arab states, which gained influence from the surging flows of petrodollars. In the 1990s and early 2000s the collapse of the Soviet Union and the transition from socialist to market-driven economies marked the establishment of the fourth major regional bank, the European Bank for Reconstruction and Development (EBRD), as well as banks founded by the post-Soviet states, such as the Eurasian Development Bank (EDB) and the New Development Bank (NDB). The fifth and current phase is marked by the creation of two China-based MDBs that specialize in support for infrastructure: the Asian Infrastructure Investment Bank (AIIB), based in Beijing, and the New Development Bank (NDB), based in Shanghai. After almost a decade with no new MDBs, this reflects the growing power of the world's emerging economies, particularly China, and their discontent with the governance of traditional MDBs, which they view as imbalanced (Humphrey et al. 2015).

2.2   Localization Spatial Patterns

The centrality of Washington, DC, in the North American IFIs system connects to the agreements reached in Bretton Woods, where the leadership role of the US as *primus inter pares* was set, that is, it follows the geopolitical decisions taken in 1944. This created a shift in the financial geography of the US as well, with Wall Street in New York forming an axis with London (Wójcik 2013).

The location of IMF and World Bank Group headquarters, as well as the composition of the boards and their braches, shows the need to concentrate these IFIs close to political and policy-making centers as they represent non-profit financial institutions seeking macroeconomic objectives. International financial institutions are thus seen to follow the same localization criteria used by central banks. In a Washington-centered system, the US government inevitably can play a leading role: the proximity to the national decision-making centers and the concentration of informationally sensitive activities (Gehrig 1998) are not only symbolic but can also drive activities, management and human resources. This concentration produces a range of agglomeration economies which complement information spillovers: this is exemplified in the non-governmental organizations, service companies, developing agencies and embassies that localize their branches or build a staff presence in Washington, DC. This concentration thus makes attracting and retaining talented and specialized labor easier (Dixon and Monk 2014) as it does informal spillovers of ideas and information.

Localization policies in Europe, in contrast, tend to be distributive because they are the results of negotiations and competitions often related to the *acquis communautaire* in the decision-making processes among European nation states. Next to the role of Switzerland, strongly related to the United Nations (UN) system and the BIS, other cities host IFIs as multilateral development banks that provide financing and/or advisory services for the purpose of economic development. Examples of this include: the European Investment Bank (EIB) in Luxembourg, which is the main financial institution of the European Union; the Council of Europe Development Bank (CEB) in Paris; the EBRD, which is headquartered in London and focused on funding projects in the post-Cold War era in Central and Eastern Europe; and the Black Sea Trade and Development Bank (BSTDB), located in Thessaloniki. Other than regional or sub-regional banking, IFIs include MFIs and other financial institutions (OFIs) focused on policy and governance, as is the case for the OECD in Paris, the European Commission in Brussels, the European Central Bank in Frankfurt and the Nordic Investment Bank in Helsinki. The latter is particularly notable in the context of sovereign wealth funds (Dixon 2017) and other global – public or partially publicly owned – fund-based financial institutions, even though they do not conform to the standard IFI definition, which is also used in this book.

Similar distributive patterns may be observed in Africa and in Central and Latin America, where, political instabilities and insecurities also affect the decision-making process of creating and locating the regional and sub-regional MDBs and MFIs.

In contrast, IFIs in Asia fall into one of three main groups: those associated with Islamic and Arab influences, those shaped by post-Soviet dynamics, and those in the Asia-Pacific area. Particularly in this area, IFIs represent not only a development strategy, but also symbolize global power, a recalibration of geopolitics and the strength of emerging economies. The rise of Islamic and Arab institutions comes largely from the recent phenomenon of petrodollars which, since the 1970s, have created large pools of public and private funds. These institutions have supported the geopolitical objectives of Arab oil-producing states seeking regional and global influence. Perhaps the most recent significant evolution in the spatial and geopolitical pattern of IFIs is the establishment of the AIIB. Launched as a response to dissatisfaction with American dominance of the World Bank, and Japanese dominance of the regional IFI, that is, the

AsDB – headquartered in Manila and founded in the 1960s – the AIIB was proposed by the Chinese President, Xi, in October 2013. The AIIB has been positioned to invest China's financial surplus in infrastructure and on large-scale, cross-border trade and investment, not only in China but in the wider Asia Pacific region, which contained several countries in need of funds for building and maintaining basic infrastructure. The AIIB can be thus closely tied with the Belt and Road Initiative; the geopolitical significance of this strategy is revealed in the unease expressed by the US and the World Bank. The US reportedly attempted to discourage allies from signing up to the project, putting pressure on South Korea and Australia. United States skepticism about the newer IFIs is reflected in statements from the White House:

> The White House national security council said the US agreed there was a pressing need to enhance infrastructure investment, but had concerns about whether the AIIB would meet 'the high standards, particularly related to governance, and environmental and social safeguards' of the World Bank and regional development banks. . . . 'People have been criticising the World Bank on exactly the same issues for decades and through all of that flak there's been significant learning.' . . . 'The new multilateral organisations do have a lot to learn from the World Bank and regional development banks on the environmental and social side – but [the existing institutions] probably have quite a lot to learn from places like China in terms of how to deal with rapid infrastructure building and so on.' (Branigan 2015)

Beijing is also a major player in the NDB being set up by the BRICS nations (Brazil, Russia, India, China and South Africa) and is providing $40 billion for the new Silk Road Fund to improve connectivity across Asia.

Other than patterns of headquartering, another notable trend is in the opening and closing patterns of the regional offices of these institutions. The World Bank Group and the IMF have a wider country and regional office network across member countries. The BIS, in the past few years, opened two Representative Offices: one for Asia and the Pacific in the Hong Kong Special Administrative Region of the People's Republic of China and one for the Americas in Mexico City. This reflects the globalization of finance, particularly the diversity of players and their relative importance, especially in Asia and Latin America. Also relevant, albeit for different reasons, was the temporary relocation of the African Development Bank, from Abidjan in Ivory Coast to Tunis.

Aside from clearly geo-localized institutions, the role of OIFIs is in the form of networks where the roles of presidency and governance are based on rotation principles. These arrangements shine a light on the dynamics of the infrastructural architecture of global finance. For instance, the composition of the G7, the G10 and, later, the G20 and G77 is politically intertwined with the geography of global powers: thus the creation of centers and peripheries that were able to either catch up – as in China – or fall behind (Parenti and Grandi 2016).

3. UNEVEN FLOWS OF CAPITALS

International financial institutions are shaping the world map of finance available for states. The fluidity of this financial geography can be observed through the evolution of the numbers of IFIs, the flows of capital and their types of policy interventions, the capacity of borrowing on international capital markets at attractive rates, taking advantage of their credit rating (often AAA) and of collecting funds from donor/member countries. In particular, the most important IFIs in terms of capital involved are the MDBs and the funds related to selected UN agencies (for example, IFAD) and some funding schemes of the IMF can be included in the MFIs typology introduced at the start of the chapter.

The size of funds – both available and committed – offered each year by IFIs, especially MDBs and MFIs, varies significantly and makes comparison difficult. Given this perspective, a ranking of MDBs and MFIs according to capital may be calculated based on the annual reports of IFIs and ODI data. A set of 30 structures has been analyzed and ranked as shown in the map in Figure 2.2. In particular, it is observed that only two IFIs' – the EIB's and the World Bank Group's – financial structures rank 5, that is with assets above US$300 billion, while more than 50 percent of the MDBs are ranked less than 2, thus with total assets less than US$10 billion. This suggests that IFI financial capacity is highly concentrated, with about 90 percent of subscribed capital in only a few structures; mainly the global and the regional IFIs, that is, the EIB and World Bank Group financial structures, IMF, IADB, AsDB, AfDB, IsDB, EBRD, AIIB and NDB.

Moreover, the governance and the membership offer further geographical insights, showing the unevenness in global and regional distribution. The map in Figure 2.3 shows that the spatial distribution of the MDB coverage varies substantially by region and sub-region. In particular, OECD countries tend to be less well served, while Central Asia (including the Caucasus), and North, West and East Africa are the regions with the largest numbers of banks operating: two main cores that cannot be explained only by gross national income (GNI) data.

The number of MDBs from which a country can borrow varies from ten (that is, in Azerbaijan, Egypt and Tajikistan) to just two, whereas, on

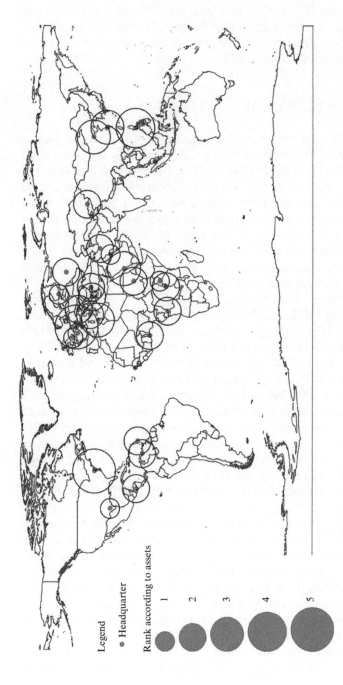

Legend

• Headquarter

Rank according to assets

1

2

3

4

5

Note: Rank 5, assets more than US$300 billion; rank 4, more than US$100 billion; rank 3, more than US$10 billion; rank 2, more than US$1 billion; rank 1, less than US$1 billion.

Source: Author's elaboration on ODI data, 2018.

Figure 2.2   Headquarters of main global, regional and sub-regional IFIs and MDBs rank according to assets

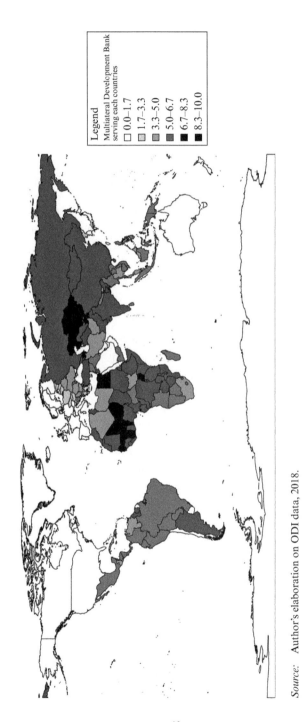

Source: Author's elaboration on ODI data, 2018.

Figure 2.3   Number of MDB coverage per country

average, each country can receive assistance from six MDBs. In general, the numbers tend to be inversely related to the wealth of the borrowing country. Thus, low-income countries are served by an average of 7.3 banks, lower-middle-income countries by 6.4 banks and upper-middle-income countries by 5.4 banks (Engen and Prizzon, 2018).

Other factors affecting the geography of IFIs include foreign policy at the state level, particularly political and regional alliances. These factors shape opportunities to become a direct member of an IFI, the level of power in the participation in decision-making boards and ability to have a significant voice in decision-making processes. These elements may explain, for instance, why states such as North Korea can borrow from only two IFIs even though economic indicators would otherwise position the Democratic People's Republic of Korea in 'other low income countries' according to the DAC List of ODA Recipients (OECD-DAC 2018). Furthermore, to explain the unevenness of borrowing from IFIs, government proficiencies and capabilities in policy planning, programming and projecting must also be taken into consideration; there is inherent, significant unevenness across countries that cannot be solved in the short term.

In general, size of the membership varies considerably, from 189 members of the World Bank – nearly universal coverage – to two in the case of the North American Development Bank (that is, the United States and Mexico). Global, regional and sub-regional membership arrangements – as outlined in the introduction to this chapter – mean that global IFIs have far larger and more geographically dispersed memberships than regional banks, which are, in turn, larger and more dispersed than sub-regional banks. According to practice, bank members are classified as regional members or non-regional members; the latter are not borrowers but donors with a strong role in boards and other decision-making processes. In this perspective, it is observed that the sub-regional African MDBs have the largest share of non-regional shareholders among their memberships, while the EADB is the only bank with a majority of non-regional shareholders in number of members but not in voting share.

Finally, another fundamental parameter to be considered relates to the financial activity performed by an IFI, assessed by considering outstanding loans, committed funds, and so on. The outstanding loans of MDBs tend to be concentrated in their respective top five borrowing countries: the data shows a strong concentration of flows of capital in few countries. To some extent, this phenomenon is expected in geographically focused and small sub-regional banks, such as the EADB, the EDB and the ETDB. However, such trends are also found in regional banks where the top five recipient countries constitute on average more than half of the outstanding loan portfolio (see Table 2.1); a similar trend is observed in the IBRD and

Table 2.1 Summary table on MDB main indicators, 2016

MDB	Largest five shareholders	Top five borrowers	Share of landing of top five borrowing countries	Headquarters city	Bank capital-size rank
IBRD	US, Japan, China, Germany, France	Indonesia, Brazil, Mexico, China, India	40%	Washington, DC	5
IDA	US, Japan, UK, Germany, France	India, Pakistan, Bangladesh, Vietnam, Nigeria	45%	Washington, DC	5
EIB	Germany, France, Italy, UK, Spain	Spain, Italy, Germany, France, Greece	65%	Luxembourg	5
IADB	US, Argentina, Brazil, Mexico, Japan	Brazil, Mexico, Argentina, Colombia, Ecuador	65%	Washington, DC	4
AsDB	Japan, US, China, India, Australia	China, India, Indonesia, Philippines, Pakistan	75%	Manila	4
AfDB	Nigeria, US, Egypt, Japan, South Africa	Morocco, Tunisia, Egypt, South Africa, Botswana	55%	Tunisia	3
IsDB	Saudi Arabia, Libya, Iran, UAE, Qatar	Turkey, Pakistan, Morocco, Iran, Indonesia	37%	Jeddah	3
EBRD	US, France, Germany, Italy, UK, Spain	Turkey, Ukraine, Russia, Kazakhstan, Poland	52%	London	3
AIIB	China, India, Russia, Germany, South Korea	Not yet active	NA	Beijing	3
NDB	Brazil, China, India, Russia, South Africa	Not yet active	NA	Shanghai	3

Note: NA = not applicable.

Source: Author's elaboration on data by Engen and Prizzon (2018), EIB (2019) and IMF annual reports.

the IDA as well, even though the share is around 40 percent. Moreover, comparing data of the largest shareholders, the top five borrowers, and the headquarters of MDB and the main MFI shows that for global or multi-regional institutions the location of the headquarters tends to be related to the first- or the second-largest shareholder. For regional and sub-regional financial institutions, the location of the headquarters is within the first three largest borrowing countries. These patterns can be explained by two overlapping reasons: in global IFIs, leadership tends to be donor driven, thus creating main shareholders' dependency unevenness, whereas in regional and sub-regional banks the proximity of the headquarters location creates significant relational and knowledge spillover that enhances awareness of the local government and other institutions of financial opportunities; thus it becomes easier to access funds, thus creating a locational renting unevenness.

4.   CONCLUSIONS

International financial institutions play a crucial role in providing finance for development – generally economic development or monetary stability – as well as in creating the global financial policies executed by states and private organizations. From a geo-historical perspective, global IFI geography could be originally depicted as two centred, in Basel and Washington, respectively (Grandi and Parenti 2019), while since the late 1960s regional and sub-regional IFIs created new patterns, leading to a multi-scalar system and multi-centrality. Next to these two cores, a set of regional IFIs has been funded as expressions of interests in, geopolitical strategies for and tentative ownership of development processes as well as in the competition to gain ascendancy in the financial geographies of power. Despite recent transformations in the global architecture of IFIs, the Elson model (Figure 2.1) has retained its relevance even as the geographical patterns of IFIs show changes in the past decade with the emergence of powerful actors such as China, Russia and the Central Asian countries (Eichengreen 1999; Kanen 2001, 2010).

Spatial analysis of the location of the headquarters of the global and regional IFIs as well as their founding phases offers substantial insights into the relationships among IFIs and the elements of political geography – namely, power, policies, politics, place, space and territory (Jones, 2016), and finance – thus advancing perspectives on geobanking and geofinance processes. Among these, two effects have been observed: main shareholders' dependency unevenness, when the leadership in the location of the headquarters is driven by the main shareholders, and locational renting unevenness, when in regional and subregional banks the proximity of the headquarters location creates significant relational and knowledge spillovers that improve awareness in local government and other institutions of financial opportunities, thus making it easier to access funds and IFI advisory services.

The growth of the IFIs – in numbers and geographical reach – indicates the widening inclusion of emerging countries and regions in the international financial institutional architecture. However, this process of expansion is still imperfect in geopolitical terms, particular because it is centered on the Bretton Woods and European Union processes; despite intentions and auspices, multicentrism is still asymmetric, uneven and unstable, thus the system remains ripe for change, but is also open to crises, inequalities, uncertainties and misalignment.

REFERENCES

Bank for International Settlements (BIS) (2005), 'This is the Bizbiz', BIS, Basel.
Boekema, F., Morgan, K., Bakkers, S. and Rutten, R. (eds) (2001), *Knowledge, Innovation and Economic Growth*, Cheltenham, UK and Northampton, MA, USA: Edward Elgar, pp. 38–56.
Branigan, T. (2015), 'Support for China-led development bank grows despite US opposition', *Guardian*, 13 March, accessed 11 July 2019 at https://www.theguardian.com/world/2015/mar/13/support-china-led-development-bank-grows-despite-us-opposition-australia-uk-new-zealand-asia.
Dixon, A. (2017), 'The state as institutional investor: unpacking the geographical political economy of sovereign wealth funds', in R. Martin and J. Pollard (eds), *Handbook on the Geography of Money and Finance*, Cheltenham, UK and Northampton, MA, USA: Edward Elgar, pp. 279–97.
Dixon, A. and Monk, A. (2014), 'Frontier finance', *Annals of the Association of American Geographers*, **104** (4), 852–68.
Dörry, S. (2018), 'Creating institutional power in financialised economies: the firm–profession nexus of advanced business services', *FinGeo Working Paper No. 12*, March, Global Network on Financial Geography, Oxford University, accessed 16 July 2019 at http://www.fingeo.net/wordpress/wp-content/uploads/2018/03/WP12_Creating-institutional-power-in-financialised-economies.pdf.
Eichengreen, B. (1999), *Toward a New International Financial Architecture. A Practical Post-Asia Agenda*, Washington, DC: Peterson Institute for International Economics Press.
Elson, A. (2011), *Governing Global Finance*, New York: Palgrave Macmillan.
Engen, L. and A. Prizzon (2018), *A Guide to Multilateral Development Banks*, London: Overseas Development Institute.
European Investment Bank (EIB) (2019), '2018 figures summary', Annual Press Conference, 29 January, Luxembourg, accessed 24 March 2019 at https://www.eib.org/attachments/general/events/apc_2019_key_data_en.pdf.
Gehrig, T. (1998), 'Cities and the geography of financial centers', CEPR Discussion Paper No. 1894, Centre for Economic Policy Research, London
Grandi, S. and Parenti, F.M. (2019), 'Does geography matter in finance? Frontiers,

polarizations, alternatives and power dynamics for financial analysis', in S. Boubaker and D.K. Nguyen (eds), *Handbook of Global Financial Markets: Transformations, Dependence, and Risk Spillovers*, Singapore: World Scientific, pp. 767–88.

Grote, M.H. (2009), 'Financial centers between centralization and virtualization', in P. Alessandrini, M. Fratianni and A. Zazzaro (eds), *The Changing Geography of Banking and Finance, Heidelberg*, Dordrecht: Springer, pp. 280–94.

Humphrey, C., Griffith-Jones, S., Xu, J., Carey, R. and Prizzon, A. (2015), *Multilateral Development Banks in the 21st Century*, London: Overseas Development Institute.

Jones, M. (2016), 'Polymorphic political geographies', *Territory, Politics, Governance*, **4** (1), 1–7.

Kanen, P.B. (2001), *The International Financial Architecture: What's New? What's Missing?* Washington, DC: Peterson Institute for International Economics Press.

Kanen, P.B. (2010), 'The substitution account as a first step toward reform of the international monetary system', Policy Brief 10-6, Peterson Institute for International Economics, Washington, DC.

Marshall, A. (1947), 'Industrial organization, continued. The concentration of specialized industries in particular localities', in A. Marshall, *Principles of Economics: An Introductory Volume*, 8th edn, London: Macmillan, pp. 267–77.

Organisation for Economic Co-operation and Development, Development Assistance Committee (OECD-DAC) (2018), DAC list of ODA recipients effective for reporting on 2018, 2019 and 2020 flows, OECD, Paris.

Parenti, F.M. and Grandi, S. (2016), 'The evolution of global finance architecture: the institutional framework', in F.M. Parenti and U. Rosati (eds), *Geofinance and Geopolitics*, Milan: Egea.

Saxenian, A.L. (1994), *Regional Advantage: Culture and Competition in Silicon Valley and Route 128*, Cambridge, MA: Harvard University Press.

Wallerstein, I. (1974), *The Modern World-System: Capitalist Agriculture and the Origins of the European World-Economy in the Sixteenth Century*, New York: Academic Press.

Wójcik, D. (2013), 'The dark side of NY–LON: Financial centres and the global financial crisis', *Urban Studies*, **50** (13), 2736–52.

Yeandle, M. (2015), 'Global Financial Center Index GFCI18', September, Z/Yen Group and Qatar Financial Center, London.

3. Shadow banking: a geographical interpretation

Gianfranco Battisti

1. INTRODUCTION

Shadow banking is a peculiar kind of business organization: a set of institutions, products and markets, closely intertwined to run credit activities partly or mainly outside the regulated banking system and to avoid regulations. Shadow banking is a core feature of contemporary financialization and manifests itself through a variety of activities carried out currently and in the past: scholars generally agree that it was operating in the 1930s (for example, Bordo and Landon-Lane 2010) and some find evidence of its existence as early as the seventeenth century (for example, Thomson and Dutta 2015). It seems that some aspects of shadow banking were established well before the institutionalization of banks as we know them. An example is a *contractumtrinius*, developed to bypass the canonical prohibition of loans during the Middle Ages.[1]

The shadow banking structure was active in the 1930s – a troubled period for global finance – but it attracted the attention of the wider public only with the outbreak of the most recent financial crisis (Kodres 2013). The first analyses of the phenomenon were made within national institutions and international bodies in the wake of the 2007–09 financial crises, thus projecting it in a negative light. Shadow banking was seen as an anomaly of the financial markets, to which it is deeply linked.

2. A PROBLEM OF DEFINITION

Charged with being an underworld sector that plunged the world into the 2007–09 financial crisis (the painful *ex post* 'discovery' of the regulators), and with appropriating the credit functions of the banks (Tett and Davies 2007), shadow banking not only reflects the transformation of the banking system but it is also entrenched in it. This is increasingly recognized by the global research community and is captured in the official stance of organizations such as the Financial Stability Board (FSB) in its monitoring reports. For instance, 'The "shadow banking system" can broadly be described as credit intermediation involving entities and activities outside the regular bank system' (FSB various, 2012 report, p. 3) and 'credit intermediation involving entities *fully or partially* outside the regular bank system' (FSB various, 2013 report, p. 1, emphasis added).

The embarrassment of regulators in tackling the subject (especially in the US, where the business reached its apex[2]) is understandable and some authorities and market participants prefer to use other terms such as market-based finance instead of shadow banking. While the use of the term shadow banking might unintentionally cast a pejorative tone on this system of credit intermediation, the FSB continues to use it as it is commonly employed and has been used in earlier G20 communications (FSB various, 2017 report, p. 1). A detailed taxonomy was published by Pozsar as early as 2008, later followed by a voluminous literature on the subject.

To identify the shadow banking (hereafter SB) system, we first need to consider the non-banking operators active in the field. Among them, the literature lists money market funds, hedge funds, private equity funds, credit investment funds, exchange-traded funds, credit hedge funds, structured investment vehicles (SIVs), special purpose entity conduits (SPEs), repurchase agreement (repo) markets, security broker dealers, credit insurance providers, securities and finance dealers.

To understand the phenomenon we also need to focus on the relationships among different actors. The template used by the FSB for data collection (FSB 2011a, p. 35) encompasses all types of financial institutions – insurance companies, investment banks, mortgage companies, and so on – and implicitly includes credit rating agencies (Hunt 2009). The latter wield immense influence on the credit market because they shape the quality of loans and debtors. All of these institutions participate in the SB system, albeit with varying levels of involvement. We may thus conclude that SB is simply a growing sector of credit intermediation carried out jointly by the regular banking system and other financial operators. Poschmann (2014, p. 16) goes even further, claiming that traditional banking 'can be regarded an integral part of the new intermediation model of shadow banking'. Also, Fein (2014, p. 13) speaks openly of 'An Integral Part of the Regulated Banking System'.

These assertions sound reasonable when comparing the financial dimension of the banking system with that historically achieved by the SB. In June 2007, just before the financial crisis erupted, market-based assets in the US were substantially larger than those held by the banks: $16.6 trillion versus $2.8 trillion. Shadow banking accounted for banks' liabilities of $22 trillion versus $14 trillion (Federal Reserve 2010). The size of SB soon contracted substantially, while total liabilities of the traditional banking

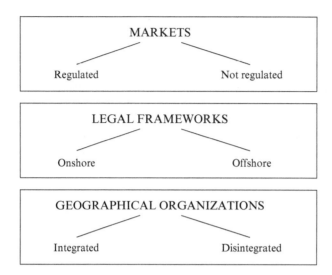

Figure 3.1, which presents three boxes labeled MARKETS (Regulated / Not regulated), LEGAL FRAMEWORKS (Onshore / Offshore), and GEOGRAPHICAL ORGANIZATIONS (Integrated / Disintegrated).

Source: Author's elaboration, 2014.

Figure 3.1   The basic spatial dichotomies

sector continued to grow throughout the crisis. In the past five years the trend has resumed in the US and globally, where the assets held by banks grew on average by 3.1 percent against 9.0 percent for the SB in its 'large measure' (see section 7 in this chapter). The investigation of SB therefore becomes an analysis of the current banking and finance system, which is formed of an array of structures carrying out new types of business.

Referring to SB implies a division or even a doubling of the credit sector within which a dichotomy has been created. Basic concepts often occur in pairs and tend to be opposites, and this can be common in the business world; see Figure 3.1. The institutional characteristics of the markets (regulated or not regulated), the legal constraints that determine their functioning according to the relevant jurisdiction (onshore or offshore) and the spatial structure of enterprises (integrated or disintegrated) represent opposing conceptions that produce different market models. This in turn gives rise to different types of economic landscapes.

3.   THE ORIGINS OF SHADOW BANKING

Far from being born covertly, behind regulators' backs, SB has been built up following their suggestions and thanks to their support (Fein 2013 [2014];

Roselli 1995, pp. 166–7). This occurred for a very good reason: to allow the system of commercial banks to survive under changed market conditions (Gorton 2010). Besides strategic errors – for instance, the Mexican loans crisis – and the consequences of the loss of competitiveness of corporate America, the banks faced a progressive erosion of their core business of financing private enterprise. The stock exchange played a crucial role among them and became the fulcrum for a generation of new financial intermediaries: investment banks, insurance companies, mutual funds, pension funds, and so on. A thorough analysis of the US credit system (Roselli 1995) reveals that, in the 1980s, national banks retreated from commercial credit to corporate America; European and Japanese institutions filled the ensuing vacuum. United States capital instead sought more profitable investments in financial markets, a sector in which industry, at home and abroad, had been struggling for at least 20 years to replace banking (Pastré 1979).

Since the economic development of America relied on an uninterrupted flow of capital from Europe, the US assumed the position of the greatest world debtor, a role it maintained up until the end of World War I. The growing role of foreign banks in the final decades of the twentieth century represented a return to the past, albeit in a very different environment. Given the pre-eminence of foreign direct investment portfolios in the hands of American firms, this might be considered an indicator of economic subordination rather than a strategic success. A considerable amount of world savings was diverted, away from productive investment in the countries where it originated, to support American businesses, thereby gaining a profit that was not considered attractive by local capitalists.[3] The latter found it more convenient to offshore their products, in order to reap the benefits of multi-nationalization. The level of profits thus accumulated was so massive that it made them autonomous, and they had no need for credit institutions.

Eventually liberated from the need to finance American enterprises, both onshore and offshore, a growing share of US capital – given corporate surpluses – approached finance, which was offering returns on investment that no other sector could guarantee. It was then only a matter of time before foreign banks followed the trend and began to speculate themselves. Indeed, in the US since the mid-1970s, deregulation and increased competition made the traditional model of banking increasingly less profitable.

4.   THE GREAT TRANSFORMATION

Shadow banking is not only the product of the financialization of the economy; it is at the core of the transformation undergone by capitalism in the final decades of the twentieth century. Through financial innovation, banks have experienced a genetic mutation. This mutation relies on five pillars: (1) retreat from financing production; (2) enlargement of the field of activity to asset management and inter-dealer brokerage; (3) splitting of the different functions developed inside the traditional banking business; (4) swift and continuous disinvestment of credits, with leveraging at all levels; and (5) a spreading out of off-balance-sheet items. These phases are analogous to the transformations undergone by corporations when they lose their original industrial or trading character to become holdings; (2) means the entry into new markets, and is related to (1), (3) and (4), which refer to the abandonment of traditional activities; (3) is also the counterpart of product-cycle disintegration, and is related to (5), namely, outsourcing of some of its phases.

All this entails conspicuous spatial fallouts. As regards the market area of credit companies, which is a typical activity considered in Christaller's (1933 [1966]) theoretical frame, phases (1), (2) and (5) bring about shifts of real activities in the physical space, at least partially. However, the deepest long-term effects are to be found in the quality of area relationships, which are disrupted and changed. The transformation from a type of bank maintaining assets on its balance sheets until their expiration, to an institution selling these assets as soon as possible, separates the economic interest of the lender from the future of the borrower, leaving the latter to his fate. This means shifting the investment perspective from long to short period, cutting the existing ties without substituting new ones. The result is an unprecedented acceleration of the creative destruction characterizing capitalism, a process that in the globalized era is no longer spatially confined.

With money being the main factor of economic development, the consequence is continuous shifts in the space of enterprises, with a destructive phase in the formerly developed areas and a swift, but ephemeral, boom in the underdeveloped areas. Such a dynamic is now active at all spatial levels, from regions to nations, continents and across the globe. What should be noted is the pace of the change affecting economic structures, which is more than the change in the distribution of wealth and economic power.

The functionalist approach interpreted the geographical space as the result of the linkages permanently established between sets of entities (Berry and Garrison 1958; Christaller 1933 [1966]; Harris 1943; Isard 1956; Juillard 1962; Loesch 1954). This seems particularly true of some activities, such as the central activities, which are molding the space around service units. In the economic space these are mainly companies, created by communities, no matter their dimension. All of them represent a decision-making center, independent of the others.

In this way the dissolution of the linkages established by firms, especially banks, triggers a process of de-structuration of geographical space the consequences of which we are currently experiencing almost everywhere in the once industrialized countries of Europe (Battisti 2014a) and North America. The most evident symptom is the scarcity of loans now plaguing the economies of countries such as Italy, which is rapidly causing the loss of the heritage of small and medium industries that made its fortune and constituted its essence.

From a historical perspective, a view of the consequences may be obtained by considering the south of Italy. Since before the unification of the state, this area has suffered from a lack of a bank network engaged in the development of local enterprises. Nowadays, the growing unavailability of capital produced locally for regional development projects everywhere moves the decisional centers farther away from the territories. The economy is estranged from local communities, which are then bound to undergo a process of neo-colonization[4] through globally raised capital.

5.   THE ECONOMIC STRUCTURE OF SHADOW BANKING

A new credit structure is replacing the waning classic commercial bank, constituted of a chain of entities, legally autonomous from each other, though in reality bound with linkages of functional interdependence. This gives birth to plenty of vehicles that in many cases are simply shell companies, like those used to transfer capital towards tax havens (Battisti 2014b).

The basic structure of this new bank model is revealed in Figure 3.2b. Central to the system are the concepts of pooling and securitization. Pools of loans, heterogeneous with respect to both origin (mortgages, student loans, advances, and so on) and originator (banks and/or finance companies) are put together and sold to a sponsor (or aggregator), usually a warehouse bank. These pools are then sold to an administrator, typically a subsidiary of a large commercial or investment bank. This creates a special purpose vehicle, namely, a company which holds the loans in its portfolio, issuing securities on this basis. The administrator sells the securities to an underwriter, generally an investment bank, which offers them to the public.

In the layout in Figure 3.2 we deliberately chose to enumerate the steps from the bottom to the top to underline that the system is more orientated to meet the demand for opportunities of financial investment than the demand for lending. In the classic model of commercial banking, in contrast (Figure 3.2a), the primary company mission is to supply money to the borrowers. As a consequence, the borrower used to become a sort

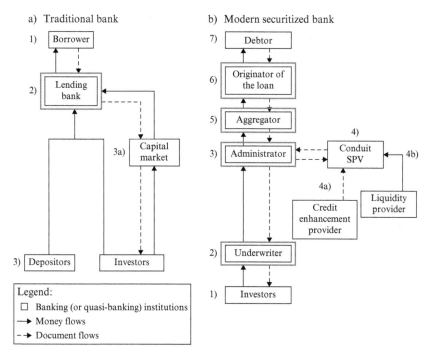

a) Traditional bank

b) Modern securitized bank

Source: Author's elaboration, 2014.

Figure 3.2   Traditional versus modern banking system

of associate of the banker, who had a direct interest in the solvency of the former. In this frame the backer (depositor, investor or the same banker with his capital) is instrumental in financing consumption/production.

In the securitized bank, the borrower remains instrumental in creating financial value for the investor only at the beginning, as it represents the connection with the real economy, but immediately afterwards the system develops from itself. Unfortunately, in the end the subprime business proved that the hole in the SB business was not a shortage of capital – which is incidental – but rather a lack of eligible borrowers: these were not abundant enough to allow the uninterrupted growth of investments.

In Figure 3.2b, four phases out of seven (2, 3, 5 and 6) are usually part of the banking system. Moreover, phases 5 and 6 may be performed inside a unique institution. However, all phases from 2 to 6 may be inside the perimeter of the same bank holding or financial firm. Even if SB is a multifaceted system, the regulated banks have deep connections with the securities business.

A comparison between the two structures, albeit an oversimplified outline, reveals a substantial lengthening of the credit chain, from three steps to seven. Considering other additional functions, such as credit enhancement and liquidity provision in Figure 3.2b and of capital market intervention in Figure 3.2a, we reach nine steps, compared with four in the previous system. From an economic point of view, this means eight more actors to be paid, compared with only two in the old system.

Over time, these additional steps gave rise to as many specialized markets: an increase in economic activity not justified by the real needs of production.[5] All the labor engaged in the system thus performs an activity useless for the bulk of the community, thus representing a parasitic sector (Lapavitas 2013). While it is true that the inherent burden is not placed directly on specific borrowers, sooner or later it will fall on the economic system as a whole, as happened with the 2007–09 financial crash. It was not merely a technical accident, it was something that had been foreseen well in advance (Lipietz 1985), and hence the crash was simply the price to be paid – at the end of the business cycle – for the anomalous growth of the system.

In light of these considerations, it is very hard to accept that SB caused an increase in banking efficiency. Also, transparency leaves much to be desired, considering the number of different subjects involved and their right to their privacy. Particularly disturbing is that the common investor is unable to know which the mind behind the games is and therefore to appreciate the level of risks he is confronted with. This might be considered of little relevance, but it is precisely the lack of confidence among financial operators that caused the catastrophic chain of insolvencies to shatter the system in 2007–09. Above all, in every kind of activity, long chains usually increase the risk of dangerous events occurring.[6]

In traditional securities transactions, the presence of multiple actors is a positive factor because it makes it possible to cumulate the guarantees offered by all underwriters. In contrast, in the particular case of SB, the risk is increased because functions are rarely developed at each step with the required level of professional skill. To this is to be added the banking nature of the activities performed by different brokers. In this field they operate outside banking regulations (unsupervised and not even monitored), but leverage may be used at all steps, thus increasing potential losses to untenable dimensions.

6.   THE NEW ORGANIZATION OF FINANCE

In a stimulating essay on financial capitalism, Gallino (2013, pp. 9–12) divides the contemporary worldwide financial system into three structural components: these are real subsystems in themselves and comprise (1) the banks, (2) shadow finance and (3) institutional investors. The last of these components, the large category of investment funds, is seen as occupying a central position between the other two. We do not share this view: in our opinion, banking, SB and institutional investors are contiguous structures having the same purpose, namely, collecting and investing community savings to make a profit. In different ways, all three perform a credit function, which means the arbitrage of financial assets in time and space.[7]

This appears evident for instance in the case of hedge funds.[8] An analysis of their activity reveals that since the beginning (Lhabitant 2006, pp. 7–9) they have been carrying out arbitrage in the financial market combining short selling with long buying, using capital from short operations to invest in long positions. If we add to this the management of client assets and leverage, we find the core of banking activity.

The key differences between the two structures are revealed in a temporal analysis of their operations and the clients they service. Shadow banking is located in the middle, linking both structures together – being part of them – and providing both with the services they require. Furthermore, Gallino himself uses the term shadow finance instead of banking, thus indicating that SB is something else, with no clear borders, instead of merely a concept parallel to that of banking.[9]

What becomes apparent then is that there is no clear divide between banking and finance, either in principle or in practice. Any differentiation may be attributed to the legislation created, on both sides of the Atlantic, following the 'great crash' of 1929. This was apparently the case for the Glass–Steagall Act, which was eventually repealed to ease the financialization of the economy; an evolution that made it impossible to maintain the separation between short- and long-term lending and borrowing as it was guaranteed, for instance, in the Italian Bank Reform of 1936.

To get to the point, we must rely on a voice from the environment where SB took its origin. Fein (2013 [2014], pp. 5–12)[10] reveals that SB is a myth, diffused by the regulators of the market to misinform public opinion, and specifically legislators, 'as to the true nature of the causes that destabilized the financial system'. Shadow banking, not called this before the emergence of the 2007–09 crisis, emerged in the regulated bank system in the 1980s and 1990s, when the traditional banking model became outmoded. It was simply part of the evolution of the business of banking and therefore was encouraged by banking regulators, so it would be misleading to call it the sick portion of banking and finance. If 'any investor investing in long-term credit products using short-term funding formed a part of the shadow banking system' (Pozsar 2008, p. 17), it must be concluded that SB is going to be the new configuration of the banking sector.

Other than the pursuit of yield, there is another reason why speculation at such a level was tolerated and encouraged. The continuous shrinking of the American productive machine has consistently reduced national income, creating the problem of how to run an economy based on mass internal consumption. It was therefore necessary to create *ex nihilo* a huge stock of means of payment to distribute in order to make the process viable.[11] This is just the function of banking. This time such a massive goal was reached by putting to work a set of entities that were not regulated and therefore not coordinated; the price paid for this was the overproduction of financial assets, technically defined as a bubble. It is worth emphasizing that by confining the price rise to real estate and financial assets, the general system, at the level of consumer prices, has been insulated from the inflation threat.

Having become accustomed to the growing role of derivatives, bankers underestimated the technical hazards of attempting to control millions of short and long positions and keep them inside markets that were specialized as well as independent. The underlying risks were enormous – emanating from procyclicality, contagion, bank run or panic, fire sales, defective credit risk transfer (CRT) – and proportionate to the profits reaped, so it is no wonder that the result is a financial system that has been globally destabilized. What determined that the crisis of the financial sector would turn out to be so catastrophic was that '(. . .) the CDO machine had become self-fueling. . . . [Financial operators] made money when the CDOs performed, but could also make money if the market crashed. These factors helped keep the mortgage market going long after house prices had begun to fall and created massive exposures on the books of large financial institutions' (Final Crisis Inquiry Commission 2011, p. 188). These practices are not unusual in the American tradition of enterprise, i.e. in a poorly regulated environment where economic activities tend to become a sort of lottery, from which, by definition, only a few come out winners. In the long run, however, the sheer dimensions of the sector[12] will make it impossible to continue separating the real economy from the virtual one.

7.   THE POST-CRISIS EVOLUTION

In the climate of the worldwide economic crisis triggered by the 2007–09 crash, Western banking and finance now face the threat of national – and supranational, as in the case of the European Union (European Commission 2014) – legislation to restrict its activity and avoid a future catastrophe. This contrasts with the interests of the industry, which is strongly opposing new regulations and bans on new financial service products. To prevent this from happening, the industry is actively lobbying in all national bodies, and trying to shift the question to a wider level, promoting new agreements within the World Trade Organization and outside it.

The first step to address this problem is data collection. In May 2010, the Federal Reserve began collecting and publishing data on part of the SB system, specifically that dealing in some types of repo lending. In 2011, the FSB conducted a global monitoring exercise to examine all non-bank credit intermediation in 11 jurisdictions.[13] The coverage was enlarged in the following years, to include 29 jurisdictions for 2016, thus totaling over 80 percent of global gross domestic product (GDP) and about 90 percent of global financial system assets. The report has been improved year by year. The effort to enlarge the statistical base and refine data has been considerable, at the same time reducing the comparability of the figures between one edition and another. Most of the statistical information now available stops at the end of 2016, but some of the data reported herein-after are referring to the 2018 edition.[14]

After the 2015 report, an economic-function approach was adopted in order to identify the activities performed by non-bank credit intermedia-tion that may pose bank-like systemic risks to the international financial system. This produced a classification of non-bank financial entities in five categories, which is currently used by the FSB.[15]

To maximize the scope and granularity of available data, at the macro level these are presented for two different samples of FSB jurisdictions. The first sample is composed of 29 individual reporting jurisdictions, while the second comprises 21 jurisdictions and the euro area (EA) as an aggregate. This means a difference in data which cannot be fully explained by its spatial coverage. The 29-group sample has a more comprehensive sector-level data granularity, while the 21+EA-group sample has a wider scope in terms of jurisdiction coverage.

In order to reduce potential problems, the data are aggregated into three main categories – monitoring universe of non-bank financial intermediation (MUNFI), other financial intermediaries (OFIs) and narrow measure – the last two being the main focus of analysis. The first category (MUNFI) is a measure of the amount of all non-bank financial intermediation, comprising insurance corporations, pension funds, OFIs and financial auxiliaries. The second category comprises the OFIs, that is, all financial institutions that are not central banks, banks, insurance corporations, pension funds, public financial institutions or financial auxiliaries;[16] a large measure of SB. The narrow measure includes non-bank financial entity types that authorities have assessed as being involved in credit intermediation that may pose financial stability risks, based on the FSB's methodology and classification guidance. At the end of 2017, the estimated size of MUNFI accounted for $184.3 trillion of estimated global financial assets of $382 trillion. The OFIs and SB in the narrow measure accounted for $116.6 trillion and $51.6 trillion respectively, the latter representing 28 percent of MUNFI and 13.7 percent of total global financial assets, an amount still significant in terms of potential risk.

This is particularly worrying as 71.2 percent of the assets in the category are represented by collective investment vehicles (CIVs) whose features make them susceptible to runs. Moreover, structured finance vehicles (SFVs) grew in 2017 for the first time since the last global financial crisis (FSB 2018, p. 5). In the period 2011–17 the dynamics of NM and MUNFI are equal (+70 percent), while a value more than double (+150 percent) is evidenced by CIVs (data processing FSB 2018, p. 9).

Between 2011 and 2016, the aggregated narrow measure increased at an average yearly growth rate of 8.8 percent, rising in relative terms from 12.1 to 13.7 percent of the total global financial assets. In 2016 total financial assets of these entities grew by 7.6 percent. Over 75 percent of their assets reside in six jurisdictions.[17] Compared with 2011, the US share declined, whereas China's and the Cayman Islands' shares increased over the same period. In 2016 the inclusion of China and Luxembourg boosted the sector by $7.0 trillion (15.5 percent) and $3.2 trillion (7.2 percent), respectively.[18]

After several years of decline, aggregate funding and credit interconnectedness between banks and OFIs at the end of 2016 were still approximately at pre-crisis (2003–06) levels. Banks' claims on OFIs amounted to $6.3 trillion at the end of 2016, while banks' funding from OFIs declined to $5.9 trillion. In some jurisdictions, however, as in the Americas, the most sizeable linkage is between OFIs and pension funds as OFIs use funding from insurance corporations and pension funds.

In most jurisdictions, banks' exposures to OFIs were below 5 percent of total bank assets, while banks' use of funding from OFIs was below 10 percent of total bank assets, with few exceptions. However, OFIs' exposure to banks 'remains large in a number of jurisdictions, at over 10% of total OFI assets in thirteen jurisdictions and over 15% of total OFI assets in seven of these jurisdictions (Belgium, Germany, Hong Kong, India, Indonesia, Italy and Russia)' (FSB various, 2017 report, p. 36).

It is important to note that in the 2018 issue the FSB report changed its title. The term 'shadow banking' has been replaced with 'nonbank financial intermediation'. Rather than emphazising 'the forward-looking of the FSB's work' (FSB 2018, p. 9), this proves, as we are supporting in this work, that the phenomenon is entirely within the official financial system, of which it accounts globally for 48.2 percent (ibid., p. 4). Clearly, at the international level it was decided to dismiss the memory of the responsibility of the banks in the crash of 2007–09.

8. CONCLUSIONS

Although this interconnectedness with banks

> may not in itself raise risks, issues could arise when banks supply short-term funding to certain investment funds or leveraged non-bank financial institutions, a potential abrupt withdrawal of such funding could, under some circumstances, precipitate funds' asset sales and contagion, and raise going-concern challenges at more leveraged institutions with acute maturity mismatches. (FSB various, 2017 report, p. 39)

As the International Monetary Fund economist Tobias Adrian noted at a Société Universitaire Européenne de Recherches Financières (SUERF)/Bank of Finland conference in 2017, although 'certain areas of reform remain outstanding', since 2007 'many of the types of activities that amplified the impact of the global financial crisis no longer pose an existential threat to financial stability' (Adrian 2018, p. 33).[19] 'Reform efforts have aimed at transforming the structural characteristics of riskier aspects of shadow banking, as well as the economic incentives. The business models of intermediaries have fundamentally changed as a result' (Adrian 2018, p. 33). Alternatively, the world of finance is a sort of living organism in continuous evolution, where new potential problems are constantly emerging, as Adrian himself points out.[20] Similarly, the need to always create new means of payment through finance remains a vital factor for the system, and from the US it has been generalized to the whole world.

This brings us back to the basic question. If SB has swollen excessively, has this occurred to compensate for the insufficiencies of production? Finance, we must never forget, having assumed a paramount role in the current world, still remains instrumental to all the other sectors of activity, and in the end it is from the real economy that the greatest risks now seem to emanate.[21] Finance and the real economy must be evaluated together, taking into account their mutual relationships. To conclude, as far as the validity of the reforms carried out and the measures undertaken to respond to emergencies are concerned, the answer cannot be found without proof of the facts, and that will only happen when global finance faces the next big crisis, whatever its origin.

NOTES

1. Under this theorization, the commercial loan was interpreted as incorporating three different contracts: a commercial partnership, insurance on the investment and a second insurance covering the profit expected from the business (James, 1959).
2. Two economists of the Federal Reserve for instance insisted on crediting SB with an increase in efficiency and even in transparency and disclosure (Noeth and Sengupta 2011, p. 13), an opinion also in the European Commission (2012) Green Paper.
3. An analysis of the Comptroller of the Currency revealed that foreign banks in the US have always had lower profits than have local banks (Nolle 1994, quoted in Roselli 1995, p. 185).
4. The term neocolonialism was initially coined with reference to the Third World's underdeveloped countries (Nkrumah 1965), but the worldwide reorganization of economy (Thrift and Leyshon 1994) enables us to generalize the concept to all scales (Biagini 2006), and to include internal colonization (Hechter 1975).
5. All this is functional for an economy centered on consuming and no longer on production, which is currently the case of the US.
6. The FSB staff focused on several dangerous segments in some of the markets involved, that is, those of security lending, leveraged investment fund, financing and security borrowing, inter-dealer repo, and repo financing (FSB 2012).
7. American economists refer to maturity transformation, quality transformation and credit risk transfer.
8. According to Gallino, they belong to the category of institutional investors. From our analysis, however, they should be considered part of the SB system (see section 2 in this chapter).
9. The language of business, especially that of finance, is generally cryptic, and this is very useful to confuse clients and treasury officials. It is made of stock phrases and words, perfectly integrated into the English language, which is perhaps not always accurate enough.
10. Melanie L. Fein is a former senior counsel to the Board of Governors of the Federal Reserve System.
11. 'Bubbling house prices were thus indispensable for driving the economy, as they were essential in making possible the increase in household borrowing that enabled the consumption and residential investment that together accounted for 98 percent of the growth of GDP that took place during the length of the business cycle' (Brenner 2009, p. 70).
12. The analysis made after the crash shows how the real dimension of the bubble was unknown to most operators. Estimates vary depending on the type of activities considered, and increase every time new phases of the process are taken into consideration. Including re-hypothecation, an International Monetary Fund staff investigation for the US revealed an amount of assets 'larger than documented', estimated at more than $10 trillion in November 2007 (Singh and Aitken 2010, p. 9). A further IMF document (Pozsar and Singh 2011) cites $27 trillion at the end of 2007, reduced to $18 trillion at the end of 2010. However, the 'American sickness', as in re-pledged collaterals, was equally shared with European banks (Pozsar and Singh 2011, p. 11). An estimate for the phenomenon at world scale for the period 2003–12 provides these figures: $26 trillion in 2002, $62 trillion in 2007 and $67 trillion in 2010 (FSB various, 2012 report, p. 3). Taking for granted that SB is a set of businesses concerning the entire banking system, a further estimate, probably in excess, based on peculiar mathematical models, peaks at more than $101 trillion in 2003 and $61 trillion in 2012 (Fiaschi et al. 2013). The FSB focuses on the historical trends mainly since 2011, owing to the data gaps in the preceding years.
13. Alternatively this tentative monitoring concerned six jurisdictions and the available data on the entire euro area. On this basis the FSB sets out its initial recommendations to enhance the oversight and regulation of the SB system in its report to the G20 in October 2011 (FSB 2011b).

14. For a review of the statistics on the size of the securitization market and its riskiness, see Nuzzo (2018).
15. Fixed income funds, mixed funds, credit hedge funds and real estate funds; finance companies, leasing companies, factoring companies and consumer credit companies; broker-dealers; credit insurance companies, financial guarantors and monolines; and securitization vehicles. The list represents only an exemplification of possible entity types.
16. Other financial intermediaries also include captive financial institutions and money lenders.
17. In the alternative classification, the US is confirmed in its dominant position (with 31 percent of the total), followed by the euro area (22 percent), China (16 percent), the Cayman Islands (10 percent) and Japan (6 percent). While assessing the position of the US we should bear in mind the role performed by tax havens (the FSB refers to these as 'jurisdictions that serve as hubs for international capital flows'; FSB various, 2016 report, p. 49).
18. Data from China and Luxembourg are included in the narrow measure in the 2017 monitoring for the first time, and this makes comparisons over time less significant.
19. 'To cite just a few areas, securitization practices have been strengthened, repo market activities have been overhauled, money market funds have been made more robust, and interconnectedness between banks and shadow banks has declined' (Adrian 2018, p. 33).
20. See also de Vries van-Ewjik (2018).
21. 'Near-term risks to global financial stability – assessed using the growth-at-risk (GaR) approach – have increased somewhat over the past six months. . . . Medium-term risks to global financial stability and growth remain elevated. A number of vulnerabilities that have built up over the years could be exposed by a sudden, sharp tightening of financial conditions. . . . Total nonfinancial sector debt in jurisdictions with systemically important financial sectors has grown from $113 trillion (more than 200 percent of their combined GDP) in 2008 to $167 trillion (close to 250 percent of their combined GDP)' (GFSR 2018, p. ix).

REFERENCES

Adrian, T. (2018), 'Shadow banking and market-based finance', in E. Jokivuolle (ed.), *Shadow Banking: Financial Intermediation beyond Banks*, Proceedings of the SUERF/Bank of Finland Conference, Helsinki, 14–15 September 2017, Vienna: Larcier, pp. 14–37.

Battisti, G. (2014a), 'Geopolitical dislocation as a product of the financialisation of economy: lessons from Europe', in M.G. Lucia and L.M. Rizzo (eds), *A Geographical Approach to the European Financial Crisis: Challenges and Policy Agenda*, Rome: Aracne, pp. 73–84.

Battisti, G. (2014b), 'Offshoring and financial markets', *Economy of Region*, **2**, 150–60.

Berry, B.J.L. and Garrison, W.L. (1958), 'The functional basis of the central place hierarchy', *Economic Geography*, **34** (2), 145–54.

Biagini, E. (2006), *Rule Britannia. The Wielding of Global Power*, Halle: Projekte-Verlag.

Bordo, M. and Landon-Lane, J. (2010), 'The banking panics in the United States in the 1930s: some lessons for today', *Oxford Review of Economic Policy*, **26** (3), 486–509.

Brenner, R. (2009), 'What is good for Goldman Sachs is good for America: the origins of the current crisis', April, Center for Social Theory and Comparative

62   *Geofinance between political and financial geographies*

History, University of California Los Angeles, accessed 24 July 2019 at https://escholarship.org/uc/item/0sg0782h.

Christaller, W. (1933), *Die zentralen Orte in Süddeutschland: eine ökonomisch-geographische Untersuchung über die Gesetzmässigkeit der Verbreitung und Entwicklung der Siedlungen mit städtischen Funktionen* (*The Central Places in Southern Germany: An Economic-Geographical Study on the Regularity of the Distribution and Development of Settlements with Urban Functions*), Jena: G. Fischer; English trans. C.W. Baskin, 1966, *Central Places in Southern Germany*, Englewood Cliffs, NJ: Prentice-Hall.

De Vries van Ewjik, S. (2018), 'Looking ahead: forthcoming financial innovations and institutions – opportunities and risks from a financial stability perspective', in E. Jokivuolle (ed.), *Shadow Banking: Financial Intermediation beyond Banks*, Proceedings of the SUERF/Bank of Finland Conference, Helsinki, 14–15 September 2017, Vienna: Larcier, pp. 73–6.

European Commission (2012), *Green Paper Shadow Banking*, Brussels, 19 March, COM (2012) 102.

European Commission (2014), *Proposal for a Regulation of the European Parliament and of the Commission on Reporting and Transparency of Securities Financing Transactions*, Brussels, 2014/0017 (COD).

Federal Reserve (2010), 'Shadow banking', Staff Report No. 458, July, Federal Reserve, New York, p. 8, accessed 7 August 2019 at https://www.newyorkfed.org/medialibrary/media/research/staff_reports/sr458.pdf.

Fein, M.L. (2013), 'The shadow banking charade', 16 February, revd 24 April 2014, accessed 20 February 2018 at http//ssrn.com/abstract=2218812.

Fiaschi, D., Kondor, I. and Marsili, M. (2013), 'The uninterrupted power law and the rise of shadow banking', Discussion Paper No. 166, University of Pisa.

Financial Crisis Inquiry Commission (2011), *The Final Crisis Inquiry Report: Final Report of the National Commission on the Causes of the Financial and Economic Crisis in the United States*, Washington, DC: US Government Printing Office.

Financial Stability Board (FSB) (2011a), 'Shadow banking: scoping the issues: a background note of the Financial Stability Board', 12 April, Basel.

Financial Stability Board (FSB) (2011b), 'Shadow banking: strengthening oversight and regulation recommendations of the Financial Stability Board', 27 October, Basel.

Financial Stability Board (FSB) (2012), 'Strengthening the oversight and regulation of shadow banking', Progress report to G20 ministers and governors, 14 April, Basel.

Financial Stability Board (FSB) (various), 'Global shadow banking monitoring report', for each year 2011–17, FSB, Basel.

Financial Stability Board (FSB) (2019), 'Global monitoring report on Non-Bank Financial Intermediation 2018', FSB, Basel.

Gallino, L. (2013), *Finanzcapitalismo: La civiltà del denaro in crisi* (*Financial Capitalism: The Civilisation of Money in Crisis*), 2nd edn, Turin: Einaudi.

Global Financial Stability Report (2018), 'A decade after the global financial crisis: are we safer?', October, International Monetary Fund, Washington, DC.

Gorton, G.B. (2010), *Slapped by the Invisible Hand: The Panic of 2007*, Oxford: Oxford University Press.

Harris, C.D. (1943), 'A functional classification of cities in the United States', *Geographical Review*, **33** (January), 85–99.

Hechter, M. (1975), *Internal Colonisation: The Celtic Fringe in British National Development*, Berkeley, CA: University of California Press.

Hunt, J.P. (2009), 'Credit rating agencies and the "worldwide credit crisis": the limits of regulations, the insufficiency of reform, and the proposal for improvement', *Columbia Business Review*, **1** (April), 1–74.

Isard, W. (1956), *Location and Space-Economy: A General Theory Relating to Industrial Location, Market Areas, Land Use, Trade, and Urban Structure*, Cambridge, MA: Wiley.

James, E. (1959), *Histoire sommaire de la pensée économique*, Paris: Editions Montchrestien.

Juillard, E. (1962), 'La région: essai de définition', *Annales de géographie*, **71** (387), 483–99.

Kodres, L.E. (2013), 'What is shadow banking?', *Finance & Development*, **50** (2), 42–3.

Lapavitas, C. (2013), *Profiting Without Producing: How Finance Exploit Us All*, London and New York: Verso.

Lhabitant, F.-S. (2006), *Handbook of Hedge Funds*, Chichester: Wiley.

Lipietz, A. (1985), *The Enchanted World: Inflation, Credit and the World Crisis*, London and New York: Verso.

Loesch, A. (1954), *The Economics of Location*, New Haven, CT: Yale University Press.

Nkrumah, K. (1965), *Neo-Colonialism, the Last Stage of Imperialism*, London: Thomas Nelson & Sons.

Noeth, B.J. and Sengupta R. (2011), 'Is shadow banking really banking?', *Regional Economist*, October, 8–13.

Nolle, D. (1994), 'Are foreign banks out-competing U.S. banks in the U.S. markets?', Economic and Policy Analysis Working Paper 94-5, Comptroller of the Currency, Washington, DC.

Nuzzo, G. (2018), 'A critical review of the statistics on the size and riskiness of securitization market: evidence from Italy and other euro-area countries', in E. Jokivuolle (ed.), *Shadow Banking: Financial Intermediation beyond Banks*, Proceedings of the SUERF/Bank of Finland Conference, Helsinki, 14–15 September 2017, Vienna: Larcier, pp. 92–7.

Pastré, O. (1979), *La strategie internationale des groupes financiers americains (The International Strategy of American Financial Groups)*, Paris: Economica.

Poschmann, J. (2014), 'The shadow banking system – an analysis of FSB proposed regulation on money market funds in respect to financial stability', PhD dissertation, Friedrich-Schiller-University, Jena.

Pozsar, Z. (2008), The rise and fall of the shadow banking system', *Regional Financial Review*, July, 13–25.

Pozsar, Z. and Singh, M. (2011), 'The non-bank nexus and the shadow banking system', IMF Working Paper WP/11/289, International Monetary Fund, Washington, DC.

Roselli, A. (1995), *La finanza americana tra gli anni Ottanta e Novanta. Instabilità e risorse* (American Finance between Eighties and Nineties. Instability and Resources), Milan: Cariplo.

Singh, M. and Aitken, J. (2010), 'The (sizable) role of rehypotecation in the shadow banking system', IMF Working Paper WP/10/72, International Monetary Fund, Washington, DC.

Tett, G. and Davies, P.I. (2007), 'Out of the shadows: how banking's secret system broke down', *Financial Times*, 16 December, accessed 7 July 2019 at https://www.ft.com/content/42827c50-abfd-11dc-82f0-0000779fd2ac.

Thomson, F. and Dutta, S. (2015), *Financialisation: A Primer*, Amsterdam: Transnational Institute.

Thrift, N. and Leyshon, A. (1994), 'A phantom state? The de-traditionalization of money, the international financial system and international financial centres', *Political Geography*, **13** (4), 299–327.

4. Spatial development and offshore financial chains

Umberto Rosati

1. INTRODUCTION

This chapter explores perspectives on financial centres in classical models of the urban concentration of banks, stock markets, insurance and financial companies: two different economic forces – centrifugal and centripetal – are seen to operate within the financial space to define the spatial structure of the financial economy. This analysis emphasizes offshoring, seen here as located in the semi-periphery; this practice plays a core role in shaping spaces, territories and local–global–local finance. Thus, offshore banking creates peculiar local systems where offshore sites are located in clusters where this form of finance is widespread.

Agnew and Corbridge's (1995) theorization of how space is mastered outside the frame of the nation state is based on the changing relationships among political geographies, geopolitical orders and the international political economy. Michiel van Meeteren (2018) notes that this framework, which describes the operationalization of the thick space conception, relies on Lefebvre's (1974 [1991]) categories of 'spatial practices', 'representations of space' and 'representational spaces' (Figure 4.1). Lefebvre's framework posits continuous interplay between how spatial practices – material spaces, circuits and flows (see Hudson 2004) – are spun over the face of the earth, representations of space through which we interpret and name these practices and representational spaces that imagine future geographies (van Meeteren 2018).

These concepts underpin the practices of spatial development and global economic integration of financial centres. A financial centre is a specific area in the centre of the city with a concentration of banks, stock markets, insurance and financial companies, linked to a high employment level in this branch (Labasse 1974). The role of a financial centre as a supranational system, able to move, control and manage the world's economic system, is captured in the geographical concept of the selective agglomeration of the functions connected to both structural and dynamic

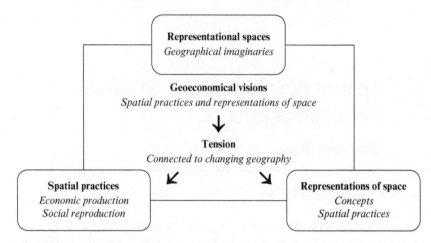

Figure 4.1   Mastering space

elements. Within this model, an international spatial hierarchical structure on an urban scale is defined.

The remainder of this chapter proceeds as follows: section 2 surveys the scholarship on localization to present a context for the economic forces – centrifugal and centripetal – that shape the geography of the financial economy. Section 3 introduces the concept and the typologies of financial clusters. Section 4 discusses the historical and spatial features of offshore financial clusters. Section 5 builds on this by drawing attention to the geographical factors in the development of offshore finance. Section 6 links this analysis to local financial systems, given that these are the entry point for international money flows.

2.   LOCALIZATION AND THE GEOGRAPHY OF THE FINANCIAL ECONOMY

Among the discrete factors of localization, connected to the choice of the physical locations to place financial assets, is the availability of human resource expertise in the financial system to optimize potential gains. Other key roles assumed by the financial institutions and players involve the processing of new financial innovations and strategic projects (Onado 1992). However, there are quantitative indications linked to the dynamics of concentration that evidence how most of the important international banks and financial companies – almost 40 and 20 per cent, respectively – are concentrated between London, New York and Tokyo. The options of localization are extended through the development of high technology, and condition the choice to form specialized districts within the financial industry.

A financial city is defined as a development centre in as much as there is a concentration of high-level financial enterprises, services and institutions. An urban district is a hub able to attract other companies, enterprises and services, that is, law firms that specialize in auditing and information technology (IT) and so on, as well as other economic branches that guarantee the efficiency of the financial district and provide jobs. The city becomes a development hub for a territory connected to a large space that overcomes the urban district boundaries. It is a specific trend that, on the one hand, is able to attract business companies and specialized workers from the surrounding areas, and, on the other, is able to outsource retail and back-office companies within the area of influence, defining a regional development.

The analysis of these topics is also connected to Paul Krugman's work on agglomeration (Krugman 1991) which observes that there are three different layers that allow for the rise of the agglomeration processes of business companies and services: (1) the job market, (2) the demand for intermediate services and (3) the technological spillover within a specific area. A favourable job market for financial branches reflects the presence of specialized professionals that advance the agglomeration process of business companies able to attract financial experts.

A key role is played by the intermediate services, that is, specialized legal services, auditing and accounting services, and efficient transport systems. These service providers share a symbiotic relationship with financial agglomeration processes since not only do companies benefit from service providers, but service providers also develop by engaging with companies from different sectors. Social, institutional and cultural factors, linked to the relationship chains between participants, rules of behaviour, reputation, reliability and binding legislation play an important role here: these factors encompass taxation, freedom of transaction and capital movement, and have the capacity to define strategies and policies that maintain the territory, that is, the embeddedness of a city's position as a financial centre.

Technological spillovers are connected to informational spillovers within the financial centre given the importance of being the first to access and exchange information at a low cost. Financial agglomeration dynamics are based on the economic strategy known as selective centralization. If a financial centre has these features, it can take on a central position within the world economic chain. Two different economic forces operate within a financial space, and they define the geographic space structure connected to the financial economy: the forces are, respectively, centrifugal and centripetal (Gehrig 2000). When centrifugal force prevails, there is a rise in the development of agglomerations within only a few cities connected to the financial command: these then have a high level of embeddedness and assume a leading role.

3.   FINANCIAL CLUSTERS AND CENTRES

A financial centre evolves with different economic phases: from a local hub to a regional hub and then an international hub as evolutionary periods change (Kindleberger 1974). Dufey and Giddy (1978) identify three types of territories connected to local financial services providers and their development status. The first links to the credit function carried out by the bank systems and the issuance of securities, as well as the lending market, subscription and placement of shares onto the financial market (Dufey and Giddy 1978). The second category is the financial market that links to institutional services, that is, monetary and stock markets which target both domestic and foreign residents. However, the capital-exporting centres are excluded from the last category. The third typology is linked to the offshore centres that have intermediate services linked to foreign users' deposits and loans, even if this service can occasionally involve domestic residents. In the latter case, there is a rule system able to divide the domestic finance and the offshore sectors. International functions are sometimes linked to the export of capital, such as the transfer of national surplus savings. International ratings are connected to the role of the financial centre's money interchange. Some studies show how the primary importance of acquiring offshore functions is to raise ratings towards a supranational market providing services exclusively for foreign clients. These services are excluded from the fiscal and legal constraints of monetary controls.

Based on functional and geographical analysis, Yoon S. Park (1982) observes that new types of financial centres develop in conjunction with the traditional centres. This approach identifies four typologies connected to the evaluation of the capital origins and destinations, as well as transaction volume and financial activity. London and New York are primary centres, that is, territorial districts with financial funds and resources that are used all over the world. Moreover, there are the booking centres where deposits and loans are registered as eurocurrency, for example, the Bahamas and the Cayman Islands. The role of funding centres is linked to the national financial brokerage, making use of offshore funds for local investments, for example, Singapore and Panama. Collecting centres provide financial services such as outward financial intermediation directing the domestic funds the funds somewhere else, for example, Bahrain.

These analyses are used to identify other typologies, that is, primary centres that operate within the industrial space, meeting both demand and supply of capital, financing centres that have the role of financial intermediaries within the national environment, and transit centres that are similar to offshore centres covering the role of the financial districts for non-residents (Park and Essayad 1989). For instance, Jao (2003) examines the financial situation in China, showing the area of influence and the historical evolution of the financial centres. Thus, sub-national centres connect to spaces that handle the brokerage of capitals for local companies within the financial centres or those nearby, for instance, Shenzhen in southern China. A financial centre can raise its profile beyond national borders to larger areas of the world, as London and New York have done, only if its decisions and strategies exert wider political and economic influence.

4. OFFSHORE FINANCIAL CLUSTERS

The term offshore is linked to markets and branches of the financial service industry that differ from each other. This English word implies a possibility to operate within a different legal system than that of the financial player's country of origin (Moore 1992). The term offshore refers to territories where there is non-binding legislation for the financial sector: thus, the geographical variable becomes a financial variable. The concept of a city state is relevant here because it describes spaces that are devoid of political borders, and their financial chains freely connect with international flows of capital. Offshore territories have these same privileges, which may be likened to the model of international free zones.

The creation of offshore centres has led to specialization in the local economy in financial services so that profits from this sector account for the largest share of national income (Zoromè 2007). These strategies are based on the spatial development of the financial economy. An offshore space is a social construction founded on the transactions of external players that have activated relationships with their respective national governments, local institutions and investors (Hudson, 1998). These spatial typologies are built on a specific relationship chain: their economic and political stability connects to the dynamics of relationships and the global context of these relationships (Massey 1993). Consensus and trust are connected to the reputation and professionalism of the local financial institutions.

The tacit aspect of the legal system is another factor linked to the development and improvement of the local economy. The territories that have the potential to become offshore spaces have a system of free movement of people, goods, capital and financial information; therefore non-binding legal and institutional systems can create less expensive market initiatives precluded elsewhere.

Because the regulatory system is linked to the financial sector, it has special importance and is relied upon up for institutions and other financial players. Offshore centres can offer more profitable services, security and anonymity compared with other financial systems (Hudson 1998). Offshore centres also have other specific characteristics, for example, historical events connected to the economic and political dynamics and international relationships. Thus, the failure of the Bretton Woods institutions, the rise of the Euromarkets, the increase in the price of energy and the internationalization of the economy have all shaped the geography of these financial centres.

> The term offshore finance is often used interchangeably with tax haven. This is clearly wrong, since what attracts financial activity offshore is much more than low or no taxation and includes laws, regulations, transparency/opacity, and other institutions and characteristics present in offshore jurisdictions [Figure 4.2]. In addition to equating offshore finance with international finance, this definition also puts pressure on small economies as offshore financial centres. Research that focuses on moving certain parts of the value chain, typically back-office operations, of financial and other services companies, refers to the phenomenon as financial and services offshoring. Thus, effectively, it also equates offshoring with internationalization, adding to the confusion around the term offshore finance. (Gordon et al. 2015, p. 241)

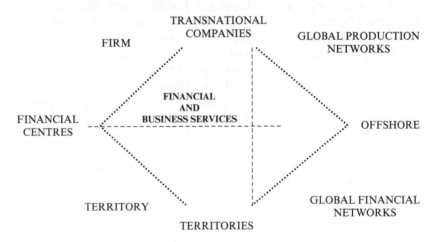

Figure 4.2   Offshore jurisdictions in the global economy

From a historical perspective, the offshore phenomenon developed in the 1970s, however, the first tax havens started between 1920 and 1930, when some states, such as the Channel Islands, which are Crown dependencies, and Panama and the Bahamas, were used to hide capital and to set up holding companies (Belchem 2000). Another historical example related to the root of the offshore activities was the establishment of the flag of convenience. The USA had the institution of US Board of Shipping, which encouraged US shipowners to register their vessels under the flag of Panama to reduce costs, as long as they agreed to put their vessels at the disposal of the USA in case of war (Carlisle 1981). A compromise was thus made between tax evasion and the avoidance of other rules and regulations linked to the security sector and labour law (Murphy 2004).

However, there are other factors connected to the birth of the offshore systems, that is, the influence exercised by the big banks and transnational corporations (TNCs),[1] particularly by US banks, which looked for non-binding economic and financial systems to produce larger profit margins. The removal of the fixed exchange rate connected to the dollar and the collapse of the Bretton Woods system allowed the introduction of monetary policies to control the national financial system and to compete at an international level. Thus, because the US Federal Reserve (the Fed) policy stipulates low interest rates for domestic banks, the credit institutes pushed for the setting up of offices in foreign countries where the legal systems were not binding. Indeed, the TNC offices take advantage of more favourable economic and financial systems, leading to bank agglomerations and the development of the offshore financial centres.

The foundations of the Euromarket system were the creation of a monetary union and a European Central Bank (ECB): these institutions facilitated the creation of offshore spaces. London is not only one of the biggest financial centres in the world; its stock market can exchange US currencies under a less binding legal system than the system in the USA. In this way, London can strengthen its international role operating as an offshore centre, and it makes financial transactions in dollars with strong security and high profit margins.

Another factor in offshoring is connected to the deposits of petrodollars from the Organization of the Petroleum Exporting Countries (OPEC) countries, which thus benefit from rising fossil fuel costs (Gennilard 1970). London has allowed non-residents to deposit money that is not governed by rigid exchange controls and bank reserve norms. The example of London reflects how difficult it is to separate the concept of offshore from onshore, because very often there are numerous different financial operations made within the same financial market.

Numerous geographical features are associated with offshore financial centres: for instance, accessibility and a time zone that can allow investors to choose where to establish their financial agglomerations. Financial centres also need the most innovative and technological infrastructures, such as transport networks, telecommunications and regulatory systems that favour non-resident investors. The offshore financial centre becomes a space for financial innovation.

5.   THE GEOGRAPHY OF OFFSHORE FINANCE

Multiple parameters may be used to define an offshore financial centre, and they are linked to categories that vary greatly and depend on the financial market in question. For example, the Cayman Islands hosts 500 banks based all over the world, but only a few of these banks can offer deposits and loans services (Roberts 1995).

Several geographical factors have a role in the setup of offshore financial centres. An analysis of geographical distributions shows how they are positioned near the biggest financial markets in the world. Another factor is time zones which allow for the continuity of financial transactions during the day. Thus concentrations of offshore financial centres occur in specific areas with different clusters connected to the most important financial markets. These clusters offer a variety of financial services and seek to meet the demands of the most influential and wealthy investors. Each financial cluster specializes in a different financial sector: financial chains thus have a complex structure as they become spaces linked to the financial industry with services connected to a specific economic region with its area of influence (Johns and Le Marchant 1993).

Analyses have focused on different financial offshore areas. One analysis is that of Risto Laulajainen (2003), which discusses financial management in the Cayman Islands, the Bahamas and the British Virgin Islands. These islands do not adopt the classic management of a financial cluster that is identified by the setting-up of companies with the same functions in a situation of interdependence and cooperation. Likewise, the centres within the British Channel Islands cannot represent a cluster as none of them are in such a leadership position to create a hub role with the respective satellite centres that are privileged spaces able to make links with the onshore financial centres (Laulajainen 2003). It must be noted that there are no inter-relationships between offshore financial centres, but there are connections between offshore financial centres and the financial centres that conditioned their setup (Figure 4.3) (Parenti and Rosati 2018).

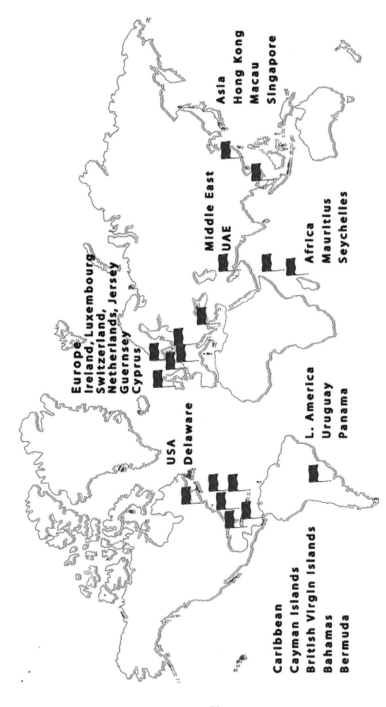

Figure 4.3   Offshore funds, top 20 players

Another factor linked to financial offshore centre agglomeration is the proximity of these spaces to the companies and institutions that have decided to localize their businesses in the offshore system, while the management remains in the country of origin. The proximity of these two environments – investors and the financial offshore centre managers – is linked to a greater frequency of contacts between them. There are some exceptions: the Cayman Islands and the British Virgin Islands, despite their geographic distance, are able to attract capital from Asian countries (Laulajainen 2003). Therefore it may be assumed that the agglomeration dynamics linked to the offshore financial system are also connected to specialization and not just distance.

Location analysis reveals that many offshore financial centres share a common past under the political influence of the UK. British common law influences all the territories that were included in the British Empire and are now dominions or Commonwealth members. This is the case for the Caribbean where important agglomerations of offshore financial centres can be found (Bardouille 2001). For instance, in Anguilla, although the local authorities have administrative powers and political responsibilities, the controls of offshore activities remain in the UK. Antigua and Barbuda are financial centres that comply with international standards, even though their treaty with the USA indicates the creation of information flows and a legal system for more transparency. The Organisation for Economic Co-operation and Development (OECD) rebuked Belize for its recycling activities. Bermuda, the British Virgin Islands, the Greater Antilles and the Lesser Antilles, the Virgin Islands and Barbados are all territories with connections to the USA, and are thus associated with political stability.

The Cayman Islands and Bermuda are the most popular centres linked to the USA's financial system: this is because of the agglomeration dynamics (Figure 4.4) of financial offshore centres which are based particularly on taxation levels, banking secrecy practices and political stability. The Dutch political landscape directly shapes the Netherlands Antilles: Aruba has obtained independence from the Netherlands and, while the other three islands have administrative autonomy, they delegate powers to the Netherlands' government. Their history as offshore financial centres dates back to the Second World War and is linked to the needs of multinational companies such as Philips and Shell.

There are also offshore financial centres in other geographical areas of the world: these later disseminated rules linked to the international regulations that drew attention to financial crimes such as money laundering (Laulajainen 2003). Landlocked states with limited resources for economic development adopted legal systems to create attractive financial settings, particularly by facilitating tax exemption for offshore finance.

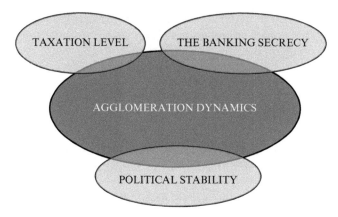

Figure 4.4   Relationships between agglomeration dynamics and some economic, financial and political factors

The Republic of Mauritius is one example of this; it became a gateway for capital coming from China, India, Europe and South Africa. Indian capital benefited from an agreement, signed in 1981, that carries fiscal advantages from investment in Mauritius. China also signed a similar agreement in 1995. The Cook Islands obtained independence from New Zealand in the 1980s and thus have a more recent origin as a financial centre. The many features of the Cook Islands include physical accessibility through air traffic networks, fiscal laws, financial expertise, political stability and a legal framework that allows for companies to be listed on Hong Kong's stock exchange. The Marshall Islands, the Solomon Islands and Tonga, Samoa and Nauru, and Niue and Vanuatu have also adopted norms to facilitate the setting up of offshore financial companies. These territories also seek to adopt international rules to improve the transparency of their legal systems and the exchange of information.

The above analysis highlights that there is a connection between the context of offshore spaces, their legal frameworks – namely, common law versus civil law – their political histories, and their economic and political structures. Particularly important is the emphasis large financial companies place on the advantages of less binding norms. Numerous financial centres specialize in various aspects of financial laws and banking norms. The establishment of financial services and infrastructure within a specific territory thus arises from the political and strategic decisions taken in the largest onshore centres (Cobb 1998).

While it is difficult to define a precise hierarchy for offshore financial centres, it is important nevertheless to emphasize that several of them are international hubs which form part of a global network of capital and are connected to the international financial chain (Roberts 1995). Competition among offshore financial centres is on both an international and a regional level, depending on their financial functions.

6. OFFSHORE FINANCIAL FLOWS AND DEVELOPMENT

After the analysis reported on the global offshore financial system in the previous section, it is important also to investigate local financial networks. These are where international capital flows land, and they underscore the relationships between financial flows and regional development, as defined in this section.

The local financial chain shapes the development of local services and industry. Since the 1980s, the financial industry in advanced capitalist countries has been restructured through reorganization processes, aggregations and bank mergers. These patterns define the ownership patterns of assets and the geography of the banking system. Numerous trends centred on new technologies – including the development of sophisticated rating techniques, the repackaging of financial risks, the standardization of numerous financial assets and the reduction of contact costs with customers – have improved competition among various banks and allowed access to new markets with different core businesses. Moreover, the deregulation of markets and intermediates with the advance of the European Monetary Union has further reduced transaction costs. In addition, the economic crises of the 1990s and 2000s triggered bank failures which were managed by the monetary authorities through acquisitions. These led to shifts in the banking system, which moved from public to private management. Other factors are connected to management strategies, that is, the execution of business policies linked to economies of scale, the growth of market power and the possibilities around fiscal advantages.

While most mergers are linked to banks within a national financial system, in Europe the corporate consolidation and integration among banking systems has occurred mainly through cross-border agreements. This financial management process is based on bank and financial institution agreements and aims to advance a unique European monetary and financial system (Berger et al. 2000; Boot 1999; Buch and De Long 2001; Eisenbeis and Kaufman 2006).

Moreover, the globalization of the credit market, bank mergers, the elimination of national barriers for bank expansion and penetration into peripheral markets are connected to two factors, that is, the integration of banking systems and developmental convergence among European regions. However, some issues remain. The first is the extent to which these patterns are related to economic and financial development. Another issue is the concern about banking institution consolidation across financial centres and peripheral areas, particularly the nature of job subdivisions among international and local banks.

NOTE

1. A multinational company organizes its activities in at least two different countries, for example the management operates from one country, while the production facilities build elsewhere, defining a supranational chain.

REFERENCES

Agnew, J.A. and Corbridge, S. (1995), *Mastering Space*, London and New York: Routledge.

Bardouille, N.C. (2001), 'The offshore service industry in the Caribbean: a conceptual and sub-regional analysis', *International Journal of Islamic Financial Services*, **31** (2), 1–9.

Belchem, J. (ed.) (2000), *A New History of the Isle of Man*, Liverpool: Liverpool University Press.

Berger, A.N., De Young, R., Genay, H. and Udell, G.F. (2000), 'Globalization of financial institutions: evidence from cross-border banking performance', Brookings-Wharton Papers on Financial Services No. 3, pp. 23–158.

Board of Governors of the Federal Reserve System, Washington, DC.

Boot, A.W.A. (1999), 'European lessons on consolidation in banking', *Journal of Banking and Finance*, **23** (2–4), 609–13.

Buch, C.M. and De Long, G. (2001), 'Cross-border bank mergers: what lures the rare animal?', paper presented at the conference of Competition, Financial Integration and Risks in Global Economy, Università di Tor Vergata, Rome, 5 December.

Carlisle, R. (ed.) (1981), *Sovereignty for Sale*, Annapolis, MD: Naval Institute Press.

Cobb, S.C. (1998), 'Global finance and the growth of offshore financial centres: the Manx experience', *Geoforum*, **29** (1), 7–21.

Dufey, G. and Giddy, I. (eds.) (1978), *The International Money Market*, Englewood Cliffs, NJ: Prentice Hall.

Eisenbeis, R.E. and Kaufman, G.G. (2006), 'Cross-border banking: challenges for deposit insurance and financial stability in the European Union', Working Paper No. 15a, Federal Reserve Bank of Atlanta, pp. 1–81.

Gehrig, T. (2000), 'Cities and geography of financial centres', in J.-M. Huriot and J.-F. Thisse (eds), *Economics of Cities: Theoretical Perspectives*, Cambridge: Cambridge University Press, pp. 415–30.

Gennillard, R.L. (1970), 'The eurobond market', in H.V. Prochnow (ed.), *The Eurodollar Market*, Chicago, IL: Rand McNally, pp. 316–47.

Gordon, L.C., Lai, K.P.Y. and Wójcik, D. (2015), 'Editorial introduction to the special section: deconstructing offshore finance', *Economic Geography*, **91** (3), 237–49.

Hudson, R. (1998), 'Placing trust, trusting place: on the social construction of offshore financial centres', *Political Geography*, **17** (8), 915–17.

Hudson, R. (2004), 'Conceptualizing economies and their geographies: spaces, flows and circuits', *Progress in Human Geography*, **28** (4), 447–71.

Jao, Y.C. (2003), 'Shanghai and Hong Kong as financial centres: historical perspective and contemporary analysis', paper presented at the International Conference, Shanghai, 12–13 September.

Johns, R.A. and Le Marchant, C.H. (eds) (1993), *Finance Centres, British Isles Offshore Development since 1979*, London: Pinter.

Kindleberger, C.P. (1974), 'The formation of financial centers: a study in comparative economic story', paper presented at the Princeton Studies in International Finance, Princeton, NJ, November.

Krugman, P.R. (1991), *Geography and Trade*, Cambridge, MA: MIT Press.

Labasse, J. (1974), *L'espace financier: Une analyse géographique* (*Financial Space: Geographic Analysis*), Parigi: Colin.

Laulajainen, R. (2003), *Financial Geography: A Banker' View*, London: Routledge.

Lefebvre, H. (1974), *The Production of Space*, English trans. D. Nicholson-Smith 1991, Oxford and Cambridge, MA: Blackwell.

Massey, D. (1993), 'Power – geometry and a progressive sense of place', in J. Birds, B. Curtis, T. Putman and I. Tickner (eds), *Mapping the Futures: Local Cultures, Global Change*, London: Routledge, pp. 59–69.

Moore, P. (1992), 'Editorial, the 1992 guide to offshore financial centres', *Euromoney Research Guide*, May, London: Euromoney Publications.

Murphy, R. (2004), *The Structure of Regulatory Competition Corporations and Public Policies in a Global Economy*, Oxford: Oxford University Press.

Onado, M. (1992), *Economia Dei Mercati Finanziari* (*Economics of Financial Markets*), Bologna: Il Mulino.

Parenti, F.M. and Rosati, U. (2018), *Geofinance and Geopolitics*, Milan: Egea.

Park, Y.S. (1982), 'The economics of offshore financial centres', *Columbia Journal of World Business*, **1** (4), 31–5.

Park, Y.S. and Essayad, M. (1989), *International Banking and Financial Centres*, Boston, MA: Kluwer.

Roberts, S. (1995), 'Small place, big money: the Cayman Islands and the international financial system', *Economic Geography*, **71** (3), 237–56.

Van Meeteren, M. (2018), 'Financial integration in Europe', FinGeo Working Paper No. 15, Global Network on Financial Geography, Oxford University, March, pp. 1–25.

Zoromè, A. (2007), 'Concept of offshore financial centres: search of an operational definition', IMF Working Paper No. IMF/WP/87, International Monetary Fund, Washington, DC.

5. Financial system and urban networks: an empirical analysis of Brazilian territory

Fabio Betioli Contel

1. INTRODUCTION

Among other authors, Dariusz Wójcik (2009, 2012, 2013) makes it explicit in some of his more recent texts that financial centers are probably the best theme to link geography to finance. The cities or metropolitan regions with the highest concentrations of commercial banks, investment banks, stock exchanges, insurance companies and clearing houses play a major role in their respective urban networks. When this concentration enables prominent international activity of these financial companies, the agglomeration is recognized as a global financial center. A city that exerts influence only in the context of neighboring countries is considered a regional (or continental) financial center; if a city only has the power to organize and serve its own urban network, it is defined as a national financial center (Roberts 1999).

This chapter analyses how the evolution of the financial primacy of São Paulo occurred in the context of the Brazilian urban network, since this agglomeration is the main national financial center – as Contel and Wójcik (2019) also argued with recent data. The primacy of São Paulo has been attained in the context of a financial system that has two main characteristics. Using the terminology of Verdier (2002), (1) it is a centralized system controlled by a small number of large commercial banks, and (2) it is more a bank-based economy, such as Japan or Germany, than a capital market economy, such as the US and England. Owing to these structural characteristics, we seek to highlight the evolution of empirical variables linked to commercial banks in the country, especially the assets and number of bank branches controlled by each institution, as well as the recent activities of the private banking sector. Hence, according to authors with different views about the geography of finance, including Jean Labasse (1974), Charles Goldfinger (1986), David Porteous (1995, 1999), Leyshon and Thrift (1997), Ron Martin (1999) and Martin Sokol (2013), variables such as the number of financial operators, the different types and degrees of internationalization, as well as the financial assets and branches that each have, are interesting indicators to analyze financial centers.

Based on these considerations, the chapter describes how the Brazilian urban network of its largest financial operators evolved, especially commercial banks. Section 2 evokes some of the main scholars of the subject to reconstruct this evolution from the context of World War II (when São Paulo's financial primacy began in the national urban network). Section 3 catalogues some empirical variables to identify the characteristics of this more recent primacy. Section 4 looks at final considerations.

2.   THE EVOLUTION OF THE BRAZILIAN BANKING AND FINANCIAL SYSTEM BETWEEN 1940 AND 1980

The 1940s witnessed a huge banking expansion in Brazil, through the creation of a large number of local banks, each with a small number of branches. According to the literature on the banking system during that period, this low proportion of the number of banks relative to the number of their branches made it difficult to create economies of scale, and this pushed up the interest rates offered by the banks and hindered financial intermediation in the country (Lopes and Rosseti 1982).

The situation started to change in the late 1950s, but it was the Reform of the National Financial System (the Reforma do Sistema Financeiro Nacional, RSFN), which occurred in 1964 and 1965, that initiated a vigorous process of banking concentration. The monetary authorities – and the Central Bank of Brazil which was created in 1964 – catalyzed this process in which larger banks absorbed smaller banks, and small banks closed. Together with the organic expansion of the branch network of some banks, which already had a significant dimension in the Brazilian banking system, the formation of the country's major financial conglomerates began in this period. As Correa (1989, p. 19) shows, 'The disappearance of small local banks first emerged, primarily regional banks, and then, as the concentration continued, some banks started to operate nationally'.

The main provision for bank concentration was the creation of the Merger and Consolidation Commission (Comissão de Fusão e Incorporação de Empresas, COFIE) in 1971, which implemented policies with the following logic: (1) bank concentration would lead to an increase in 'economies of scale' in the sector; (2) economies of scale would reduce the operational costs of banks; and (3) these lower costs would allow lower interest rates for borrowers (Tavares and Carvalheiro, 1985, p. 10). In just over ten years, the total number of banks declined by about 70 percent. At the same time, the aforementioned financial conglomerates were formed, under the leadership of existing large commercial banks, and with a concerted process of growth (Tavares and Carvalheiro 1985, p. 10).

This process of banking conglomeration occurred during a period of significant transformation in Brazilian geoeconomics; in 1945, the territory began a vigorous industrialization and urbanization process, which required significant reformulation of the national financial system. As Tavares and Carvalheiro (1985, p. 30) state, 'the banking system expanded considerably after the war, mainly due to the growth of the country's urban income, which was a consequence of the industrial expansion itself, that is, due to the displacement from the agrarian-exporting pole to the urban-industrial'. Therefore, this new type of economic development, based on vigorous processes of industrialization and urbanization, also altered the financing needs in the country and forced the creation of new credit institutions in the national financial system.

During this period, São Paulo emerged as the main gravitational center for the national economy, superseding Rio de Janeiro, both in financial assets and the banking network it controlled. São Paulo stood out as the primary location for headquarters of large financial and non-financial national companies. Also, it increased its importance by becoming the country's main gateway city for most of the sub-headquarters of transnational companies that settled in Brazilian territory beginning in the 1960s. In relation to the distribution of bank branches, of a total of 15070 units existing in the country in 1985, São Paulo controlled 6208, equivalent to 41 percent of the national total (Correa 1989, p. 20). As a gateway city, the number of representative offices of foreign banks was distributed as follows: São Paulo had 140 of the 223 existing units in 1985, while Rio de Janeiro had 81 (Correa 1989, p. 20).

At that time, the following hierarchy of territorial management centers existed, taking into account the network of bank branches in each capital: first was São Paulo; second was Brasilia (because it was the headquarters of Banco do Brasil S.A., the largest state-owned bank in the country); the third was Curitiba; fourth Belo Horizonte; fifth Salvador; sixth Porto Alegre; and seventh Rio de Janeiro with 387 branches under its control (Correa 1989, p. 20).

From the perspective of the banking economy, the rise of São Paulo in the Brazilian urban network takes three main forms: (1) the incorporation of smaller and/or economically unsuccessful banks; (2) the creation of new agencies by existing banks (organic growth); and (3) the relocation of the headquarters of several banks from a given city to São Paulo. This relocation is related to the search by banks for corporate services of all kinds, which were already concentrated in São Paulo. As Correa (1989, pp. 28–9) notes, the relocation of the headquarters from a given city to São Paulo, in search of a more central location, endowed with quaternary activities including headquarters of large industrial, commercial and financial services companies, consulting and corporate auditing, contributed to the role of São Paulo as the most important management center.

3. SOME RECENT DIMENSIONS OF THE BRAZILIAN FINANCIAL SYSTEM AND THE CENTRALITY OF SÃO PAULO

This bank concentration process occurred in the 1960s, 1970s and 1980s; then, in the 1990s, other important changes took place in the equity structure and topology of Brazilian banks, which enhanced the importance of São Paulo as the main national financial center. The main transformations that occurred in the 1990s were implemented in a context of economic liberalization; key changes were implemented mainly during the two governments of President Fernando Henrique Cardoso (1994–2002). In this period, the three main public policies aimed at transforming the Brazilian banking and financial system were the Plano Real, PROER and PROES.[1] With these, banks started a strong process of rationalizing their internal structures and began vigorously expanding their credit portfolios (Metzner and Matias 2015). Also, during this period, several public regional banks were privatized, which led to even more concentration in the sector.

Concomitantly with these normative measures, in the 1990s the construction of a series of informational support-networks in the territory increased the transmission of information and corporate data in the national space to make it more efficient and cheaper (Bernardes 2002). In addition, the installation of new communication channels through satellites, fiber optic networks, and telephone and television infrastructures consolidated the diffusion of computer, Internet and cellular/mobile technologies. These new elements of information technology, that not only make up the major infrastructures of the territory but are also for personal/individual use, are mostly responsible for increasing the reach of banking activity, a scope that can be named *hypercapillarity of finance* given its strength and breadth (Contel 2009, 2011). The centrality that São Paulo acquired as the main hub of most of these informational networks helped to further increase its primacy in the Brazilian urban network, transforming the city into the main informational and financial metropolis of the country (Santos 1994).

How can this recent primacy of the São Paulo Metropolitan Region in the context of the Brazilian urban network be measured? Table 5.1

Table 5.1 *Recent evolution of financial centrality: São Paulo, Rio de Janeiro, Brasilia, Porto Alegre and Belo Horizonte (selected variables, R$000s, 2000–2016)*

	2000	2010	2016
São Paulo			
Number of credit institutions	290	253	230
Total assets	492 962 274	2 225 945 530	3 988 806 665
Agencies	9045	11 002	12 453
Number of foreign institutions	55	59	61
Brasilia			
Number of credit institutions	31	28	21
Total assets	267 224 588	1 153 098 586	2 713 298 681
Agencies	4693	7385	9043
Number of foreign institutions	0	0	0
Rio de Janeiro			
Number of credit institutions	167	105	83
Total assets	116 842 281	593 758 605	1 028 699 943
Agencies	240	127	104
Number of foreign institutions	7	6	5
Porto Alegre			
Number of credit institutions	63	60	55
Total assets	12 335 272	69 241 284	151 913 613
Agencies	421	477	578
Number of foreign institutions	2	6	2
Belo Horizonte			
Number of credit institutions	84	71	45
Total assets	6 273 697	37 841 147	38 513 336
Agencies	243	214	258
Number of foreign institutions	0	0	0
Sum of the 5 largest cities			
Number of credit institutions	635	517	434
Total assets	895 638 112	4 079 885 152	7 921 232 238
Agencies	14 642	19 205	22 436
Number of foreign institutions	64	71	68
Brazil (totals)			
Number of credit institutions	1 782	1 786	1 445
Total assets	962 217 202	4 335 030 701	8 253 635 081
Agencies	17 275	20 922	23 425
Number of foreign institutions	74	137	81

Source: Banco Central do Brasil IF data, selected data from supervised entities (several years) (accessed 15 March 2018 at https://www3.bcb.gov.br/ifdata/).

demonstrates the recent evolution of four important empirical variables of the national financial system: the number of credit institutions (commercial and investment banks), the total assets of these institutions, the number of agencies they run and the number of offices or sub-offices of foreign credit institutions in the Brazilian territory. Table 5.1 divides these variables by the five main capital cities of the Brazilian urban network in terms of financial centrality, arranged by the amount of total financial assets that each commands: first is São Paulo, second Brasilia, third Rio de Janeiro, fourth Porto Alegre and fifth Belo Horizonte. It should be remembered, from the outset, that no statistics are available for important capital cities in the North and Northeast regions of the Brazilian territory, as these areas have historically had a lower economic and financial dynamism than the areas where these five major cities are located.

When analyzing the first variable indicated in Table 5.1, note the disproportion between the number of credit institutions existing in São Paulo in relation to the other Brazilian capitals; in 2016, São Paulo had 230 credit institutions, from a total of 1445 existing in the entire Brazilian territory (therefore, representing 16 percent of the total). The second most important city – Rio de Janeiro, with 83 institutions – housed only 5.7 percent of the total (almost three times fewer units than São Paulo). Another important figure that Table 5.1 shows is the reduction in the total number of institutions in the country, which decreased from 1782 to 1445. This is linked to a process of banking consolidation, which is still in progress: larger institutions continue to buy smaller institutions, aiming to increase their market power and capillarity in the territory.

However, the more precise dimension of the primacy exercised by São Paulo appears mainly in the second indicator shown in Table 5.1, the total assets that each city commands. In 2016, São Paulo was responsible for handling R$3 988 806 665 representing 48 percent of the total financial assets of credit institutions in the country. Importantly, this indicator is not decreasing in value, but increasing. Therefore, São Paulo held almost half of the national wealth in banking assets, while in previous years it had a similar proportion: 51.2 percent in 2000 and 51.3 percent in 2010.

In the other two indicators, this primacy of São Paulo is even clearer in relation to the other cities in the urban network indicated in Table 5.1. Although bank branches lose their prominence as a channel for providing financial services, they are still the main form that banks use to communicate and sell their services and products. In Table 5.1, São Paulo had 12 453 branches under its command in 2016, corresponding to 53.2 percent of the total in Brazil; Brasilia, in second place, owned 39 percent of the total, or 9043 units. The other three major cities in the country, in financial terms, had 940 branches under their responsibility, about 4 percent of the total.

*Table 5.2   Brazilian private banking: geographical distribution by state/
metropolitan region (R$ billions, 2010–16)*

	2010		2012		2014		2016	
	R$ billion	%	R$ billion	%	R$ billion	%	R$ billion	%
São Paulo	198.1	55.4	297.5	56.4	363.5	56.4	474.2	57
Metropolitan region of São Paulo	178.8	50	258.6	49	311	48.2	406.8	48.9
Rest of the state	19.3	5.4	38.9	7.4	52.5	8.1	67.4	8.1
Rio de Janeiro	64.8	18.1	93.7	17.8	106.6	16.5	128.3	15.4
Minas Gerais/Espírito Santo	20.2	5.7	27.3	5.2	36	5.6	48.2	5.8
South region	46.8	13.1	64.2	12.2	82.8	12.8	105.9	12.7
Midwest region	6.7	1.9	12.3	2.3	16.3	2.5	21.5	2.6
Northeast region	19.5	5.5	30.5	5.8	36.4	5.6	48.4	5.8
North region	1.1	0.3	1.9	0.4	3.3	0.5	5	0.6
Brazil (total)	357.3	100	527.3	100	645.1	100	831.6	100

Source: ANBIMA (2014, 2015, 2017).

Another noteworthy indicator of the central financial role of São Paulo in the national urban network is that the city holds at least 61 of the 81 foreign financial institutions. This corresponds to 75.3 percent of the total existing in the Brazilian territory, which indicates São Paulo's role as a gateway city and demonstrates its greater functional complexity in relation to the other cities at the top of this territorial division of labor.

A final indicator of the Brazilian financial system also allows us to understand the primacy of the Metropolitan Region of São Paulo in relation to the other metropolitan regions of the country. This indicator is the amounts transacted in the private banking market, which has grown significantly in Brazil. Table 5.2 shows the client's home state or region, and how much of each area of the territory moved with this criterion.

The Brazilian banking market consists of three main customer segments: (1) private banking, (2) the high-income banking market and (3) the retail market (ANBIMA 2019). The wealthiest in society use private banking services and individuals or families with very high incomes seek investment banks – as well as some commercial banks with special portfolios – to manage their fortunes. In February 2019, the private banking market reached a transaction value of R$1.12 trillion, according to data from the Brazilian Financial and Capital Markets Association (Associação Brasileira das Entidades dos Mercados Financeiro e de

Capitais, ANBIMA), and between 2010 and 2016 it evolved as in Table 5.2.

The state of São Paulo alone accounts for no less than 57% of the total invested through private banking in the territory, which in 2016 represented R$474.2 billion. The second largest market is the Metropolitan Region of São Paulo, which moved in the same year at least R$406.8 billion, almost half (48.9 percent) of the total traded in Brazil. As Table 5.2 also illustrates, this market, since 2010, has tended to increase concentration, another element that seems to also confirm that the financial primacy of São Paulo has grown recently in the Brazilian urban network.

Another important aspect shown by the data is the weak participation by the rest of the national territory in relation to the financial movements of this type. Apart from the state of Rio de Janeiro (where 15.4 percent of national totals were handled) and the southern region of the country, which includes the states of Rio Grande do Sul, Paraná and Santa Catarina (with 7 percent of total movement), all other regions moved together only 14.8 percent, almost three times less than the São Paulo Metropolitan Region.

4.   FINAL CONSIDERATIONS

As has long been identified in urban geography, agglomerations that grow at higher rates than other cities in their urban network become primary cities. This growth, in turn, tends to become a self-sustaining process, since the very complexity of the agglomeration becomes an element to attract more high-skilled professionals and more capital, increasing the scale of business and the liquidity of the financial center in question. Under the mechanism described by Gunnar Myrdal (1957), the growth of financial centers creates a cumulative causation process, which tends to be self-reinforcing, and installs a territorial division of labor typical of underdeveloped countries, with a very active dynamic center, but with most of the other cities and productive regions of these countries facing serious difficulties in development.

As Myrdal (1957) suggests, this process of cumulative causation cannot be reversed – or moderated – if the national state does not act firmly to create conditions for other agglomerations and productive regions to attract to their own arenas this economic and financial dynamism. However, solutions that involve the state are increasingly distant from the contemporary Brazilian political scene, especially after the 2018 elections, which elected an extreme right-wing president and converted to the principles of neoliberalism.

Although São Paulo is also creating external diseconomies at the heart of the functional complexification of the firms installed here, the locational advantages offered by the metropolis reduce the chances of other financial centers developing which might advance national development outside the state of São Paulo, and the Southeast region of the national territory. Thus, regional, economic and social inequalities are likely to persist in the country, further distancing the possibility of creating more a socially and financially equitable, and fair, territory.

NOTE

1. The Real Plan, implemented in February 1994, was a macroeconomic plan aimed at controlling inflation rates, through the exchange of the national currency (from the Cruzeiros Reais to the Real), and a severe control of monetary and fiscal policy. The control of inflation enabled a concomitant internationalization of the national economy, just as the entire banking sector underwent fundamental changes (mainly because banks' profits were no longer directly related to inflation rates). The Program to Stimulate Restructuring and Strengthening of the National Financial System (O Programa de Estímulo à Reestruturação e ao Fortalecimento do Sistema Financeiro Nacional, PROER) was initiated in 1995 and lasted until 2001. It aimed to make financially healthy the national private banking system and to provide greater solidity to all these institutions in the country. In practice, it served as a powerful mechanism for bank concentration, because this instrument permitted the closure and/or the purchase of some local and regional banks by national and international banks. The Incentive Program for the Reduction of the State Public Sector in Banking Activity (*Programa de Incentivo à Redução do Setor Público Estadual na Atividade Bancária*, PROES) started in 1996, and its main function was to finance the states of the Brazilian federation through cleaning up their respective state banks. At the time, it was understood that state-owned public banks were one of the main causes of fiscal imbalances of the states as a whole, and this fiscal profligacy was also the main accelerator of inflation in the country. From a practical point of view, and for the purposes of our discussion, PROES served as a mechanism of banking privatization, which led to an even greater concentration of the sector in the Brazilian territory. Initiated through Provisional Measure no. 1,514 of 7 August 1996, it was responsible for the closure, privatization and/or internationalization of state banks located throughout the country (Contel 2011).

REFERENCES

Associação Brasileira das Entidades dos Mercados Financeiro e de Capitais (ANBIMA) (2014), 'Private banking report ano IV', no. 6, September, accessed 12 January 2017 at https://www.anbima.com.br/data/files/39/B4/34/E9/3A7675106582 A275862C16A8/BoletimPrivateBanking_201409_1_.pdf.

Associação Brasileira das Entidades dos Mercados Financeiro e de Capitais (ANBIMA) (2015), 'Private banking report ano V', no. 7, January, accessed 12 January 2017 at https://www.anbima.com.br/pt_br/informar/relatorios/varejo-private-e-gestores-de-patrimonio/boletim-de-private-banking/investimento-do-pr ivate-em-previdencia-cresce-27-7-no-ano-2CA08A9A632885AD01632F20E9D C10B7.htm.

Associação Brasileira das Entidades dos Mercados Financeiro e de Capitais (ANBIMA) (2017), 'Private banking report ano VI', no. 9, April, accessed 12 January 2017 at https://www.anbima.com.br/pt_br/informar/relatorios/varejo-private-e-gestores-de-patrimonio/boletim-de-private-banking/patrimonio-do-seg mento-private-tem-alta-de-16-7-no-ano-2CA08A9A632885AD01632F20F60810 CE.htm.

Associação Brasileira das Entidades dos Mercados Financeiro e de Capitais (ANBIMA) (2019), 'Novos modelos de distribuição, segurança cibernética e conduta desafiam reguladores e autorreguladores em todo o mundo' ('New distribution, cyber security and conduct models challenge regulators and self-regulators worldwide'), *Informativo Anbima*, no. 112, February, accessed 13 March 2019 at https://www.anbima.com.br/pt_br/institucional/publicacoes/informativo/novos-modelos-de-distribuicao-seguranca-cibernetica-e-conduta-desafiam-reguladores-e-autorreguladores-em-todo-o-mundo.htm.

Bernardes, A. (2002), 'São Paulo, produção de informações e reorganização do território brasileiro' ('São Paulo, information production and reorganization of the Brazilian territory'), PhD thesis, University of São Paulo.

Contel, F.B. (2009), 'Espaço Geográfico, Sistema Bancário e a Hipercapilaridade Do Crédito No Brasil' ('Geographic space, banking system and credit hypercapillarity in Brazil'), *Caderno CRH*, **22** (55), 119–34.

Contel, F.B. (2011), *Território e Finanças: Técnicas, Normas e Topologias Bancárias no Brasil* (*Territory and Finance: Banking Techniques, Norms and Topologies in Brazil*), São Paulo: Annablume.

Contel, F.B. and Dariusz Wójcik (2019), 'Brazil's Financial Centers in the Twenty-first Century: Hierarchy, Specialization, and Concentration', *The Professional Geographer*, pp. 1–11. DOI: 10.1080/00330124.2019.1578980.

Correa, R.L. (1989), 'Concentração bancária e os centros de gestão do território' ('Bank concentration and territorial management centers'), *Revista Brasileira de Geografia*, **51** (2), 17–32.

Goldfinger, C. (1986), *La Géofinance. Pour Compreendre la Mutation Financière*, Paris: Seuil.

Labasse, J. (1974), *L'Espace Financier* (*The Financial Space*), Paris: Armand Colin.

Leyshon, A. and Thrift, N. (1997), *Money/Space: Geographies of Monetary Transformation*, London and New York: Routledge.

Lopes, J.C. and Rosseti, J.P. (1982), *Moeda e Bancos: Uma Introdução* (*Money and Banks: An Introduction*), São Paulo: Atlas.

Martin, R. (1999), 'The new economic geography of money', in R. Martin (ed.), *Money and the Space Economy*, New York: Wiley and Sons, pp. 1–27.

Metzner, T.D. and Mathias, A.B. (2015), *O Setor Bancário Brasileiro de 1990 a 2010* (*The Brazilian Banking Sector from 1990 to 2010*), São Paulo: Manole.

Myrdal, G. (1957), *Economic Theory and Underdeveloped Regions*, New York: Gerald Duckworth & Co Ltd.

Porteous, D. (1995), *The Geography of Finance. Spatial Dimensions of Intermediary Behaviour*, Aldershot: Ashgate.

Porteous, D. (1999), 'The development of financial centres: location, information externalities and path dependence', in R. Martin (ed.), *Money and the Space Economy*, New York: Wiley and Sons, pp. 95–114.

Roberts, R. (1999), *Inside International Finance: A Citizen's Guide to the World's Financial Markets, Institutions and Key Players*, London: Orion.

Santos, M. (1994), *Por uma economia política da cidade: O caso de São Paulo* (*For a Political Economy of the Cit: The Case of São Paulo*), São Paulo: Hucitec.
Sokol, M. (2013), 'Towards a "newer" economic geography? Injecting finance and financialisation into economic geographies', *Cambridge Journal of Regions, Economy and Society*, **6** (3), 501–15.
Tavares, M. and Carvalheiro, N. (1985), *O setor bancário brasileiro: alguns aspectos do crescimento e da concentração*, São Paulo: FIPE/USP.
Verdier, D. (2002), *Moving Money: Banking and Finance in the Industrialized World*, Cambridge: Cambridge University Press.
Wójcik, D. (2009), 'Geography of stock markets', *Geography Compass*, **3** (4), 1499–514.
Wójcik, D. (2012), 'Where governance fails: advanced business services and the offshore world', *Progress in Human Geography*, **37** (3), 330–47.
Wójcik, D. (2013), 'The dark side of NY–LON: financial centres and the global financial crisis', *Urban Studies*, **50** (13), 2736–52.

PART II

The State–Bank–Firm Nexus in the Finance
Semi-Peripheries

6. Italian banks and business services as knowledge pipelines for SMEs: examples from Central and Eastern Europe*

Christian Sellar

INTRODUCTION

The literature on postsocialist transformation highlights the central role of foreign direct investments (FDIs) in the restructuring of Central and Eastern European firms (Bandelj 2008; Broadman 2006; Pavlinek 2008; Pickles et al. 2006; Smith et al. 2008). Recent work on the global financial crisis also shows that the financial sector has become overly dependent on Western European sources of credit (Myant and Drahokoupil 2012; Smith and Swain 2010). How did such a 'fragile' development model come into being during the years of transition preceding the crisis? With very few exceptions (Kamaras 2001), there are no systematic analyses of the relationships between Western manufacturers and financial and service institutions in Central and Eastern Europe. This chapter investigates this nexus through an analysis of foreign investment and outsourcing practices in Italian financial institutions and manufacturing firms. The focus of this chapter is on one major banking group (Unicredit), a smaller banking group (Italo Romena), one consortium of consultancies (IC & Partners), and a collection of small and medium-sized textile and clothing producers. These businesses established operations in several regions of Central and Eastern Europe, and the author conducted interviews in three of them: Bratislava (Slovakia), Timis County and Bucharest (both Romania), and Sofia (Bulgaria). As banks and consultancies have common organizational structures, visions and strategic approaches throughout Central and Eastern Europe, the result is a macro-regional analysis.

The following questions are addressed: (1) what were the investment strategies of Italian banks and business services in the region? (2) How did conditions in Italy and Central and Eastern Europe affect those strategies? (3) What kind of relationships did they establish with Italian small and medium-sized enterprises (SMEs) operating in the region? In answering these questions, the chapter argues that banks and service firms act as knowledge pipelines between Italian small and medium-sized enterprises (SMEs) and the local communities hosting them. In practice, Unicredit, Italo Romena and IC & Partners play the role of cultural mediators, providing manufacturers with information about local norms and customs, and facilitating labor relations and business opportunities.

Theoretically, the chapter contributes to the literature on the internationalization of SMEs. Specifically, it adapts the Uppsala internationalization process model (Johanson and Vahlne 1977; Luostarinen 1980) to explain the connections between some Italian manufacturers, business services and banks. It also contributes to the debate on clusters and innovation systems in which scholars have examined whether or not Italian firms abroad reproduce the thick web of relationships typical of Italian industrial districts, and to what extent Italian firms transfer knowledge and professional culture abroad (Chiarvesio et al. 2006b; Corò and Volpe 2006; Dunford 2006; Rullani 2002; Sabel 2003). The chapter takes an intermediate position on this issue: while I found no evidence of a reproduction of the district system in the three areas investigated, I also show that Unicredit, Italo Romena, IC & Partners and some manufacturers have established a loose relationship based upon the provision of Italian language business services and knowledge of place that allow resource-scarce SMEs to thrive in foreign environments.

The chapter is organized as follows. The next section focuses on issues specific to the internationalization of Italian SMEs within the framework of clusters and innovation systems, as well as the relatively recent internationalization of retail banks. The third section describes the reasons why the postsocialist environment attracted Unicredit and Italo Romena to Central and Eastern Europe, and the reasons why conditions in Italy led to the internationalization of banks in the 1990s. The fourth section analyzes how the manufacturing firms involved in this research have intensified their commitment to Central and Eastern Europe since the 1990s. The fifth section discusses how the relationships between banks and manufacturers have evolved since 2000 and how they are explained by an adaptation of the Uppsala model. The final section describes the internationalization of a large consortium of business consultancies known as IC & Partners and its focus on providing place-specific knowledge to Italian firms. Together, these consultancies and banks provide Italian firms with cultural services that allow knowledge spillovers between these firms and Central and Eastern European regional economies.

The research is based on 85 semi-structured interviews with Italian manufacturers, local partners, Italian banks, government officials at national, regional and local levels, and trade unions which were undertaken between 2005 and 2006 in Slovakia, Romania, Bulgaria and the western part of Ukraine.[1] Using a case study method (Yin 2003), the chapter uses part of this research: western Ukraine is excluded because during the research period it was at the margins of Italian outsourcing. Only a handful of Italian manufacturers were working there, there was no major Italian banking group operating in western Ukraine, and there was only one independent business consultant (for more information on the geography of Italian outsourcing, see Sellar 2009). The author also collected information at IC & Partners' headquarters in Italy, and at its branches in Bratislava, Sofia, Timisoara and Bucharest. Interviews with Unicredit were conducted in Bratislava and Sofia, while Bank Italo Romena was interviewed in Timisoara. In Romania, Slovakia and Bulgaria, the author interviewed officials at 40 textile and clothing firms (30 Italian-owned firms and ten local suppliers of Italian firms). Information on events after 2006 is derived from Unicredit's and IC & Partners' websites. Open-ended questions focused on how banks and services decided to invest in Eastern Europe, the changes in their customer base and how a sample of Italian firms made decisions about financing and the use of services.

THE INTERNATIONALIZATION OF SMES AND BANKS

Following the seminal work of Raymond Vernon, transnational firms are portrayed in the literature as large and powerful (Vernon 1971, 1972, 1985, 1998) with sufficient resources to access any information needed. They may invest nearly anywhere in the world and have sufficient political influence to access the highest levels of any government administration. However, is it possible to conceptualize such enterprises differently? Gibson-Graham (1996, 2006), for example, portrayed the capitalist system as contested and limited. In doing so, they laid the theoretical foundation for 'alternative social representations, in which non-capitalist economic practices proliferated, gender identities were renegotiated and political subjects actively resisted industrial restructuring, thereby influencing its course' (Gibson-Graham 1996, p. viii). When extended to transnational firms, Vernon's assumption is still valid for large transnational firms, but it does not apply to SMEs. Indeed, the latter often lack resources, have limited investment capabilities and have difficulty accessing government administrations. Equally, even though one cannot construe giants such as Exxon or Microsoft as small and weak, there is empirical evidence that at least some multinational firms are not giants capable of influencing governments. For example, Aspelund and Butsko (2010), Calof and Viviers (1995), Kalogeresis and Labrianidis (2010a, 2010b), and Welch and Loustarinen (1988) have described case studies of successful internationalization of SMEs in Norway, South Africa, Greece and the UK. For those SMEs, issues which many large corporations take for granted may become serious problems. For example, how do firms with sparse human and financial resources deal with geographically distant headquarters, unfamiliar language and business practices, and unknown legislation? Nina Bandelj (2008, p. 218) describes FDI in Central and Eastern Europe as the product of 'social structures, power and culture, and negotiated by practical actors'. Taking Bandelj's argument further, large corporations occupy a position of power when they negotiate their inclusion into the normative and institutional framework of Central and Eastern European states; SMEs do not.

Notwithstanding their inherent weaknesses, in some cases SMEs have been at the forefront of internationalization. For example, Kalogeresis and Labrianidis (2010b) demonstrated that small Greek firms pioneered investments in the Balkans in the 1990s. Italy also provides an excellent case study of the internationalization of SMEs in Central and Eastern Europe because the Italian system of SMEs, the aptly named industrial districts or Third Italy, is well known (Becattini 1979; Locke 1995; Piore and Sabel 1984; Storper 1997) and Central and Eastern Europe is the most important investment location for several key Italian industrial districts (Coro and Volpe, 2006). Such districts are 'dense concentrations of interdependent small and medium enterprises in a single sector and in auxiliary industries and services' (Dunford 2006, p. 27; Marshall 1919). In the 1980s and 1990s, district firms supplied locally; in the mid-1990s and early 2000s, they expanded abroad, establishing new contracting relations and/or FDIs (Chiarvesio and Micelli 2006; Corò and Micelli 2006; Di Maria and Micelli 2006; Rabellotti 2001). Some firms were so successful in their foreign operations that both Italy's academic and popular press defined them as *multinazionali tascabili* – pocket multinationals (Bonomi 1997).

Studies on Italian industrial districts are part of an international literature that focuses on worldwide regional economies (Marshall 1919; Martin and Sunley 2003; Markusen 1996; Porter 1990; Scott and Storper 1987). This literature partially pinpoints innovation and knowledge to explain the success of clusters of firms. Revamping and deepening Schumpeter's interest in innovation (1942), since the late 1980s the literature has highlighted the progressively beneficial cycles of development among research institutions, companies and infrastructures (Perrin 1993). Innovation is considered a source of success in both high-technology regions such as Silicon Valley and Route 128 in the USA (Markusen 1986; Saxenian 1994), and traditional sectors such as the mechanical or textile districts in Italy (Becattini et al. 2003; Brusco 1986; Rabellotti et al. 2009). The literature on regional economies identifies two main sources of knowledge and innovation. The first is the industrial atmosphere or local buzz (Marshall 1919; Storper 1997) in which face-to-face interactions and shared culture generate specific professional cultures and developmental trajectories within regions. Some claim that the region is not the only source of innovation but rather that innovation requires sustained social relationships and social capital, or the 'social structure that enables social actions' (Bourdieu 1986; Dolfsma 2008, p. 19; Granovetter and Swedberg 2001; Putnam et al. 1993). Using the concept of social capital, scholars have shown that innovation systems depend on social structures which, in turn, encompass nations, regions and sectors (Cooke et al. 2004; Freeman 1987; Malerba 2004; Nelson 1993). A second source of innovation is the use of knowledge pipelines through which firms acquire knowledge and process innovation through sustained relationships with partners or suppliers located in distant areas (Gertler 2008; Malmberg 2003; Moodysson 2008; Powell and Grodal 2005).

According to Italian scholars, 'pocket multinationals' acted as knowledge pipelines and brought the professional culture of Italian districts to foreign locations (Chiarvesio et al. 2006a, 2006b; Corò and Volpe 2006). In doing so, they had to acquire sufficient local knowledge to establish good partnerships, provided in some cases by Italian banks and services. In turn, following a worldwide trend of internationalization in the banking sector, banks acquired knowledge about Central and Eastern Europe through their significant investment in the region. In the 1980s, Tschoegl argued that since proprietary knowledge is difficult to protect from imitation, 'there is no reason to expect foreign banks to have any particular advantage over domestic banks familiar with their local environment' (Tschoegl 1987, p. 67; see also Guillen and Tschoegl 2000). In spite of this argument, by the late 1990s large banking groups began to enter the general commercial and mass retail markets of developing countries at an increasing pace. It has been a global process, but one that occurred earlier and with a stronger intensity in Western Europe than in North America. The European Monetary Union (EMU) has led to the further consolidation of the European banking system and mergers of pre-existing groups (De Paula 2002; Padoa-Schioppa 1999). At the same time, normative and economic changes at the global level have facilitated acquisitions by European banks outside the EMU. For example, Brazil has allowed the 'gradual flexibilisation of legal restrictions with respect to the presence of foreign banks' (De Paula 2002, p. 59).

The following sections analyze the interaction and overlapping geographies of internationalization in relation to Unicredit, Italo Romena, IC & Partners and selected manufacturing firms. The Uppsala internationalization process model is used in this analysis to explain the emergence of a systemic, but imperfect and limited, relationship among these actors. In the Uppsala (or stage) model, internationalization has a sequential nature, from lighter to deeper degrees of commitment abroad (Johanson and Vahlne 1977; Luostarinen 1980). It is an experience/knowledge-based model: the more experience firms gain abroad, the more they will commit. Davidson (1980) identified two forms of intensification of commitment. One is spatial, that is, firms will invest first in culturally and geographically close countries, and when sufficiently experienced they will move further afield. The other concerns the amount of capital and human resources deployed abroad; progressively moving from exporting, to distribution, to joint venture manufacturing and, finally, to wholly owned manufacturing. Summarily, the Uppsala model identifies four stages of internationalization, repeated in two phases of international expansion (see Table 6.1). In the first phase, firms first begin exporting to, or sourcing from, countries culturally and geographically close to their headquarters (stage 1). In the second stage, they establish permanent distribution networks. Together, these two stages correspond to light forms of commitment as they do not entail large investment or technology transfer. Stages 3 (joint-venture manufacturing) and 4 (wholly owned manufacturing) are considered strong forms of commitment as firms are required to use a larger amount of resources and take greater risks. In the second phase of the model, the same sequence is repeated in culturally and geographically distant places.

Table 6.1   Uppsala or stage model

	Phase 1	Phase 2
	Internationalization to geographically and culturally proximate countries	Internationalization to geographically and culturally further countries – repeats the stages as phase 1
Light commitment	Stage 1: export/import Stage 2: distribution/ acquisition network	Stage 1 Stage 2
Strong commitment	Stage 3: joint venture Stage 4: wholly owned manufacturing	Stage 3 Stage 4

Source: Author's elaboration of Johanson and Vahlne (1977) and Davidson (1980).

It should be noted, however, that firms do not necessarily complete all four stages of phase 1 before starting phase 2.

In developing the model, Barkema et al. (1996) argued that the progressive acquisition of information plays a key role in shifting from one stage to the next as it reduces uncertainty, thereby enabling firms to make better evaluations of future expansion potential. Similarly, Henisz and Delios (2001) argued that the accumulation of international experience reduces the barriers to skills and knowledge, thus furthering international expansion. They critiqued and expanded the stage model to include the influence of political hazards on corporate expansion, revealing that 'firms that have followed a sequential process of international expansion exhibit lower sensitivity to the deterring effect of political hazards'. However, they also noted the existence of 'a robust relationship between the extent of policy uncertainty and FDI entry rates' (Delios and Henisz 2003, p. 1162). Another critical study found that the Uppsala model was more suited to explaining the behavior of small manufacturing firms rather than large firms or services, as large firms have enough resources to jump-start internationalization and service firms must locate near their customers and cannot increase or decrease their commitment (Cattani and Tschoegl 2002). The following sections conclude that Cattani and Tschoegl are correct within separate analyses of each Italian service provider and manufacturer, but not when the interactions between them are considered.

THE STRATEGY OF UNICREDIT AND ITALO ROMENA: FROM CUSTOMER FOLLOWING TO MARKET SEEKING, FROM AN ITALIAN INDUSTRIAL DISTRICT TO THE WIDER WORLD

One of the largest Italian banking groups, Unicredit, adopted an internationalization strategy that does not appear to follow the Uppsala model. In particular, since its formation in 1998, the group has focused on a strategy involving 'the acquisition of the largest bank in each Eastern European country' (interview with high-level manager, Bulbank, 22 May 2006). However, this section shows that the Uppsala model acquires explanatory power when the history of the group and the conditions in one industrial district (Treviso) are considered.

In 1998 Cassamarca, a leading bank in Treviso, merged with several local banks based in northeastern Italy and established Unicredito. In the same year, Unicredito merged with the state-owned, large firm orientated bank Credito Italiano, forming Unicredito Italiano. Around the same time, changes in the Italian banking regulations made foreign acquisitions easier (interview with high-level manager, Bulbank, 22 May 2006). Thus, in 1999 Unicredito Italiano began its acquisition campaign – becoming Unicredit Group. By 2007, it had become the largest bank in both Italy and Central and Eastern Europe. In spite of considerable problems in managing the newly acquired subsidiaries (Ambos et al. 2009), and in spite of the 2008–09 financial crisis, up until 2012 the group maintained investments. A manager working for Bulbank (Bulgaria's largest bank, part of Unicredit Group) summarized the reasons why the group invested so heavily in postsocialist Europe:

> Those countries have . . . a GDP growth much higher than Western Europe, and banking activity used to be low, if not very low. Thus, there were good chances of development for our sector. . . . the banks we acquired through privatization were sold at reasonable prices, which allowed us to invest without going into debt and putting our Italian investors at risk.. . . There were episodes that reminded us of the impossibility of further growth in Italy. . . . [Also], in these countries there was not much interest from American or, in general, non European banks. (Interview high level manager, Bulbank, 22 May 2006)

In his view, the combination of the perceived lack of opportunities in the homeland, low-cost acquisitions through privatization, economic growth in Central and Eastern Europe, and the absence of strong North American competitors shaped the geography of Unicredit's expansion. Figure 6.1 shows the Western European core of the group and the Eastern European acquisitions in the banking sector, while it omits the most recent expansion in Central Asia and the acquisition of financial institutions in North America.

Unicredit is similar to other case studies reported in the business literature. Spain's Banco Santander shares similar origins to Unicredit; that is, being rooted in provincial banks and demonstrating a push towards internationalization owing to competitive pressure (Guillén and Tschoegl 2008). Similar to the case of Norwegian banks, legislation in the homeland influenced the processes of internationalization (Jacobsen and Tschoegl 1997); however, it is the particular relationship with Italian manufacturers in the context of postsocialist Europe that makes Unicredit unique. Taken together, the eastward expansion of manufacturers, as well as Unicredit, follows the pattern of the Uppsala model. In doing so, they built knowledge pipelines between Italy and Central and Eastern Europe.

Geoeconomic circumstances during the 1990s shaped the behavior of Unicredit and manufacturers. First, postsocialist transformations created opportunities that were attractive to Italian firms. Both Unicredit and Italian manufacturers focused their overseas investments in Central and Eastern Europe. Indeed, half of all employment generated by Italian

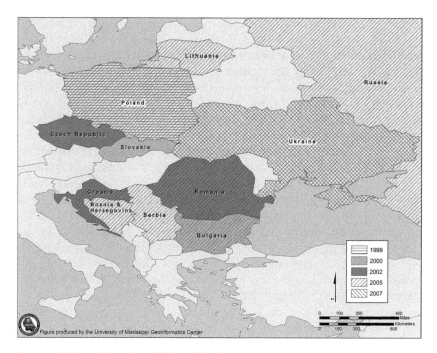

Source: Author elaboration of Unicredit's webpage.

Figure 6.1 Expansion of Unicredit in Central and Eastern Europe

manufacturers abroad is in Central and Eastern Europe (Corò and Volpe 2006). Such geographical overlap between manufacturing and finance is uncommon (Buckley et al. 1992; Hellman 1996), but not unique. In particular, Kamaras (2001) and Kalogeresis and Labrianidis (2010b) suggest a similar pattern for Greek manufacturers and banks in the Balkans. In both cases, banks followed their customers and found a welcoming environment thanks to the aggressive promotion of foreign investment by Central and Eastern European governments (Bandelj, 2008).

Second, conditions within Italy in the 1990s pushed Italian firms to invest abroad. In the 1980s, Piore and Sabel (1984) had noted that the close connection between manufacturers, services and banks being cemented by local institutions had been one of the key factors behind the success of small Italian firms. Thus, not surprisingly, many of the regional banks that in 1998 merged into Unicredit came from the northeast; the area with the highest level of internationalization in Italy (Cainelli and Zoboli 2004; ICE 2006a; Rabellotti 2004). Even more strikingly, a single town, Treviso, was home to the most internationalized textile and clothing district in

Italy – firms employed two people overseas for every one employee in Treviso (Corò and Volpe 2006, p. 15 – as well as the first two local banks to invest in Central and Eastern Europe: Cassamarca Trevigiana (now part of Unicredit) and Banca Italo Romena.

In Treviso, internationalization has characterized the whole district across both the manufacturing and the financial sectors owing to the close relationship between economic actors. When, as a group, manufacturers began to increase their commitment in Central and Eastern Europe, the demand for financial support began to change. Banks in Treviso initially reacted with suspicion to requests for loans for international projects. However, ultimately the tradition of cooperation between local banks and manufacturers prevailed, thereby transforming the whole district. In describing the banking sector's initial resistance to financing the international operations of local firms, a former manager of Cassamarca Trevigiana stated: 'If a customer came to my bank in Treviso asking for money to go to do business in Slovakia, it was very difficult to grant him credit. It sounded like a dangerous adventure' (interview with high-level manager, Unibanka, 28 June 2006).

Over time, however, the bottom-up pressure of long-term corporate customers grew. Business owners increasingly complained that they could not be competitive against other foreign investors because 'other foreigners had support from their governments and banks, while they were alone' (interview with high-level manager, Unibanka, 28 June 2006). Finally, Cassamarca decided to acknowledge this customer input, and in 1996 established a joint venture in Slovakia, consisting of an exchange of shares with the Slovak bank, Polnobanka. The goal of the joint venture was 'to know this market and help commercial relations between our customers and Polnobanka customers' (interview with high-level manager, Unibanka, 28 June 2006). In 2000, Unicredit acquired Polnobanka, and renamed it Unibanka.

Another leading bank from Treviso, Veneto Banca, internationalized by following a pattern similar to that of Cassamarca. In both cases, local manufacturers pushed their banks to establish some presence in Central and Eastern Europe. Veneto Banca targeted Romania, the country with the largest presence of firms from the Veneto region. It opted for a stronger involvement than Cassamarca and, in the late 1990s, acquired a pre-existing Italian-Romanian joint venture, Banca Italo Romena. This was an attempt to deepen the existing networks. In the 1980s, during the socialist era, the Commercial Bank of Romania and three Italian banks formed Banca Italo Romena to bolster the already strong commercial ties between the two countries. Again, bottom-up pressure from corporate clients played a key role in influencing the acquisition, because:

Almost the entire body of subcontractors from the Veneto region moved to Romania to produce here . . ..Veneto Banca perceived the need of entrepreneurs from Veneto to have a bank that could act as contact point between Veneto and Romania. Thus, the acquisition of Italo Romena is essentially due to the outsourcing from Italian entrepreneurs. (Interview country manager, Banca Italo Romena, 7 April 2006)

In this interview excerpt, the Italo Romena country manager draws direct connections between the changing geography of manufacturing in Treviso and the surrounding areas, and the decision to invest in Romania. In the 1990s, the large number of investments in Central and Eastern Europe created demand for financial support that pushed Italo Romena and Cassamarca to invest in the region. Thus, their customer-following investment strategy was due to manufacturers which, as a group, affirmed the patterns predicted by the Uppsala model. However, between 2000 and 2010, the strategies of both banks changed. Cassamarca 'was very strong in northeastern Italy, but not strong enough to support [large] investments abroad' (interview with high-level manager, Polnobanka, 28 June 2006). Rooted in a close-knit and relatively small community, the bank was equipped to listen to the demands of local businesses. However, as soon as Cassamarca and other banks merged into Unicredit, the group adopted a large-scale market-seeking strategy, independent from Italian manufacturers. Even the smaller Italo Romena shifted its focus away from Italian customers: 'We came at the end of the 1990s. We have been here for six years already, and we had great satisfaction. Essentially, we began following Italian entrepreneurs, and year by year our customers became more and more heterogeneous' (interview country manager, Banca Italo Romena, 7 April 2006).

Therefore, in spite of their initial role in pushing the internationalization of Italian banks, Italian entrepreneurs soon became a minority among the customers of Unicredit and Italo Romena, among others.

THE STRATEGY OF MANUFACTURERS: FROM 'LIGHT' TO 'DEEP' COMMITMENT TO CENTRAL AND EASTERN EUROPE

The existing literature on economic change in Italy suggests that the Uppsala model is applicable beyond the firm level and that it can be extended to sector and district levels. For example, in analyzing the textile and clothing industry, Dunford (2006, p. 56) explained the mechanisms underlying an intensification of FDI in the past decade: a handful of service firms located in Milan led the entire industrial sector and they consciously induced outsourcing as a cost-containment strategy. Manufacturers responded with a progressive intensification of their commitment abroad, from subcontracting to foreign investment. Italian scholars have made similar arguments concerning the internationalization of single industrial districts, as well as the SME sector as a whole. For example, a report from the Italian Trade Commission (ICE) showed that there is a correlation between firms' internationalization and industrial districts, and that the highest degree of internationalization is found in some of the districts in northeastern Italy (ICE 2006a). Other studies have identified a specific time frame for the internationalization of the Italian economy. For example, Federico showed that Italian firms began to relocate abroad in the mid-1980s, following a pattern consistent with the Uppsala Model, first establishing subcontracting relations, and then pursuing acquisitions (Federico 2004; see also Graziani 1998). Sellar (2009, p. 338) noted that within two decades Italians 'became permanent residents of Slovakia and Romania in order to control their investments'[2] and began to consider those countries their homes. In doing so, investors increased their stakes in host countries. Italians formed associations and chambers of commerce to lobby local governments (Sellar 2009), especially in Timisoara, Romania, where they became an elite group that contributed to the postsocialist transformation of the city (Sellar 2011).

Firms interviewed in this research clearly followed the pattern identified by Federico (2004) and by Sellar (2009). Not only did firms intensify their commitment over time, but their geographical distribution also changed according to the Uppsala model. Western Romania, geographically the closest to Italy and speaking a Romance language related to Italian, is to date the area with the largest concentration of Italian FDI (Sellar 2011). According to interviewees, the quality of investment has changed significantly over time. An entrepreneur in the customs and logistics sector, working in Romania since 1994, described the change mercilessly:

> Italians came in large numbers, in waves. The first who came were attracted purely by cheap labor. . . . They had no margins in Italy anymore, so they came here. The good times didn't last. Very few remain of those who came in 1994. Those who had a counterpart, a parent company in Italy survived; all the others are gone. So, there were those desperately hoping to solve their problems here, and then there were adventurers hoping to come here with a few coins and buy a palace. I do not have a good vision of our presence in Romania, because as usual, we were dispersed, with no direction, with no support from institutions. (Interview Italian entrepreneur, anonymous, Timisoara, 10 April 2006)

In sum, this interviewee argues that there has been a shift from a migration of entrepreneurs who came to Romania as a last resort to avoid bankruptcy, to foreign investment by more established firms. Accordingly, the other firms interviewed for this research were mostly foreign subsidiaries of an Italian company, all established in the late 1990s or later. There were only two cases of diasporic entrepreneurs (Kamaras 2001). One of them established Frara in 2005, after leaving the management of a foreign company (interview entrepreneur, Frara Ricami 11 April 2006). Frara Ricami is important because it is an example of how entrepreneurs in the apparel sector intensified their activity in Romania. After a sufficient number of producers were established, a market opportunity emerged for firms that provided Italian-speaking, high-technology services for apparel producers. Frara Ricami uses laser cutters to provide a specialized product previously unavailable in Romania.

Similarly, Intercolor is a large professional washing and dyeing service firm, active in Italy since 1987, that decided to establish a factory in Romania in 1999. Intercolor followed its main customer (a jeans producer) and established a facility near Timisoara with the help of an expatriate entrepreneur (interview entrepreneur, Intercolor, 11 April 2006). The other firms interviewed followed a more traditional form of intensification. For example, after several years of subcontracting to Romanian producers, a company named CHP established a small logistics center to coordinate its operations more effectively and to provide technical support to their Romanian subcontractors (interview entrepreneur, CHP, 12 April 2006). The other firms interviewed began working with Romanian subcontractors, and later established facilities in Romania to enhance their control over the production process. All these firms' output and employment grew rapidly, thanks to the low cost of labor in Romania. In some cases, firms that employed 20 or 30 workers in Italy could employ several hundred in Romania for the same cost (interview entrepreneur, anonymous, Romania, 14 April 2006).

Firms interviewed in Slovakia followed a very similar pattern to those in Romania, but with a smaller number of firms involved. The author found no evidence of Italian firms similar to Frara or Intercolor, because there were not enough Italian producers in Slovakia to support them. However, Italian firms in Slovakia grew rapidly in terms of employment, output and quality of product. The firm Twista, for example, located in eastern Slovakia, is part of a large Italian group that at the time of the interview had production sites in both Italy and Slovakia. This firm: 'officially began manufacturing in Slovakia on February 15, 1999, with twenty-five workers producing about 15,000 kilograms of yarn per month; now we have 270 workers producing a half million kilograms per month. The trend is still growing' (interview entrepreneur, Twista, 28 June 2006).

Compared with Romania and Slovakia, Italian investments in Bulgaria were, on average, larger and came to the country later. Two conditions attracted them: new, pro-business laws following a financial crisis in 1997, and the acquisition of Bulgaria's largest bank by Unicredit (interview Chief Economic Officer, Italian Embassy in Bulgaria, 4 November 2005). In the textile sector, one large company, Miroglio, constitutes the largest share of Italian investment. This company followed closely the pattern predicted in the Uppsala model in that it had already established a small company in Bulgaria in the 1980s, a logistics firm that coordinated the work of local subcontractors. This company was crucial for future investment, because, in the words of Miroglio's country manager, 'In fifteen years of activity of this company, we got to know normative, geographical, even personal aspects of Bulgaria. We established a good number of personal relationships and contacts that turned out to be important when we decided to invest' (interview country manager, Miroglio, 7 May 2006).

Miroglio owned similar logistics firms in other countries as well, including Romania, but eventually chose Bulgaria for expansion because of the political situation after the crisis in 1997:

> The decision to invest was taken in late 1997. It had been an extremely important year for Bulgaria; in my opinion it was the year in which the new Bulgaria was founded. In 1997 IMF came. . . . The political climate totally changed, and the political and institutional premises for investments were created. (Interview country manager, Miroglio, 7 May 2006)

After an initial investment of €45 million in 1998 that led to the establishment of the first factory near Sofia, Miroglio progressively added new facilities, peaking at investment of around €200 million in 2006. Later, the growth of wages in Bulgaria and the financial crisis led Miroglio to disinvest from several plants (follow-up interview, 25 June 2009).

To summarize, in the 1990s, the internationalization of both banks and manufacturers originated within the culture of the industrial districts and, when analyzed together, followed the pattern of the Uppsala model. Italian firms then intensified their investments in Bulgaria, Slovakia and Romania as predicted by the Uppsala model. In the early 1990s, western Romania quickly became the preferred region for SME investment, owing to a combination of cheap labor, geographical proximity with northeastern Italy and a language related to Italian. At the same time, Slovakia attracted a smaller number of firms owing to higher wages and a different (Slavic-based) language (interview with Italian entrepreneur, anonymous, Slovakia, 9 July 2006). Bulgaria, farther geographically than Romania and Slovakia, began to host significant investments later and by larger firms (interview with Chief Economic Officer, Italian Embassy in Bulgaria, 4 November 2005). Banks followed suit. The smaller banks in this study had already invested in Romania and Slovakia in the 1990s, and when the large

Unicredit Group was established they reached Bulgaria in 2000. Did banks and manufacturers maintain a systematic relationship when the former increased their investments with large acquisitions? The following section reveals the weak relationship between Italian banks and manufacturers, based upon the specific needs of SMEs to establish flows of knowledge between Italy and Central and Eastern Europe.

RELATIONSHIP BETWEEN BANKS AND MANUFACTURERS: THE IMPORTANCE OF CULTURAL SERVICES

The literature on regional economies emphasizes the need for social capital and sustained social interactions to produce innovation and notes that repeated interactions along global pipelines are effective in reaching that goal (Moodysson 2008). However, José-Luis Hervas-Oliver and José Albors-Garrigos (2009) have shown that the internal capabilities of firms are crucial in accessing external knowledge. That is, firms require resources to establish the relationships they need to be competitive and innovative. The Italian banks interviewed in this research were attractive to Italian manufacturers because they could provide resources helpful in establishing many types of relationships in a foreign environment, from offering a staff fluent in Italian to providing a link with the Italian credit system. In doing so, banks created the preconditions necessary for effective knowledge pipelines. In practice, Italian banks provided Italian manufacturers with cultural support: manufacturers received information about credit conditions, as well as information on trustworthy service providers, all in their native language. Moreover, Italian banks had the expertise and information to interpret the financial conditions of their Italian corporate customers better than non-Italian banks could, and were therefore able to avoid situations such as presented in the following statement:

> If a foreign company establishes a 'daughter' here, to evaluate the 'mother' is more important than to evaluate the daughter. However, when entrepreneurs came showing balances written in Italian, using . . . [a system] different from the Slovak, then you may well understand that the Slovak colleague could not understand the one sitting in front of him or her. (Interview high level manager, Unibanka, 28 June 2006)

Currently, culture is the key service provided by Italian banks: they provide Italian manufacturers with the means to respond to 'first, the language barrier; second, the different legislation, third, the different banking system' (interview with high-level manager, Unibanka, 28 June 2006).

Unicredit has institutionalized its function of cultural support to Italian firms by establishing a department named a New Europe Desk[3] in each of its Eastern European-controlled banks. Each New Europe Desk addresses the specific needs of the foreign (and therefore, mostly Italian) customers of the group. The head of the New Europe Desk in Bulbank, for example, described the reasons for the establishment of the desks as follows:

> [We established New Europe Desks] first, because of the link between Unicredit and local banks. Second, although we are a European level bank, Italy is our most important market. Thus it is our interest to support the internationalization of Italian companies . . . because often our group finances these companies' headquarters in Italy. (Interview high level manager, Bulbank. 22 May 2006)

Unicredit has kept a large percentage of the management involved in the mergers. Also, Unicredit's largest corporate market is still Italy. Providing support to Italian-owned firms in Central and Eastern Europe thus directly contributes to the financial health of the group's corporate customers in Italy.

However, support in establishing knowledge pipelines has not necessarily led to an exclusive relationship between Italian banks and firms. Manufacturers interviewed often chose not to work with Italian banks. According to interviewees, this is a characteristic that distinguishes Italians from other Western Europeans, who tend to 'live and die together with their bank' (interview country manager, Banca Italo Romena, 7 April 2006). Instead, Italians 'come [abroad] by themselves, and look around for the best offer. There is no loyalty at all' (interview with high level manager, Unibanka, 28 June 2006). Italian firms explore investment options without explicit agreements with their banks in Italy and then look for financial support locally. Therefore, firms respond to the weak contracting powers of the banks by exhibiting a lack of loyalty.

The non-exclusive link between Italian banks and manufacturers is not free of conflicts. Bank managers expressed frustration with the time spent advising entrepreneurs, only to see those same entrepreneurs signing loans with their competitors:

> An Italian coming here for the first time needs everything. We tell him 'look, if you want to go to a good consultant, we have five or six names, if you want to go to a notary, we have a few names too.' . . . Thus, Italians come first to us, we talk, discuss, help, then, clearly, they go around. They check where they can find the best conditions and the best rates. (Interview country manager, Italo Romena, 7 April 2006)

In this interview excerpt, the Italo Romena manager highlighted not only the power of his bank to attract Italian customers, thanks to the language connection, but also the uncertain character of the relationship between banks and firms. Similarly, manufacturers perceived an existing tension within business communities even sharing the same language, especially concerning trust; sometimes expressed in the bitter language of disillusion-ment: 'Obviously, an Italian entrepreneur goes to the Italian bank because he thinks he will have a more direct and familiar relationship. Oftentimes this is an illusion' (interview Italian entrepreneur in Bucharest, Romania, 20 March 2006); and '[Banks] don't help us much. People talk about an "Italian team," of joint efforts, but these are words, not facts. Quite the opposite: here banks ask for more guarantees than in Italy, therefore they give firms a harder time' (interview Italian entrepreneur in Timisoara, Romania, 10 April 2006).

Italo Romena and Unicredit played an important role in supporting the establishment of knowledge pipelines between Italian manufacturers and local business and legal environments. As a result, banks and manu-facturers did not necessarily re-establish the same close-knit relationships as in Italy's industrial districts. Instead, banks have offered manufacturers a less pervasive, arm's-length relationship, based on the provision of cultural services, which is not free of conflict. The following section discusses the case of IC & Partners Group, the largest Italian consultancy in Central and Eastern Europe. The case reveals that: (1) the group reinforces a system of manufacturer support based on cultural services; (2) the causality of the Uppsala model is in some instances reversible, that is, according to the model, firms increase their commitment because they acquire sufficient knowledge of the foreign market and, inversely, Italian firms began to demand more knowledge because they decided to increase their investments; and (3) such a system is geographically bound to Central and Eastern Europe, since postsocialist transformation offered favorable conditions to Italian firms.

THE STRATEGY OF IC & PARTNERS GROUP: CULTURAL SERVICES AS A CONNECTION BETWEEN SERVICES AND MANUFACTURERS

Analyzing the internationalization of Finnish banks and insurance companies, Pasi Hellman demonstrated that 'banks tended to move to international banking centers, whereas the internationalization patterns of insurance companies followed more closely the internationalization of manufacturing companies' (Hellman 1996, p. 191). However, the geogra-phies of IC & Partners and Unicredit are very similar (Figure 6.2) owing to the importance of Central and Eastern Europe for Italian manufacturers

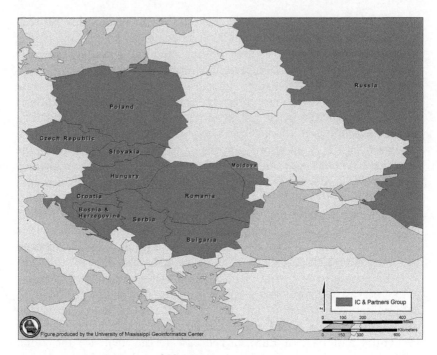

Source: Author's elaboration of IC & Partner's webpage.

Figure 6.2   Countries covered by IC & Partners

as well as the relationships within Italian industrial districts. The IC & Partners Group started as an association and in 2000 formed a consortium. It all started as an initiative of five chartered accountants, each owning at least one firm in Italy and one in Central and Eastern Europe. By the mid-2000s, with the exception of Central Asia, IC & Partners was active in the same countries as Unicredit.

From the start, the goal of IC & Partners has been to create synergies and a common brand to provide homogeneous services across the area (interview Chairman, IC & Partners Group, 10 October 2006). The logic behind this decision was that several firms had interests in more than one Central and Eastern European country and they needed a network of chartered accountants to support them. As in the case of Italian banks, a combination of conditions within Italy and opportunities in Central and Eastern Europe shaped the choices of IC & Partners. Specifically, the average small size of Italian accountancy firms channeled their expansion toward Eastern Europe. The chairman of the IC & Partners group describes the situation as follows:

Here, in this office, we have twelve professionals; it means we are a large firm [for the Italian standard]. The situation is very different with respect to, for example, Northern Europe. I had a partnership with a German firm with 550 chartered accountants; overall they have 2000 employees in 150 offices throughout Germany. (Interview Chairman, IC & Partners Group, 10 October 2006)

In this interview excerpt the chairman singles out the structural weakness of service firms in Italy in comparison with Germany. On average much smaller than their northern European counterparts, Italian accountancy and business services firms do not have the financial means to enter northern European markets, where they would be obliged to compete with larger and more established local firms. The geographical proximity of Central and Eastern Europe, together with the particular conditions of the market in the early phases of the 1990s postsocialist transformation, provided the low costs and low competition necessary for the internationalization of the group (interview Chairman, IC & Partners Group, 10 October 2006).

IC & Partners has a strategy similar to that of Unicredit, centered on providing cultural services to Italian firms, although the two companies understand culture and cultural services in a slightly different way. Unicredit focuses on the provision of information (in Italian) about credit conditions and about trustworthy business services. IC & Partners adopted a broader focus, providing knowledge of spoken and unspoken rules of professional behavior. The range of services provided by IC & Partners, together with the reasons underlying its internationalization strategy, suggests that the implied causality in the Uppsala model can be reversed. Barkema et al. (1996) and Henisz and Delios (2001) argued that the progressive accumulation of knowledge about foreign markets leads firms to further investment. On the contrary, the relationship between IC & Partners and its customers suggests that Italian firms tend to seek information after deciding to increase commitment. Specifically, when Italian investments shifted from short term and speculative to long term and relatively stable, they had to transform subcontracting relationships into joint ventures or acquisitions. In doing so, they had to acquire new knowledge, ranging from organization of the facilities and their relationships with local labor to the legal details of the contracts. Thus, they turned to their own consultancies and tax advisors in Italy for help:

Twelve or thirteen years ago the approach of the Italian entrepreneurs was – and mostly still is – not very organized. They go [abroad], they do business, and they face problems afterwards. This is not a complaint; this is just what it is. Some of our clients (very few at that time) went abroad to invest, and found troubles. Then, they asked us to follow and solve their problems. (Interview Italian chartered accountant, Boscolo & Partners Bucharest, 30 March 2006)

This unflattering excerpt highlights both the weaknesses and the strengths of the Italian system for small firms. Although many firms did not have sufficient resources to internationalize, they could turn to the support networks within their own industrial districts in Italy.

The origin of IC & Partners within the environment of the Italian industrial districts clearly influenced the activity of the group. IC & Partners' members followed their customers to Central and Eastern Europe, providing services and a structure that reproduced the Italian standard. This was not simple, especially before Central and Eastern European countries became EU members and introduced new laws. For example, an IC & Partners representative in Romania described the work undertaken as follows:

> We reproduced our Italian model. We are a fully fledged '*studio dottori commercialisti*' [chartered accountancy firm] even though this professional qualification does not exist in Romanian law. Here we became '*expert contàble*' and were enrolled in the chamber of auditors. With time, we became a structure similar to the one we have in Italy. (Interview Italian chartered accountant, Boscolo & Partners Bucharest, 30 March 2006)

Thus, in order to provide 'Italian' services in Romania, IC & Partners' members had to combine the qualifications of two different professional categories.

Since IC & Partners targets knowledge-seeking SMEs as their main customers, it is not surprising that the group's mission statement focuses on local knowledge and cultural mediation: 'IC & Partners Group has the goal of reconciling the expectations of economic operators and the reality of the markets in which they want to make their way' (IC & Partners website). In Slovakia, the firm EDAS is the IC & Partners Group local member. In the vision of EDAS founder and owner, cultural mediation is at the heart of the firm's work: '70% of EDAS work is not to help Italian entrepreneurs build a copy of their business in Italy, but to create new entities adapted to thrive in Slovakia' (interview entrepreneur, EDAS, 26 September 2005).

Examples of the cultural support provided by EDAS to Italian firms abroad are primarily aimed at 'organizing the human resources in a correct way' (interview entrepreneur, EDAS, 26 September 2005) in order to help entrepreneurs understand spoken and unspoken rules in the organization of the labor force. To do so, EDAS insists on listening to input from local people. Secondly, EDAS provides detailed information on local norms and customs, highlighting the importance of continuity with the past.

> For example, in Slovakia contracts of employment specify in detail employees' duties, while in Italy they tend to be much less detailed. . . . [Italian firms should]

balance continuity with the past and innovation, retaining the positive aspects of the old system, re-using them in a more modern way. [EDAS suggests initiatives such as] medals for excellent employees, prizes for senior workers, feasts organized for the village, health assistance beyond what is required by law. (Interview entrepreneur, EDAS, 26 September 2005)

EDAS advisors highlight the relationship of Italian firms with the socialist past of the host countries: socialist legacies must be used to support capitalist production. The examples provided here of continuity with the socialist past are instrumental in gaining employee loyalty.

In the EDAS owner's words, 'the objective is to motivate employees, to let them share the goals of the enterprise' (interview, 26 September 2005). More precisely, Italian entrepreneurs must be able to organize the technology, structure and goals of their enterprises, while at the same time manage personnel in a way familiar to local workers in an effort to minimize any friction between the Italian management and local labor.

The structural limitations of Italian capitalism, and especially the predominance of small firms, explains why the causality of the Uppsala model can be reversed: the customers of IC & Partners did not decide to internationalize because they acquired more knowledge through their subcontracting relationships. On the contrary, the decision toward internationalization created a demand for local knowledge. Rooted in the tradition of the industrial districts in Italy, service firms such as IC & Partners and banks such as Unicredit and Italo Romena aided in the survival of Italian firms outside the districts. In doing so, IC & Partners attempted to reproduce the relationships it has within its districts by providing Italian standards in Central and Eastern Europe. However, banks which were less dependent on Italian customers provided cultural services but did not attempt to establish exclusive relationships with Italian firms. This peculiar relationship between Unicredit, Italo Romena, IC & Partners and manufacturers is geographically centered in Central and Eastern Europe owing to a window of opportunity opened by postsocialist transformation, which established an environment favorable to foreign investments in both the manufacturing and financial sectors. Geographical proximity with Italy also allowed small firms to invest, thereby creating a demand for cultural services as fulfilled by banks and service firms.

CONCLUSION

The literature on postsocialist transformation highlights the crucial role of FDI in the restructuring of the economies of Central and Eastern Europe. However, few analyses have considered the interactions between investors in the financial and service sectors with investors in manufacturing. Moreover, there are few studies concerning the role of the country of origin in shaping investment, with the exception of work on Greek firms in the Balkans (Kalogeresis and Labrianidis 2010a, 2010b; Kamaras 2001). This chapter explored both issues, discussing the internationalization of two Italian banks (Unicredit and Italo Romena), a consortium of consultancies (IC & Partners) and a sample of SMEs in Central and Eastern Europe.

The Uppsala internationalization process model provided the theoretical framework to discuss both the internationalization of banks, services and manufacturers, as well as their relationships. This model assumes that firms progressively increase their international commitments, shifting from subcontracting to joint ventures and FDI, and from geographic and cultural proximity to more distant places. The increase in commitment is a function of knowledge; the more experience firms acquire abroad, the more ready they are to shift to a higher commitment. Building on interviews and secondary literature, this research has argued that the Uppsala model applies not only at the firm level but also at the level of (some) sectors and industrial districts. In Italy, internationalization depended upon conscious decisions of the leaders of the textile and clothing industry, as well as conditions in the national economy, and within industrial districts. As a result, a large number of firms internationalized in a similar time frame and in a way that is consistent with the Uppsala model. Interviews in Romania, Slovakia and Bulgaria confirmed that Italian firms intensified their commitment in various ways. In the 1990s, Italian textile and clothing SMEs invested in large numbers in Romania, which is both the closest geographically and culturally to Italy. Slovakia, also geographically close, attracted a smaller number of investors. Bulgaria, more distant than Romania or Slovakia, became a popular site of investment later, after a financial crisis in 1997 led to pro-market reforms that attracted larger firms on average.

The analysis of banks and services presented here also suggests that the causality of the Uppsala model can be reversed. According to the model, firms increase their commitment abroad after they gain enough knowledge of foreign markets. However, some Italian SMEs decided to increase their commitment abroad first and sought knowledge afterwards. Not having enough resources to gain such expertise on their own, these firms pushed the internationalization of their banks and service providers, which became knowledge pipelines between Italian firms and Central and Eastern European regional economies.

These findings contribute to the literature on internationalization of SMEs and particularly to the debate on the reproduction of industrial districts outside of Italy. This chapter demonstrated that the conditions within Italian districts (especially Treviso) shaped the patterns of internationalization of Italian firms, connecting the decisions of manufacturers, banks and services. However, once located in Central and Eastern Europe, these firms established at best a loose connection with each other, based on the provision of cultural services, that is, knowledge of local languages, norms and customs. Similar to the Greek case (Kalogeresis and Labrianidis 2010b), the resulting geographies of internationalization of Italian firms were shaped by the postsocialist transformation of Central and Eastern Europe. Both the Greek capitalist diaspora and Italian district firms were followed by banks in the late 1990s (Kamaras 2001, p. 55). While the Greeks initially focused on the Balkans, Italian banks and consultancies invested in a broader area as mergers in Italy and postsocialism offered them unique opportunities. From the mid-1990s to early 2000s, the lack of competition and the low cost of intellectual labor allowed IC & Partners and other consultancies to enter Central and Eastern European markets, notwithstanding their small size and limited financial means. In the early 2000s, large-scale privatization and lack of interest from American competitors, together with the resources acquired in Italy through mergers, allowed Unicredit to acquire major banks in the whole region. At this time (2012), notwithstanding the financial and sovereign debt crisis affecting both Italy and most economies of Central and Eastern Europe, Unicredit, Italo Romena and IC & Partners are still major players in their respective markets.

NOTES

* This chapter is based on a paper that was first published in *European Urban and Regional Studies* as Sellar, C. (2015), 'Italian banks and business services as knowledge pipelines for SMEs: examples from Central and Eastern Europe', *European Urban and Regional Studies*, **22** (1), 41–60.
1. A Doctoral Dissertation Improvement Grant from the National Science Foundation, an Off Campus Dissertation Research Fellowship from the Graduate School of the University of North Carolina (UNC) at Chapel Hill, a Doctoral Research Travel Award from the University Center for International Studies (now the Center for Global Initiatives) of the UNC-Chapel Hill, and a Dissertation Completion Fellowship from the Graduate School of the UNC-Chapel Hill funded this project entitled 'The relationship between the processes of outsourcing of Italian textile and clothing firms and the emergence of industrial districts in Eastern Europe'.
2. This is a very different phenomenon from the Greek 'capitalist diaspora' identified by Kamaras (2001) and Kalogeresis and Labrianidis (2010b), according to whom a large number of Greek SMEs fully relocated to the Balkans, especially in the early 1990s, and were later followed by larger firms establishing FDIs. In the Italian case, the literature presents no evidence of a large-scale migration of firms. Most of the firms interviewed in this study maintained headquarters in Italy, and sent one of the owners, or a close associate,

to live permanently or semi-permanently in Central and Eastern Europe. There was a minority of expatriate entrepreneurs, mostly former directors of Italian-owned companies.
3. All New Europe Desks were renamed International Desks following the merger between Unicredit and the Austrian group HVB in 2005. This chapter maintains the old name, New Europe Desk, to be consistent with the content of the interviews.

REFERENCES

Aliber, R.Z. (1984), 'International banking: a survey', *Journal of Money, Credit and Banking*, **16** (4), 661–712.

Ambos, T., Schlegelmilch, B., Ambos, B. and Brenner, B. (2009), 'Evolution of organisational structure and capabilities in internationalising banks: the CEE Operations of UniCredit's Vienna Office', *Long Range Planning*, **42** (5–6), 633–53.

Aspelund, A. and Butsko, V. (2010), 'Small and medium-sized enterprises' offshoring production: a study of firms' decisions and consequences', *Tijdschrift voor Economische en Sociale Geografie*, **101** (3), 262–75.

Bandelj, N. (2008), *From Communists to Foreign Capitalists: The Social Foundations of Foreign Direct Investment in Postsocialist Europe*, Princeton, NJ: Princeton University Press.

Barkema, G., Bell, J. and Pennings, M. (1996), 'Foreign entry, cultural barriers, and learning', *Strategic Management Journal*, **17** (2), 151–66.

Becattini, G. (1979), 'Dal "settore" industriale al "distretto" industrial: alcune considerazioni sull'unità d'indagine dell'economia industriale' ('From "industrial sectors" to "industrial districts": reflections upon the units of analysis in industrial economics'), *Rivista di economia politica e industrial*, **5** (1), 7–21.

Becattini, G., Bellandi, M. and Sforzi, F. (2003), *From Industrial Districts to Local Development: An Itinerary of Research*, Cheltenham, UK and Northampton, MA, USA: Edward Elgar.

Bonomi, A. (1997), *Il capitalismo molecolare: La società al lavoro nel nord Italia* (*Molecular Capitalism: Society and Work in Northern Italy*), Turin: Einaudi.

Bourdieu, P. (1986), 'Forms of capital', in J. Richardson (eds), *Handbook of Theory and Research for the Sociology of Education*, New York: Greenwood Press.

Breschi, S. and Malerba, F. (eds) (2005), *Clusters, Networks and Innovation*, Oxford: Oxford University Press.

Broadman, L. (2006), 'From disintegration to reintegration: Eastern Europe and the former Soviet Union in international trade', accessed 1 March 2009 at http://go.worldbank.org/6WKTRSQMS0.

Brusco, S. (1986), 'Small firms and industrial districts: the experience of Italy', *Economia Internazionale*, **39** (2–3–4), 85–97.

Buckley, P.J., Pass, C.L. and Prescott, K. (1992), 'The internationalization of service firms: a comparison with the manufacturing sector', *Scandinavian International Business Review*, **1** (1), 39–56.

Cainelli, G. and Zoboli, R. (eds) (2004), *The Evolution of Industrial Districts: Changing Governance, Innovation and Internationalisation of Local Capitalism in Italy*, Berlin and Heudelberg: Springer Science & Business Media.

Calof, J. and Viviers, W. (1995), 'Internationalization behavior of small- and medium-sized South African enterprises', *Journal of Small Business Management*, **33** (4), pp 71–9.

Cattani, G. and Tschoegl, A. (2002), 'An evolutionary view of internationalization: Chase Manhattan Bank, 1917 to 1996', Working Paper No. 02-37, Wharton School of the University of Pennsylvania, Philadelphia, PN, accessed 13 July 2010 at http://fic.wharton.upenn.edu/fic/papers/02/p0237.html.

Chiarvesio, M. (2005), 'Internazionalizzazione, innovazione e performance delle PMI dei distretti industriali' ('Internationalization, innovation, and performance of SMEs in industrial districts'), *Argomenti*, **15** (December), 24–61.

Chiarvesio, M. and Micelli, S. (2006), 'Tecnologie di rete e innovazione nei distretti industriali' ('Web technologies and innovation in industrial districts'), in D. Marini (eds) *Nordest 2006. Rapporto sulla società e l'economia*, Venice: Marsilio.

Chiarvesio, M., Di Maria, E. and Micelli, S. (2006a), 'Global value chains and open networks: the case of Italian industrial districts', paper presented at the Eighteenth Annual Meeting of the Society for the Advancement of Socio-Economics, Trier, 30 June–2 July.

Chiarvesio, M., Di Maria, E. and Micelli, S. (2006b), 'Modelli di sviluppo e strategie di internazionalizzazione delle imprese distrettuali italiane' ('Development models and internationalization strategies of Italian districts' firms'), in G. Tattara, G. Corò and M. Volpe (eds), *Andarsene per continuare a crescere*, Rome: Carocci, pp. 139–57.

Chiarvesio, M., Di Maria, E. and Micelli, S. (2006c), 'Strategie e modelli di internazionalizzazione delle imprese distrettuali italiane' ('Strategies and internationalization of Italian districts firms'), *Economia e politica industrial*, **3**, accessed 13 July 2010 at http://www.francoangeli.it/riviste/sommario.asp?anno=2006&idRivista=13.

Cooke, P., Heidenreich, M. and Braczyk, H. (2004), *Regional Innovation Systems: The Role of Governance in a Globalized World*, London: Routledge.

Corò, G. and Micelli, S. (2006), *I nuovi distretti produttivi: innovazione internazionalizzazione e competitività dei territori* (*The New Productive Districts: Innovational, Internationalization and Territorial Competitiveness*), Venice: Marsilio.

Corò, G. and Volpe, M. (2006), 'Local production systems in global value chains: the case of Italian industrial districts', paper presented at the Global Value Chains Workshop 'Industrial Upgrading, Offshore Production, and Labor', Duke University, Durham, NC, 9–10 November.

Davidson, W. (1980), 'The location of foreign direct investment activity: country characteristics and experience effects', *Journal of International Business Studies*, **11** (1), 9–22.

De Paula, L.F. (2002), 'Expansion strategies of European banks to Brazil and their impacts on the Brazilian banking sector', *Latin American Business Review*, **3** (4), 59–92.

De Rosa, F. (2006), 'Maxi-fusione Intesa-San Paolo: Nasce la prima banca italiana' ('Maxi-merger Intesa-San Paolo: the first Italian bank is born'), *Corriere della Sera*, 25 August, p. 25.

Delios, A. and Henisz, W.J. (2003), 'Political hazards, experience and sequential entry strategies: the international expansion of Japanese firms, 1980–1998', *Strategic Management Journal*, **24** (12), 1153–64.

Di Maria, E. and Micelli, S. (2006), 'Districts leaders as open networks: emerging business strategies in Italian industrial districts', paper presented at the Global Value Chains Workshop 'Industrial Upgrading, Offshore Production, and Labor', Duke University, Durham, NC, 9–10 November.

Dolfsma, W. (2008), *Knowledge Economies. Organization, Location and Innovation*, London and New York: Routledge.

Dunford, M. (2006), 'Industrial districts, magic circles, and the restructuring of the Italian textile and clothing chain', *Economic Geography*, **82** (1), 27–59.

EDAS website, www.edas.sk (accessed 23 July 2019).

Federico, S. (2004), 'L'internazionalizzazione produttiva italiana e i distretti indus-triali: un'analisi degli investimenti diretti all'estero' ('Italian internationalization and industrial districts: and analysis of foreign direct investments'), in Banca d'Italia (eds), *Economie Locali, modelli di agglomerazione e apertura internazion-ale*, Rome: Banca d'Italia, pp. 107–35.

Feenstra, R.C. (1998), 'Integration of trade and disintegration of production in the global economy', *Journal of Economic Perspectives*, **12** (4), 31–50.

Freeman, C. (1987), *Technology Policy and Economic Performance: Lessons from Japan*, London: Frances Pinter.

Gertler, M. (2008), 'Buzz without being there? Communities of practice in context', in A. Amin and J. Roberts (eds), *Community Economic Creativity and Organization*, Oxford: Oxford University Press, pp. 203–27.

Gibson-Graham, J.K. (1996), *The End of Capitalism (As We Knew It): A Feminist Critique of Political Economy*, Malden, MA and Oxford: Blackwell.

Gibson-Graham, J.K. (2006), *A Postcapitalist Politics*, Minneapolis, MN: University of Minnesota Press.

Granovetter, M. and Swedberg, R. (eds) (2001), *The Sociology of Economic Life*, Cambridge, MA: Westview.

Graziani, G. (1998), 'Globalization of production in the textile and clothing indus-tries: the case of Italian foreign direct investment and outward processing in Eastern Europe', Working Paper No. 128, Berkeley Roundtable on the International Economy, University of California, Berkeley, CA, accessed 16 February 2010 at http://escholarship.org/uc/item/5cr30690.

Guillén, M. and Tschoegl, A. (2000), 'The internationalization of retail banking: the case of the Spanish banks in Latin America', *Transnational Corporations*, **9** (3), 63–99.

Guillén, M. and Tschoegl, A. (2008), *Building a Global Bank: The Transformation of Banco Santander*, Princeton, NJ: Princeton University Press.

Hellman, P. (1996), 'The internationalization of Finnish financial service compa-nies', *International Business Review*, **5** (2), 191–208.

Henisz, W.J. and Delios, A. (2001), 'Uncertainty, imitation, and plant loca-tion: Japanese multinational corporations, 1990–1996', *Administrative Science Quarterly*, **46** (3), 443–75.

Hervas-Oliver, J.L. and Albors-Garrigos, J. (2009), 'The role of the firm's internal and relational capabilities in clusters: when distance and embeddedness are not enough to explain innovation', *Journal of Economic Geography*, **9** (2), 263–83.

IC & Partners website, accessed 7 December 2006 at www.icpartnersgroup.net.

Istituto per il Commercio Estero (ICE) (2006a), 'Osservatorio sull'Internazional-izzazione dei Distretti Industriali' ('Observatory on the internationalization of industrial districts'), 1 July, ICE, Rome.

Istituto per il Commercio Estero (ICE) (2006b), *Economia 2005. Banato e Transilvania. Distretto di Timis* (*Economy 2005, Banat and Transylvania. Distict of Timist*), Rome: Istituto per il Commercio Estero.

Jacobsen, F. and Tschoegl, A. (1997), 'The international expansion of the Norwegian banks', Wharton Working Paper No. 97-38, Wharton School of the University of Pennsylvania, Philadelphia, PN, accessed 13 July 2010 at http://fic.wharton.upenn.edu/fic/papers/97/p9738.html.

Johanson, J. and Vahlne, J.E. (1977), 'The internationalization process of the firm: a model of knowledge development and increasing foreign market commitments', *Journal of International Business Studies*, **8** (1), 23–32.

Kalogeresis, A. and Labrianidis, L. (2010a), 'Delocalization and development: empirical findings from selected European countries', *Competition and Change: The Journal of Global Business and Political Economy*, **14** (2), 100–123.

Kalogeresis, A. and Labrianidis, L. (2010b), 'From spectator to walk-on to actor: an exploratory study of the internationalisation of Greek firms since 1989', *European Journal of Comparative Economics*, **7** (1), 121–43.

Kamaras, A. (2001), 'A capitalist diaspora: the Greeks in the Balkans', Discussion Paper No. 4, Hellenic Observatory, European Institute, London School of Economics and Political Science.

Krugman, P., Cooper, R.N. and Srinivasan, T.N. (1995), 'Growing world trade: causes and consequences', *Brookings Papers on Economic Activity*, **1**, 327–77.

Letta, E. (2001), 'Prefazione' ('Preface'), in Ministero del Commercio con l'Estero (ed.), *Banche e imprese: it sistema Italia nel mercato globale*, Rome: Bancaria.

Locke, R. (1995), *Remaking the Italian Economy*, Ithaca, NY: Cornell University Press.

Luostarinen, R. (1980), *Internationalization of the Firm*, Helsinki: Helsinki School of Economics.

Malerba, F. (2004), *Sectoral Systems of Innovation*, Cambridge: Cambridge University Press.

Malmberg, A. (2003), 'Beyond the cluster: local milieus and global connections', in J. Peck and H. Yeung (eds), *Remaking the Global Economy*, London: Sage, pp. 145–59.

Markusen, A. (1986), *Profit Cycles, Oligopoly and Regional Development*, Cambridge, MA: MIT Press.

Markusen, A. (1996), 'Sticky places in slippery space: a typology of industrial districts', *Economic Geography*, **72** (3), 293–314.

Marshall, A. (1919), *Industry and Trade: A Study on Industrial Techniques and Business Organization; and of Their Influences on the Conditions of Various Classes and Nations*, London: Macmillan.

Martin, R. and Sunley, P. (2003), 'Deconstructing clusters: chaotic concept of policy panacea?', *Journal of Economic Geography*, **3** (1), 5–35.

Moodysson, J. (2008), 'Principles and practices of knowledge creation: on the organization of "buzz" and "pipelines" in life science communities', *Economic Geography*, **84** (4), 449–69.

Myant, M. and Drahokoupil, J (2012), 'International integration, varieties of capitalism, and resilience to crisis in transition economies', *Europe-Asia Studies*, **64** (1), 1–33.

Nelson, R. (1993), *National Innovation Systems*, Oxford: Oxford University Press.

Padoa-Schioppa, T. (1999), 'EMU and banking supervision', *International Finance*, **2** (2), 295–308.

Pavlínek, P. (2008), *A Successful Transformation? Restructuring of the Czech Automobile Industry*, Heidelberg: Physica-Verlag.

Perrin, J.C. (1993), 'Pour une révision de la science régionale: l'approche en termes de milieu', Notes de recherché 148/3, Centre d'économie régionale, Aix-en-Provence.

Pickles, J., Smith, A., Roukova, P., Begg, R. and Bucek, M. (2006), 'Upgrading and diversification in the East European industry: competitive pressure and production networks in the clothing industry', *Environment and Planning A*, **38** (12), 2305–24.

Piore, M. and Sabel, C. (1984), *The Second Industrial Divide: Possibilities for Prosperity*, New York: Basic Books.

Porter, M. (1990), *The Competitive Advantage of Nations*, New York: Free Press.

Powell, W.W. and Grodal, S. (2005), 'Networks of innovators', in J. Fagerberg, D.C. Mowery and R. Nelson (eds), *The Oxford Handbook of Innovation*, Oxford: Oxford University Press, pp. 56–85.

Putnam, R., Leonardi, R. and Nanetti, R. (1993), *Making Democracy Work: Civic Traditions in Modern Italy*, Princeton, NJ: Princeton University Press.

Rabellotti, R. (2001), 'The effect of globalisation on industrial districts in Italy: the case of Brenta', IDS Working Papers No. 144, Institute for Development Studies, Brighton, accessed 26 October 2006 at http://www.ice.gov.it/editoria/bollettino/studi/Rabellotti.pdf.

Rabellotti, R. (2004), 'How globalisation affects Italian industrial districts: the case of Brenta', in H. Schmitz (ed.), *Local Enterprises in the Global Economy: Issues of Governance and Upgrading*, Cheltenham, UK and Northampton, MA, USA: Edgar Elgar, pp. 140–73.

Rabellotti, R., Carabelli, A. and Hirsch, G. (2009), 'Italian Industrial districts on the move: where are they going?', *European Planning Studies*, **17** (1), 19–41.

Rullani, E. (2002), 'Dallo sviluppo per accumulazione allo sviluppo per propagazione: piccole imprese, clusters e capitale sociale nella nuova Europa in formazione' ('From development by accumulation to development by propagation: small enterprises, clusters and social capital in the new Europe in formation'), paper presented at East West Cluster Conference, Udine, 28–31 October.

Sabel, C. (2003), 'The world in a bottle or window on the world? Open questions about industrial districts in the spirit of Sebastiano Brusco', paper presented at the Conference on Clusters, Industrial Districts and Firms: The Challenge of Globalization, Modena, 12–13 September, accessed 16 February 2012 at http://www2.law.columbia.edu/sabel/papers.htm.

Saxenian, A. (1994), *Regional Advantage. Culture and Competition in Silicon Valley and Route 128*, Cambridge, MA: Harvard University Press.

Schumpeter, J. (1942), *Capitalism, Socialism and Democracy*, London: George Allen & Unwin.

Scott, A. and Storper, M. (1987), 'High technology industry and regional development: a theoretical critique and reconstruction', *International Social Science Journal*, **112**, 215–32.

Sellar, C. (2009), 'Geographical imaginaries of the "New Europe" and the "East" in a business context: the case of Italian investors in Slovakia, Romania, and Ukraine', *Journal of Cultural Geography*, **26** (3), 327–48.

Sellar, C. (2011), 'Europeanizing Timisoara: neoliberal reforms, continuity with the past, and unexpected side effect', *GeoJournal*, **78** (1), 1–19, doi:10.1007/s10708-011-9421-y.

Smith, A., Pickles, J., Bucek, M., Begg, R. and Roukova, P. (2008), 'Reconfiguring "post-socialist" regions: cross-border networks and regional competition in the Slovak and Ukrainian clothing industry', *Global Networks*, **8** (3), 281–307.

Smith, A. and Swain, A. (2010), 'The global economic crisis, Eastern Europe, and the former Soviet Union: models of development and the contradictions of internationalization', *Eurasian Geography and Economics*, **51** (1), 1–34.

Storper, M. (1997), *The Regional World: Territorial Development in a Global Economy*, New York: Guilford.

Tschoegl, A.E. (1987),' International retail banking as a strategy: an assessment', *Journal of International Business Studies*, **19** (2), 67–88.

Unicredit website, accessed 13 July at www.unicreditgroup.eu.

Vernon, R. (1971), *Sovereignty at Bay: The Multinational Spread of US Enterprises*, New York: Basic Books.

Vernon, R. (1972), 'Influence of national origins on the strategy of multinational enterprise', *Revue économique*, **23** (4), 547–62.

Vernon, R. (1985), 'This week's citation classic. Sovereignty at bay: the multinational spread of U.S. enterprises', *Current Contents (CC)*, **3**, 21 January, 18, accessed 13 July 2010 at http://www.garfield.library.upenn.edu/classics1985/A1985TZ13200 001.pdf.

Vernon, R. (1998), *In the Hurricane's Eye: The Troubled Prospects of Multinational Enterprises*, Cambridge MA: Harvard University Press.

Welch, L.S. and Luostarinen R. (1988), 'Internationalization: evolution of a concept', *Journal of General Management*, **14** (2), 34–55.

Yin, R.K. (2003), *Case Study Research: Design and Methods*, Newbury Park, CA: Sage.

7. Spatial aspects of the Russian banking system: transformation and access to credit for small Russian firms*

Svetlana Ageeva and Anna Mishura

1. SPATIAL TRANSFORMATION OF THE BANKING SECTOR: GLOBAL TRENDS AND THE CASE OF RUSSIA

The geographical unevenness of Russian financial development has political and institutional causes. This chapter considers the spatial transformation of the Russian banking system from observations on regularities and trends revealed in the modern financial geographies of other countries. We thus examine the role of the Russian banking system in the allocation of financial resources to Russian regions, with particular attention given to the problem of financing small and medium-sized enterprises (SMEs). In Russia, SMEs are embedded in local markets and tied to specific locations: the geography of financial institutions is thus very important. Moreover, bank loans are a main source of external financing for SMEs, which have limited ability to attract funds from the stock market. These firms are thus particularly sensitive to the geography of banking in a region or a country.

Most national banking systems in the past few decades have undergone processes of centralization that have led to geographical concentration (McCauley et al. 2010; Tickell 2000). As the number of independent banks is seen to decrease, large banking networks – often with a global presence – concentrate their head offices in large financial centers. This is an extension of the financial liberalization and processes of the 1980–90s and has been spurred on by access to new information and financial technologies. In addition, the global financial crisis of 2008–09 was followed by a tightening of regulations which has been to the advantage of larger banks (Alessandrini et al. 2016), albeit to varying extents depending on the specific national context. In Europe, banking nationalism has contributed to the strengthening of large banks, while in the United States there is a different regulatory regime for small and large banks (for example, Dymski 2016). However, in some European countries, such as Germany and Italy, the role of small regional banks is still an important institutional feature and policies of a country can either stimulate or hinder financial concentration and centralization (see Flögel and Gärtner 2018).

From this it can be seen that these processes are general; furthermore, several theoretical and empirical studies reveal potential negative consequences of banking sector concentration and centralization:

1. Large banking networks headquartered in other regions do not sufficiently finance the regional economy, especially SMEs. They redistribute capital from peripheral regions to central regions where head offices of banks are located, especially during periods of crisis (Klagge et al. 2017; Presbitero et al. 2014).
2. Large network banks usually have complex hierarchical structures. These structures make them less suited to work with SMEs, especially in remote regions (Papi et al. 2017; Udell 2009).

In contrast, small regional banks tend to work in connection with the regional economy and regional SMEs, providing them with better access to credit and protecting them against external shocks. These banks are involved in the local context and suffer less from information asymmetry and moral hazard problems. The difficulty is that regional banks are subject to local shocks, have less liquid and diversified assets and fewer economies of scale. Thus, it is not evident what model and size of bank is most appropriate for regional economies. Is it reasonable to support decentralized local and small financial institutions? We apply these issues to the case of the Russian economy and consider the extent to which banking concentration affects access to credit in various Russian regions. More specifically, could large Russian multiregional banks, mostly headquartered in Moscow, meet the needs of other regions?

In the 2000s, a steady decline in the number of Russian banks has occurred owing to concentration and consolidation processes taking place globally across this industry. In addition, the Central Bank of Russia's (CBR's) cleansing policy in the banking sector intensified from the second half of 2013, purging the banking sector of unsustainable and unscrupulous banks. The policy seeks to improve the efficiency and viability of the banking system. The fewer banks in the system, the easier they are to regulate; also, monetary control is enhanced. While the connection between concentration in the sector, competition and stability is ambiguous (see Makinen and Solanko 2018), CBR assumes that competition in the sector is robust and that improved stability in banking will strengthen small and medium-sized banks and undermine the monopoly of large banks. Similarly, the reform of bank licensing to establish different regulatory regimes for small and larger banks was carried out in 2018, but its results are not yet clear. An alternative view is that this policy is directed towards the actual liquidation of both private banks in favor of banks with state participation and regional banks in favor of Moscow-based banking networks. The Association of Russian Banks has criticized the mass revocation of licenses: the formation of a highly centralized and largely state-owned banking system can hardly be desirable for any modern market economy (Claeys et al. 2016). However, the approach thus far has created a Moscow-centered and state-oriented banking system with large banking networks, at the expense of private smaller and regional banks.

Given these concerns, this chapter examines the role of the Russian banking system in the allocation of resources across Russian regions. Using data from the CBR, the role of Moscow-based banking networks in lending to regional economies outside Moscow is investigated and concludes that a centralized banking system naturally complements a very specific Russian centralized economy. Large network banks, headquartered mainly in Moscow, provide a regular flow of financial resources concentrated in the capital for lending needs of other regions. These 'flight to home' and 'flight to quality' effects (Degryse et al. 2018) during the crisis period after 2014 reveal that lending to SMEs remains especially vulnerable in these situations.

2.   MULTIREGIONAL BANKS AND LENDING TO THE RUSSIAN REGIONS

The objective of this section is to analyze the geography of the Russian banking system. The methodological approach is as follows: information from the CBR website is used to investigate the role of Moscow-based banking networks in lending to regional economies outside Moscow; this includes information on the loan portfolio and customer funds raised by the banks in the regions.[1] The data reveals a regional structure containing the locations of offices where money for deposits and accounts were accepted and the location of borrowers, but without indicating whether or not the bank is regional or national. The main source of bank liabilities is client funds (individuals, firm and state organizations). The largest asset is loans, thus regions where this money was deposited and where loans were issued are observed. In particular, note that there are substantial regional differences in Russian regions: in 2010–17 in most regions, except Moscow

Table 7.1   The amounts of loan portfolio based on borrowers' location and
clients' funds based on offices' location, by the end of the year
(trillions of rubles)

	2010	2011	2012	2013	2014	2015	2016	2017
Moscow region								
Clients' funds	12.2	15.8	17.9	20.6	26.0	31.3	28.7	30.2
Loan portfolio	6.7	8.5	10.0	11.4	14.4	15.2	14.7	15.6
Clients' fund minus loan portfolio	5.6	7.3	7.9	9.2	11.7	16.1	14.0	14.6
Russia outside Moscow region								
Clients' funds	9.1	10.8	12.6	14.7	16.6	20.3	21.4	22.8
Loan portfolio	11.0	14.1	17.3	20.8	24.7	25.3	24.3	25.7
Clients' fund minus loan portfolio	−1.9	−3.3	−4.7	−6.1	−8.1	−5.0	−2.9	−2.9
Assets (liabilities) of regional banks	4.6	5.0	5.7	6.4	6.6	7.6	7.6	7.9

Source: Authors' elaboration based on www.cbr.ru data (accessed 11 February 2018).

and the Moscow region, the amounts of loans given to the regional
economy are larger than clients' funds accepted in those regions. At the
same time, the opposite is observed in Moscow and the country as a whole
(see Table 7.1).

Could regional banks cover the gap between loan portfolio and clients'
money in Russian regions outside Moscow? They may use their own
capital, issue securities, and use interbank loans and CBR funds. However,
the data show that it is very unlikely that they can plug the gap, since, first,
regional banks not only credit local clients, but also use money for other
purposes such as buying securities, cash, interbank loans, reserves in the
CBR and other assets. Second, the total amount of their liabilities (assets)
is insufficient and in 2014 was less than the gap between loans and the
funds raised in the regions (see Table 7.1). According to CBR data, a small
part of the loans is received by regional borrowers directly in the offices
of banks located in other regions, mainly in Moscow. Table 7.1 shows that
the regional economies are getting loans through the Moscow banking
networks or directly from Moscow offices. So they are receiving funds
from Moscow, and net transfers from head offices (the passive balance of
settlements between regional branches and headquarters) are one of the
important sources of funds for the regional banking sector. These transfers
reached a maximum in 2014 when they could provide up to a third of

loans issued in the regions. However, this should be considered taking into account another very important feature of the spatial organization of the Russian economy. That is, Moscow contains the head offices of the major non-financial companies of the whole country, so their financial resources, as well as state financial resources, are concentrated there. From CBR data we can see that in Moscow about 70 percent of clients' money fund companies and organizations, and only 30 percent are in household deposits, while in the rest of Russia there is the opposite ratio (30 percent and 70 percent, respectively). In this situation, the Russian banking system complements and partly compensates for the super-concentration of finance in the capital, while returning some part of the money to other regions in the form of loans.

After the global financial crisis of 2008–09 some researchers (for example, Degryse et al. 2018) used the terms flight to home or flight to headquarters for a disproportionate reduction in lending by large network banks in regions that are remote from their headquarters or in other countries (in the case of transnational banks). The phenomenon drives an overall shift in lending in favor of banks headquarter/home regions at the expense of remote regions, especially for SMEs in such regions. Contrasting examples are the highly centralized financial system of the UK and the less centralized system of Italy (Klagge et al. 2017; Presbitero et al. 2014). Alternatively, in the more decentralized German banking system, during the crisis, lending to small regional borrowers did not suffer as small local banks were doing relatively well and even received an inflow of clients' money (Klagge et al. 2017).

The Russian banking system is highly centralized and still recovering from the shock of the crisis in 2014. The 2014–17 financial crisis in Russia was the result of the collapse of the Russian ruble, beginning in the second half of 2014. The crisis stemmed from at least two main sources: the fall in the price of oil in 2014[2] and the result of international economic sanctions imposed on Russia following Russia's annexation of Crimea and the so-called Russian military intervention in Ukraine. For the period since 2014, the CBR provides more information than for previous years, which enables a study of whether there have been any flight-to-home effects in Russia. In particular, Table 7.1 shows that, since 2014, net transfers of large-bank head offices to regional economies diminished but remained positive. At the same time at first glance, the lending dynamics in Moscow and other regions did not significantly differ from each other. The reduction in the amount of funds transferred from the head offices to regional offices was mainly owing to the growth of client funds in banking institutions when the size of loan portfolios was stagnating both in Moscow and outside the capital. Client funds in the banks increased in 2015 for several reasons:

(1) the revaluation of accounts in foreign currency, (2) the intention of households to protect savings from inflation and (3) the withdrawal of firms' money from their businesses as a reaction to the crisis. This increase in clients' money in the banks was slightly more pronounced in the regions outside Moscow owing to the growth of households' funds. Despite the crisis, the loan portfolio of the banking system increased slightly in 2015, mainly owing to the revaluation of debts in foreign currency, and then slightly decreased in 2016. It remained relatively stable in Moscow and other regions. Thus, the need for net transfers from the banks' headquarters to the regions probably significantly decreased.

However, looking more closely at firms' lending, the dynamics of the firms' loan portfolio in Moscow show a better trend compared with other regions. Figures 7.1 and 7.2 show the share of regional borrowers (those outside Moscow region) in the firms' loan portfolio and in SMEs' loan portfolio for all banks and for the 30 largest banks based on asset size. The top 30 banks are the backbone of the Russian banking system. They provide 80 percent of firms' lending and about 60 percent of SME lending in the country. As we see from Figures 7.1 and 7.2, they are active in lending in the regions outside the capital, especially to SMEs.

Figure 7.1 shows since 2014 about 3 percent of the firms' loan portfolio shifts are in favor of the Moscow region at the expense of other regions mainly owing to the largest banks. In Figure 7.2 we can see the shift in

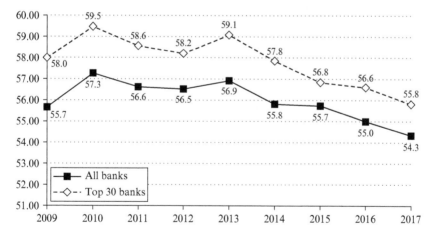

Source: Authors' elaboration based on www.cbr.ru data (accessed 11 February 2018).

Figure 7.1 *Was there a shift of firms' loan portfolio in favor of Moscow? Share of regional firms in total firms' portfolio (percentage at the end of a year)*

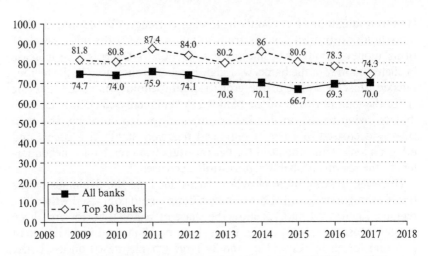

Source: Authors' elaboration based on www.cbr.ru data (accessed 11 February 2018).

Figure 7.2   *Was there a shift of SMEs' loan portfolio in favor of Moscow?*
Share of regional SMEs in total SMEs' loan portfolio
(percentage at the end of a year)

SME lending of the top 30 banks in favor of the capital during 2014–17.
The size of the shift is about 12 percent of the top 30 banks' loans to
SMEs. For all Russian banks, the effect is not so pronounced. Since the
2014 crisis began, SME lending has declined significantly (see below), and
large banks have reduced lending to SMEs in the regions outside Moscow
to a larger degree than in Moscow.

During the crisis period, the dynamics of firms' loan portfolio appeared
to be slightly better in the Moscow region, but the difference is not so significant. We conclude that there is not a very pronounced flight-to-home
effect especially concerning the loans to large companies. The Russian
economy is dominated by large companies and these companies in regions
away from Moscow are still either subsidiaries of Moscow-based organizations, have Moscow-based owners or have other close ties with Moscow
firms and organizations. Also, many large companies are operating in
the regions but are registered in Moscow. Therefore, regional economies
are not remote from the center in an institutional sense, despite the long
distances. Nevertheless some flight to home is also typical for the overall
Russian economy during the crisis period, as it is for other countries with
centralized banking systems.

3. LARGEST BANKS, REGIONAL BANKS AND LENDING TO SMES

In Russia the SME sector is insufficiently developed and lags developed (and not so developed) countries even though small and new enterprises are seen as driving innovation, employment and economic activity all over the world (see Lukács 2005). The current contribution of SMEs to the Russian economy is about 20 percent of GDP: the 'Strategies for the development of small and medium-sized businesses in the Russian Federation for the period up to 2030' of the government of the Russian Federation in 2016 notes that this should rise to 40 percent.

One of the main ways to achieve SME development is to stimulate lending to the sector (Ruchkin et al. 2017). The expansion of subsidized state lending programs is proposed as a remedy for SMEs because SMEs cannot afford commercial credit products. This plan is partially realized. Since 2008 there has been a federal law on the development of small and medium-size entrepreneurship in the Russian Federation. In different regions, special state funds were established which provide loan guarantees for SMEs (EIB 2013). In 2015, the Federal Corporation of Development of Small and Medium-sized Entrepreneurship was established and it began to provide loan guarantees for SMEs. Within this corporation a specialized development bank was created (Chepurenko and Vilenski 2016), the SME Bank, which provides credits at subsidized interest rates through commercial banks. Program 6.5 is an example developed by the corporation, in cooperation with the Ministry of Economic Development and the CBR, that provides participating banks with money to lend to SMEs at 6.5 percent interest rate.

Small and medium-sized enterprises, especially in regions outside Moscow, are often perceived as a 'factory for laundering of illegal money'.[3] The state's fight against money laundering, tax evasion schemes and the cleansing policy in the banking sector led to tighter requirements for banks in servicing SMEs. In the case of small businesses, there are several obstacles to loan issuance, including complexity of asset evaluation, informational opacity and high heterogeneity of small firms, and higher risks and transaction costs per unit of credit. Therefore, banks often prefer to reduce work with the sector as was the case during the crisis period from 2014.

Data from the CBR on SME lending in Russian regions[4] by regional banks and bank offices from other regions (mainly from Moscow) shows that, since 2014, SME lending has been declining both in absolute and relative terms (Figures 7.3 and 7.4) despite growth of the total loan portfolio of Russian banks in 2014, 2015 and 2017. The reasons for these declines

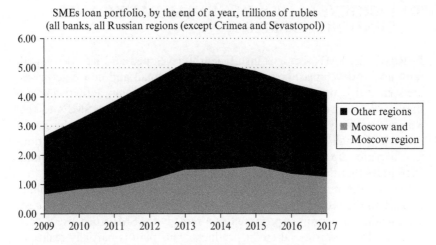

SMEs loan portfolio, by the end of a year, trillions of rubles
(all banks, all Russian regions (except Crimea and Sevastopol))

Source: Authors' elaboration based on www.cbr.ru data (accessed 11 February 2018).

Figure 7.3 SME lending in Moscow and in other regions

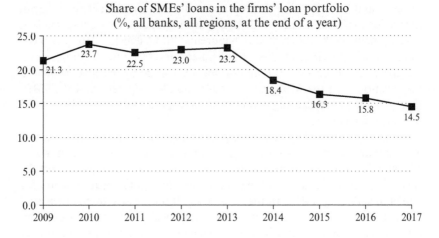

Share of SMEs' loans in the firms' loan portfolio
(%, all banks, all regions, at the end of a year)

Source: Authors' elaboration based on www.cbr.ru data (accessed 11 February 2018).

Figure 7.4 Lending to SMEs in Russia

are macroeconomic instability, the collapse of the national currency and a sharp increase in the central bank's interest rate at the end of 2014. When, in July 2015, the criteria for classifying enterprises as SMEs changed this did not improve the dynamics. Banks argue that demand for loans from

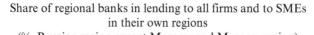

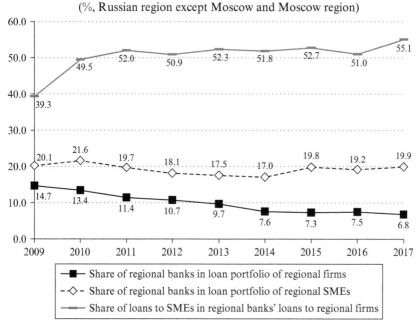

Share of regional banks in lending to all firms and to SMEs
in their own regions
(%, Russian region except Moscow and Moscow region)

Source: Authors' elaboration based on www.cbr.ru data (accessed 11 February 2018).

Figure 7.5 Regional banks in regions outside Moscow

SMEs and number of reliable borrowers has fallen, while risks and level of overdue debts have risen (up to 14–15 percent of loan portfolio in the SME sector). Entrepreneurs blame high interest rates and collateral requirements. Outcomes are reflected in Figure 7.3. In regions outside the capital, the decline in SME lending started earlier.

We examine the role of the largest banks and regional banks in the shrinkage of SME lending. Figure 7.5 shows the role of regional banks (those registered in regions outside Moscow) in lending to all firms and SMEs in their own regions. Their share in lending to SMEs is higher than their share in lending to all firms. Despite the reduction in number and share of regional banks as a result of the CBR's cleansing policy, their role in SME lending in their own regions did not decrease in 2015 but grew. The share of SME loans in the firms' loan portfolios is consistently high (about 50 percent). So regional bank lending to the local economy is biased in favor of SMEs.

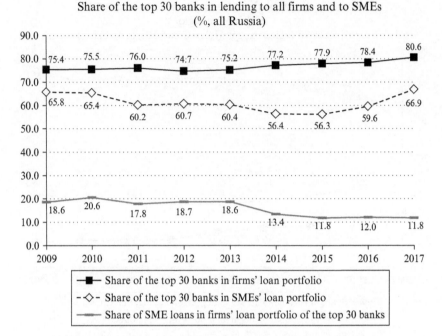

Source: Authors' elaboration based on www.cbr.ru data (accessed 11 February 2018).

Figure 7.6   The largest banks and SME lending in Russia

The 30 largest banks whose role in the economy is growing all the time (Figure 7.6) are relatively less involved in lending to SMEs compared with other banks (see the shares of SME loans in firms' loan portfolio in Figures 7.4 and 7.6). However, they provide more than half of the total amount of credit to the sector (Figure 7.6). Few of them are formally regional banks but operate nationwide, while most are large banking networks registered in Moscow.

In Moscow the largest banks also lend to SMEs relatively less than do other banks (see Figure 7.7), even though their head offices are mostly located in Moscow. This indicates the importance of hierarchical distance and institution size in each bank's suitability to serve SMEs, and not only geographical distance between offices and headquarters.

Another concept that appeared in the post-crisis period after 2009 is flight to quality or the redistribution of credit in favor of large and economically strong firms (Presbitero et al. 2014). First, when banks' credit resources are decreasing, large banks prioritize their large and established

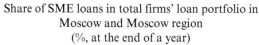

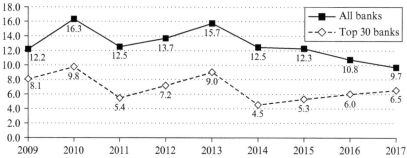

Source: Authors' elaboration based on www.cbr.ru data (accessed 11 February 2018).

Figure 7.7   Lending to SMEs in the Moscow region

clients. In unstable crisis periods risks become higher, and banks can no longer rely on standardized lending procedures (such as the credit factory): individual approaches to risk assessment for every small or new firm are not feasible, especially in remote regions.

In Italy and Germany the phenomenon of flight to quality was not evident because SMEs are more often served by local, small regional banks. In the United Kingdom, this situation was reversed. We examine this issue in the case of Russia and show that the highly centralized Russian banking system demonstrated flight-to-quality effects; the geography of borrowers also was a significant factor.

Central Bank of Russia data shows that, first, in 2014 only the largest banks reduced their lending to SMEs (see Figures 7.8 and 7.9). Access to external capital markets became limited and risks in the SME lending segment increased, so that banks drastically cut SME lending and shifted their lending focus to large companies which also suffered from limited access to foreign capital markets. In the crisis period, banks had to move from standardized assessments of borrowers to individual assessments; for large banks this entailed a significant increase in costs per transaction.

Medium and small banks in most cases made their decisions on SME loan applications on an individual basis even before the crisis. They also received an inflow of SME clients from the largest banks. So they increased their SME loan portfolio in 2014 (see Figure 7.9), but this did not compensate for the overall decline in lending to the sector in 2014 (see Table 7.2).

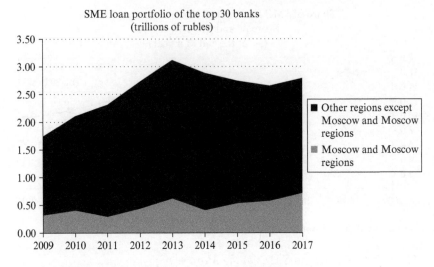

Figure 7.8   Lending to SMEs by the top 30 banks

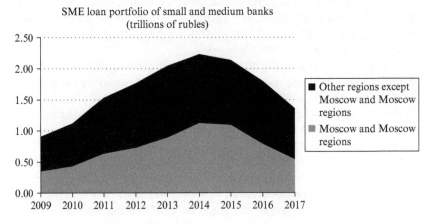

Figure 7.9   Lending to SMEs by small and medium banks

Since 2015, a new trend in SME lending has emerged. The largest banks have access to cheaper state credit resources in comparison with other banks. Their interest in SME lending increased owing to the state's stimulating measures and support. As a result, there was an increase in SME lending in Moscow by the largest banks that participated in state incentive programs for SME lending. Figure 7.7 shows how since 2015 the patterns of SME lending by the top 30 banks and other banks in the Moscow

Table 7.2   SMEs' loan portfolio, at the end of a year (trillions of rubles)

	2009	2010	2011	2012	2013	2014	2015	2016	2017
All banks									
All Russia	2.65	3.23	3.84	4.49	5.16	5.11	4.88	4.45	4.16
Moscow region	0.67	0.84	0.93	1.17	1.51	1.53	1.62	1.36	1.26
Russia without Moscow region	1.98	2.39	2.92	3.33	3.65	3.58	3.25	3.09	2.89
Regional banks									
Russia without Moscow region	0.40	0.52	0.57	0.60	0.64	0.61	0.64	0.59	0.55
Top 30 banks									
All Russia	1.74	2.11	2.31	2.73	3.12	2.88	2.74	2.65	2.79
Moscow region	0.32	0.41	0.29	0.44	0.62	0.41	0.53	0.58	0.72
Russia without Moscow region	1.42	1.70	2.02	2.29	2.50	2.48	2.21	2.08	2.07

Source: Authors' elaboration based on www.cbr.ru data (accessed 11 February 2018).

region diverged. The SME loan portfolio of the 30 largest banks in Moscow is the only line in Table 7.2 that grew since 2015. In other regions, the SME loan portfolio of the top 30 banks continues to decline. Finally, in 2017, the total SME loan portfolio of the largest banks grew. However, the portfolio of SME loans of all banks continues to decline both in the capital and outside it. Thus state support for the sector working through large banks has not reversed the overall negative trend. Those small businesses served by small and regional banks are faced with difficulties in revoking licenses from these banks. The decreasing number of regional banks has reduced SME lending since 2016 (Table 7.2) but remains focused on this sector (Figure 7.5).

Thus the collapse of SME lending initially occurred primarily because of the flight-to-quality effect in large banks. The process started in Moscow and spread to other regions (see Table 7.2). Nevertheless, since 2016, the concentration of SME lending in the largest banks has been increasing (Figure 7.6) largely owing to Sberbank and other major banks which are participating in government programs for SME support. Also, for the largest banks, it is easier than it is for smaller banks to meet the CBR's requirements for servicing SMEs.

4. ARE REGIONAL AND SMALL BANKS BETTER FOR SMES IN RUSSIA?

Although small and regional banks can be closer to customers, larger banks can serve them more efficiently and cheaply owing to their scale, centralized organization, risk tolerance, larger network of offices and new technologies. Large banks (with various forms of ownership) may also be interested in SME lending, although they have a different approach to lending (Beck et al. 2011, 2013). Within the new SME lending paradigm, it is argued that banks of different types and sizes are able to serve SMEs using different approaches and technologies. They can develop appropriate services including leasing, factoring, asset valuation systems and credit scoring. In Russia, there was also great enthusiasm for the introduction of these technologies in SME lending, especially until 2014. Small and medium-sized enterprises often want to communicate personally with bank managers, but banks often prefer to communicate with small businesses based on digitalization, remote channels and automated processes to increase the number of clients per manager. Some researchers argue that modern credit-scoring systems allow transforming 'soft' information received in the process of personal communication and knowledge of local features into a standardized 'hard' form, thereby easing the transmission of information between hierarchical levels of large banks (Berger 2015; Petersen and Rajan 2000; Udell, 2015). Other authors argue that it is impossible to remove the problem of informational asymmetry completely. Therefore, the distance between the local and head offices of banks continues to influence significantly the behavior of bank employees and the number of loans issued (Filomeni et al. 2016; Flögel and Gartner 2018).

In Russia, it is also easier for large banks to use government support for SME lending than it is for smaller banks to do so. Large state-owned banks can also have less reliable borrowers and cheaper loans relying on state support than this is the case for the smaller banks. Almost all authors agree that institutional differences between developed and developing countries, such as law and contract enforcement, cost of registering property, protection of property rights, transparency and openness of businesses, access to information and ease of firms' registration, are more important in SME lending (Beck et al. 2011). In developing countries, banks give relatively fewer SME loans for investment purposes, and offer worse conditions. However, note that this argument does not favor small banks. Small banks should have the advantages of close and stable relationships with borrowers based on trust and accumulated social capital.

5. CONCLUSION

We conclude that a very centralized banking system naturally complements the Russian centralized economy. Large network banks headquartered mainly in Moscow provide a regular flow of financial resources concentrated in the capital to lending firms and households in other regions. A reduction of this flow during the crisis period after 2014 was mainly due to the increase in raised deposits of banks' customers in the regions, but not to flight to home and unwillingness to lend in remote regions. Large companies dominate the Russian economy and many of these large companies operating in the regions are registered in Moscow or have other close ties with the center. Therefore, regional economies are not remote from the center, despite the lengthy geographical distances. However, some flight to home is also typical for the Russian economy during a crisis period, as it is for other countries with centralized banking systems.

Lending to SMEs and new enterprises remains very vulnerable in this situation, and is largely dependent on government support programs and the CBR's requirements for banks in servicing SMEs. The latest crisis shows that SME lending suffers most during crisis periods, especially outside the Moscow region. It is difficult to improve the institutional environment quickly in Russia to boost SME lending, but perhaps a more feasible approach is to change the policy in the banking sector. Thus, to strengthen medium, small and regional banks could be a solution. The super-concentration of businesses and finance in the capital would make such policy implementation complicated owing to the prominent role of the large Moscow banks in distributing finance from the capital to other regions. In such a situation, SME lending and the regional economic development are held hostage to the overall concentration of finance in the capital. Under this arrangement, the successful development of SMEs in Russia and an increase in their share of the GDP is unlikely.

NOTES

* The research for this chapter was carried out with the plan of research work of IEIE SB RAS, project XI.172.1.1.(0325-2019-0006), 'Integration and interaction of sectoral systems and markets in Russia in its Eastern regions: limitations and new opportunities', No. AAAA-A17-117022250132-2.
1. This information was available on the CBR website (www.cbr.ru data, accessed 24 July 2019) from the end of 2010.
2. Crude oil, a major export of Russia, declined in price by nearly 50 percent between its yearly high in June 2014 and 16 December 2014.
3. Statement of the head of the largest Russian bank, Sberbank, G. Gref.
4. For comparability excluding Crimea and Sevastopol.

REFERENCES

Alessandrini, P., Fratianni, M., Papi, L. and Zazzaro, A. (2016), 'Banks, regions and development after the crisis and under the new regulatory system', *Credit and Capital Markets*, **49** (4), 535–61.

Beck, T., Demirguc-Kunt, A. and Martinez Peria, M.S. (2011), 'Banking financing for SMEs: evidence across countries and bank ownership types', *Journal of Financial Services Research*, **39** (1), 35–54.

Beck, T., Demirguc-Kunt, A. and Singer, D. (2013), 'Is small beautiful? Financial structure, size and access to finance', *World Development*, **52** (c), 19–33.

Berger, A. (2015), 'Small business lending by banks: lending technologies and the effects of banking industry consolidation and technological change', in A.N. Berger, P. Molyneux and J.O.S. Wilson (eds), *The Oxford Handbook of Banking*, 2nd edn, Oxford: Oxford University Press, pp. 292–311.

Chepurenko, A. and Vilenski, A. (2016), 'SME policy of the Russian state (1990–2015): from a "generalist" to a "paternalist" approach', Working Paper No. WP1/2016/02, Higher School of Economics, National Research University, Moscow, accessed 25 October 2017 at http://www.zbw.eu/econis-archiv/bitstream/handle/11159/123/WP1_2016_02_____.pdf?sequence=1.

Claeys, S.A., Vandervennet, R. and Schoors, K. (2008), 'The sequence of bank liberalisation: financial repression versus capital requirements in Russia', *Comparative Economic Studies*, **50** (2), 297–317.

Degryse, H., Matthews, K. and Zhao, T. (2018), 'SMEs and access to bank credit: evidence on the regional propagation of the financial crisis in the UK', 3 June, accessed 11 December 2017 at https://ssrn.com/abstract=2655561.

Dymski, G. (2016), *The Bank Merger Wave: The Economic Causes and Social Consequences of Financial Consolidation*, New York: Routledge.

European Investment Bank (EIB) (2013), 'Small and medium entrepreneurship in Russia', accessed 1 December 2017 at https://www.eib.org/attachments/efs/econ_study_small_and_medium_entrepreneurship_in_russia_en.pdf.

Filomeni, S., Udell, G.F. and Zazzaro, A. (2016), 'Hardening soft information: how far has technology taken us?', CSEF Working Paper No. 455, Centre for Studies in Economics and Finance, University of Naples.

Flögel, F. and Gärtner, S. (2018), 'The banking systems of Germany, the UK and Spain form a spatial perspective: lessons learned and what is to be done?', IAT Working Paper No. WP/18/01A), Institut Arbeit und Technik, Westfälische Hochschule, University of Applied Sciences, Gelsenkirchen.

Klagge, B., Martin, R. and Sunley, P. (2017), 'The spatial structure of the financial system and the funding of regional business: a comparison of Britain and Germany', in R. Martin and J. Pollard (eds), *Handbook of Geographies of Money and Finance*, Cheltenham, UK and Northampton, MA, USA: Edward Elgar, pp. 125–56.

Lukács, E. (2005), 'The economic role of SMEs in world economy, especially in Europe', *European Integration Studies*, **4** (1), 3–12.

Makinen, M. and Solanko, L. (2018), 'Determinants of bank closures: do levels or changes of CAMEL variables matter?', *Russian Journal of Money and Finance*, **77** (2), 3–21.

McCauley, R.N., McGuire, P. and Von Peter, G. (2010), 'The architecture of global banking: from international to multinational?', *BIS Quarterly Review*, March, 25–39.

Papi, L., Sarno, E. and Zazzaro, A. (2017), 'The geographical network of bank organ-izations: issues and evidence for Italy', in R. Martin and J. Pollard (eds), *Handbook of Geographies of Money and Finance*, Cheltenham, UK and Northampton, MA, USA: Edward Elgar, pp. 156–96.

Petersen, M. and Rajan, R.G. (2000), 'Does distance still matter? The information revolution in small business lending', Eleventh Annual Utah Winter Conference, Salt Lake City, UT.

Presbitero, A.F., Udell, G.F. and A. Zazzaro (2014), 'The home bias and the credit crunch: a regional perspective', *Journal of Money Credit and Banking*, **46** (s1), 53–85.

Ruchkina, G., Melnichuk, M., Frumina, S. and Mentel, G. (2017), 'Small and medium enterprises in the context of regional development and innovations', *Journal of International Studies*, **10** (4), 259–71.

'Strategies for the development of small and medium-sized businesses in the Russian Federation for the period up to 2030 and the action plan ("road map") for its implementation on June 2, 2016', No. 1083-p, 2016, accessed 31 January 2018 at https://www.garant.ru/products/ipo/prime/doc/71318202/#1000.

Tickell, A. (2000), 'Finance and localities', in G.L. Clark, M.P. Feldman and M.S. Gertler (eds), *The Oxford Handbook of Economic Geography*, Oxford: Oxford University Press, pp. 230–52.

Udell, G.F. (2009), 'Financial innovation, organizations and small business lend-ing', in P. Alessandrini, M. Fratianni and A. Zazzaro (eds), *The Changing Geography of Banking and Finance*, New York: Springer, pp. 15–26.

Udell, G.F. (2015), 'SME access to intermediated credit: what do we know, and what don't we know?', paper presented at the 'Small Business Conditions and Finance' Conference, School of Business Indiana University, Bloomington, IN, 18–20 March.

8. Bulgaria's banking system: outside and inside the financial geography of Europe

Elena Stavrova

1. INTRODUCTION

This chapter is a commentary on financial transformation in Bulgaria, and it demonstrates how global pressures to create a neoliberal banking system are mediated and domesticated by national regulations. Banking system development in the Republic of Bulgaria commenced with the 1989 transition from a centrally planned command economy to an economy based on the principles of a free market. This transition was characterized by stability and growth, as well as crises which entailed bank panics and bouts of triple-digit inflation.

Given Bulgaria's communist-centric past, the challenge for reformers was to overcome the embedded social relations of the centrally administered economy. Policies had to be quick, efficient and carry the lowest cost possible for society. This is the setting – characterized by differences and specifics, with advantages and disadvantages – in which the nature of the transition has been shaped. Despite being in a similar position at the same time as other former communist states, the Bulgarian economy was less successful, in terms of growth and stability, than its counterparts. For instance, Poland, the Czech Republic, Hungary and Romania underwent similar processes of market restructuring of economics but achieved very different results.

Bulgarian reform is an extension of the globalization of banking in the 1990s that led to an explosion in trade and capital flows. In Central and Southeast European countries, cross-border credit flows were spurred by the rapid widening and deepening of new banking subsidiaries and branch networks as Western European banks began to establish themselves there. This strategy was seen to improve financial sector efficiency and enhance risk management (Domanski 2005). These same strategies also led to financial crises, the response to which was a hastening of liberalization to recapitalize and consolidate the banking system.[1] This strategy deepened financial intermediation. In Bulgaria, the percentage share of bank assets relative to gross domestic product (GDP) has remained relatively modest by international, and even by Central and Eastern European (CEE), standards. Nevertheless, despite increased competition and lower interest margins, the efficiency and return ratios of invested resources were higher than those observed in the EU-15 countries (Tochkov and Nenovsky 2011).[2]

Bulgaria exemplifies the complexities associated with global financial integration when reforms are complicated by domestic factors. The remainder of this chapter proceeds as follows. Section 2 identifies the salient features that shaped the Bulgarian banking system's transition from state owned to market based and dominated by foreign investments. Section 3 discusses the responses of the financial sector to internal and external risks, particularly those that became evident following the global financial crisis of 2008–09. Section 4 presents the Bulgarian banking system as a unit of global value chains. Section 5 considers the role of international financial institutions in shaping the Bulgarian banking system. Finally, section 6 offers concluding remarks.

2. STATES, MARKETS AND FOREIGN BANKS: OWNERSHIP SHIFTS IN BULGARIAN BANKING

The story of financial transformation in Bulgaria is about how a relatively stable banking system, in a command economy, came to be regularly beset by financial crises, as foreign capital from globalization became increasingly integral to Bulgarian banks. Why was foreign capital a priority for this sector? Four potential reasons are suggested: (1) the potential benefits for managers of state-owned enterprises from opaque transactions; (2) technology transfer opportunities from foreign investment in information infrastructure; (3) national pressures to draw in foreign investment; and (4) a highly fragmented banking system comprising institutions with weak capital bases. These reasons are discussed next in the context of what may be described as five distinct historical stages in Bulgarian banking: fragmentation, consolidation, crisis, consolidation and crisis again.

Stage 1: Fragmentation

The first stage begins in the command-administered economy, when the banking system of Bulgaria comprised three banks: the National Savings Bank (DSK), the Bulgarian Foreign Trade Bank (for foreign economic affairs), and the Bulgarian National Bank (BNB), which performed the functions of a central bank with branches across the country. Caporale et al. (2002) describe this arrangement as a state-operated monobank:

> The central bank combined issue and credit functions, and implemented the 'cash and credit plan' which formed part of the general economic plan. The Bulgarian National Bank (BNB) was under the direct control of the government. Besides the BNB there were only two other banking institutions, each with strictly limited functions. The State Savings Bank (SSB), established in 1951, was the only financial institution permitted to hold the accounts of individuals. The Bulgarian Foreign Trade Bank, created in 1964, handled all foreign exchange operations. (Caporale et al. 2002, p. 223)

This structure remained in place until 1981 after which seven commercial banks concerned with servicing specific industries were established. While these were not permitted to hold deposits, they drew in capital from the enterprises of various sectors which were shareholders. This led to a mixed ownership structure in which the lending operations of these privately owned banks were nevertheless funded by the BNB: the BNB provided credit to these banks which they then loaned to enterprises in the relevant sector. This mixed ownership structure was not conducive to a distribution of productive assets. It was necessary nevertheless as a source of convertible currency for energy and natural resource imports from the Soviet Union.

Between early 1989 and late 1990, 59 new commercial banks were established in what had been the branches of the BNB (Yonkova and Alexandrova 2001). Some of these banks were established with small amounts of capital and through statutory changes to allow for the use of private equity. Despite an inflationary environment, shares were sold at par value, based on the book value of authorized capital at inception. In many cases, the capital used for the creation of new banks and purchase of shares of existing banks was extended in the form of credit by the BNB and the DSK. Some banks were also created through the submission of fictitious documents for accumulated capital through the purchase of external debt and its betting or resale to third parties, as well as other mechanisms.

For the period 1990–95, the DSK alone, the only functioning savings institution, had disbursed more than BGN70 billion in loans. Most of this was used for the creation of private banks and companies. This advanced the creation of a shadow banking sector as the central bank granted licenses to non-bank financial institutions, such as financial brokerage firms, and created a system which operated parallel to the conventional banking system. In 1990–91, as a result of substantial bank failures and the passive approach to banking supervision, sizable financial resources were withdrawn from the system in the form of uncollateralized loans.

During the same period, newly formed commercial banks issued shares on the stock market at nominal values disconnected from the financial valuations of these intuitions.

Stage 2: Consolidation

The second stage described here has two features: (1) it was a response to the fragmentation described earlier, and (2) it set the tone for the financial crisis that occurred in 1996–97. The focus of the second stage was on consolidation and restructuring: 10 state-owned and 35 privately owned banks were established through the consolidation of state-owned banks. Funds mainly came from the unreformed real estate sector and the DSK, which held the savings of the general population. In accordance with World Bank recommendations, the Bank Consolidation Company was created as a government body and shareholder in the banking system (Bogetic and Hillman 1995). World Bank experts assumed that this would result in a quick privatization-driven restructuring of the banking system and reduce the total number of banks to less than 10. At the same time, however, and outside this consolidation process, many new private banks entered the Bulgarian banking market. Given inadequate regulatory control, these banks operated in an environment with limited oversight implemented by institutions based in and geared for developed market economies. In many cases, the financial resources for the establishment of these private banks were borrowed from state-owned banks or from elsewhere – often unidentified sources. These origins played a key role in shaping the future strategies of these private banks and contributed to the financial crisis in 1996–97.

The period between 1991 and 1995 was dominated by BNB policies, which encouraged the formation of large private banks while restricting the entry of foreign banks into the Bulgarian banking market. The total number of banks declined as the Bank Consolidation Company encouraged small state-owned banks to merge. The total number of state-owned banks decreased from 72 in 1991 to 12 in 1995. During that same period, 25 small private Bulgarian banks entered the market. At the start of the reforms, foreign banks were not authorized to open branches in Bulgaria. In 1994 two foreign banks, – the Greek Xios and the Dutch ING Bank – set up branches in Sofia. By the end of 1995, two other banks – the National Bank of Greece and the Yonian Bank – opened branches and three foreign banks – Reifeisen Bulgaria, BNP-Dresdner Bulgaria and Bayerishe-Bulgarishe Handelsbank – received licenses from the Bulgarian regulator to open branches. However, these banks were very specialized and limited their activity to international settlements (Table 8.1).

Table 8.1   Transformation in banking sector structure

	1990	1991	1992	1993	1994	1995	1996	1997	1998	2000
Large banks	3	4	6	9	9	6	6	6	7	8
Small banks	75	76	34	29	28	19	22	20	20	19
State	69	65	19	6	3	1	1	1	2	1
Private	6	11	15	23	25	18	21	19	18	18
Bulgarian	75	76	34	29	25	14	14	12	11	10
Foreign	0	0	0	0	0	3	5	8	9	9
Branches of foreign banks	0	0	0	2	4	4	5	7	7	8
Saving banks	1	1	1	1	1	1	1	1	0	0
Total	79	81	41	41	42	30	34	4	34	35

Source: BNB (www.bnb.bg, accessed 4 August 2019).

Given their relative advantages, including reputation, resources, international networks and staff expertise, these foreign banks had the opportunity to exert significant competitive pressure on the Bulgarian banks already operating in the market. It was of particular importance for the BNB to limit the penetration of foreign banks in the Bulgarian market. Bulgarian banks needed time to become competitive by acquiring resources and purchasing technologies. The BNB was aware that an uncontrolled market penetration process creates a competitive environment detrimental to local banks, and thus allowed banks to enter only on the condition that they offer only a limited range of services.

This stage of admission of foreign investments in the banking sector of Bulgaria coincided with a period of economic recovery and capital inflows from the common European financial market. The adoption of the Banking Law by the BNB in 1991[3] effected new rules for operating of the banking system: a two-pronged structure of management, independence from the government and responsibility for the stability of the national currency. In accordance with the International Monetary Fund (IMF) rules, limitations were imposed on credit ceilings. Over the course of negotiations with the IMF, Bulgaria's government opted for the 'shock therapy' approach, the same approach previously implemented by Leszek Balcerowicz in Poland[4] and characterized by: the sudden release of control over prices and currency; withdrawal of state subsidies; the immediate liberalization of trade; a comprehensive privatization of state assets; and an increase of as much as 300 percent in the interest rate on outstanding credit and on the basic interest rate. The effect of these actions was the exponential growth of sovereign debt payments, accounting for between 70 percent and 80 percent of total government expenditure.

These processes of financial liberalization accompanied by limited banking supervision transformed Bulgarian banking from a state-centralized system to a system dominated by information asymmetry and institutional inefficiencies. According to Minasyan (1999) the liberalization of the balance of payments and the perception of market behavior by the financial institutions are prerequisites for the integration of the country into the European and world economic structures, with the expected consequences for its structure.

During the 1991–95 period, state-owned companies lost viability as economic ties with former socialist-bloc countries were ruptured. Their drastic capital losses transferred the burden from the banking system to the fiscal sector, and the decapitalization of the banking and industrial sectors caused a loss of competitiveness in the economic system as a whole. The banking system's potential as an effective mediator between savings and investment was thus compromised. Instead, the primary role of banks was the absorption of income transfer losses through persistent credit expansion and the accumulation of nonperforming loans (NPLs). This tendency, as Ganchev (2010) observes, was typical also for other transition countries undergoing similar crises; in Bulgaria it underpinned a set of comprehensive risks taken on by the government and the BNB, and exerted a lasting influence on policy.

Balance of payments liberalization played a key role in the integration of the Republic of Bulgaria into European and global economic structures. The rapid pace of restructuring of the real and financial sectors had created uncertainty, a loss of confidence in the local currency, and currency outflows (Table 8.2). Steps taken to overcome these issues included privatization, reduction of bureaucracy, and the creation of market based entities. The Bulgarian economic reality was a set of painful processes which carried high social costs for the general population. Despite commitments made to the IMF, the process of ownership change, like in other Eastern European countries, did not give a satisfactory outcome. As Tanzi (1999) noted, the creation of national wealth and revenues from privatization in

Table 8.2   Nonperforming loans (NPLs) in percentage terms

	1993	1994	1995	1996	1997
BGL	34.2	39.8	39.5	11.5	16.6
Currency	40.2	29.4	35.3	69.1	83.4

Source: BNB (www.bnb.bg, accessed 4 August 2019).

Eastern European countries was heterogenous. The privatization process in the Bulgarian banking sector took place in a complex political and financial environment; coinciding with global financial volatility, crises in Russia and Asia, and the break-up of neighboring Yugoslavia.

Stage 3: Crisis

The third stage is marked by (1) financial and economic crisis as 15 banks declared bankruptcy in the autumn of 1996, and (2) the introduction of a currency board arrangement as a stabilization measure, through which Bulgaria's national currency was fixed to the Deutsche Mark.[5]

The main features of this crisis are as follows: embezzlement; distorted incentives for economic agents; a weak institutional environment with inadequate protection for property rights and especially creditor rights; lack of accounting transparency; ineffective or missing banking supervision; errant credit expansion leading to an accumulation of NPLs; Ponzi schemes; volatile interest rates; exchange rate volatility as a result of information asymmetry; short-horizon planning; prolonged banking panics; and large-scale capital flight.

Until the beginning of 1996, banks of all sizes had liquidity challenges and fell into a state of temporary insolvency until they were revived through financial injections from the BNB. The decapitalization process was particularly intense by late 1996 and early 1997. On 23 September 1996, nine banks were placed under special supervision. Two of them – Balkan Bank and the Agricultural Bank (BZK) – were of systemic importance for the Bulgarian economy. As Vucheva (2001) notes, this measure pushed the financial system towards collapse as 31 percent of savings and 23 percent of company current accounts were held in these banks.

The currency board was introduced as a comprehensive measure to manage both public finances and money supply, offering a similar system to those already introduced in several other countries. Bulgaria's currency board was set up in July 1997 and closely followed the lead of two other small economies in transition: Estonia in 1992 and Lithuania in 1994. In many ways, the Bulgarian currency board was a triumph. From hyperinflationary levels in February 1997, inflation fell to one-digit levels in 1998 and 1999; price stabilization was thus a success. The choice of the Deutsche Mark as reserve currency and the exchange rate to the Bulgarian Lev at the ratio of 1:1.95583 allowed a smooth exchange of currency. The US dollar had previously been used as a reserve currency but the choice of German currency was made in the anticipation that the European continent was moving towards building a unified European market. The main objectives – stabilizing the economy, rehabilitation of the banking institutions and improving the credibility of the national currency – were thus achieved.

The basic principles of the currency board as a system are an Issue Department with an autonomous balance and foreign exchange holdings in the peg currency as well as in other major currencies such as those of Great Britain, France and others. Under a currency board, the transmission function of monetary policy is limited; the central bank is prevented from financing fiscal deficits and is not permitted to engage in open market operations.

These measures were taken to stabilize the financial system and attract international investors for economic growth and sustainable development. A basic principle of the currency board, to ensure smooth transactions between the peg currency and the local currency, is that monetary policy is dictated by the country which issues the peg currency. Accordingly, interest rates and inflation in the country adopting the currency board system depend on interest rates and inflation in the reserve country. Therefore, it is important for the peg to be based on a stable international currency. The currency board arrangement also restricts national sovereignty by limiting the scope for fiscal and monetary authorities to intervene in crisis situations to stabilize the system; the BNB was thus no longer able to intervene as a lender of last resort and to refinance liquidated commercial banks.

The currency board arrangement allowed the BNB to emphasize its regulatory function. From being known for declaring a moratorium on its public debt payments in 1990 and for interest rates of up to 300 percent, Bulgaria eventually made its private sector appealing for foreign investors. The majority of the invested capital came from European economies, including Germany, France, the Netherlands, Italy, Greece, Turkey, Hungary, the Czech Republic and Romania. The European Bank for Reconstruction and Development (EBRD) was directly involved in the recovery of the Bulgarian banking system through purchasing stakes in three major Bulgarian Banks: UniCredit, First Investment Bank and the CCB. The international financial community was thus directly involved in the recovery of the Bulgarian banking system. Table 8.3 shows the breakdown of ownership of bank intermediaries by country, which includes countries in Europe, Asia and North America.

Stage 4: Consolidation

Stage 4 is characterized by stabilization, consolidation and the growth of foreign direct investment in the banking system from Europe, Asia and North America. By 2000 the market share of investments from European Union (EU) countries was about 75 percent of the banking

Table 8.3   Foreign ownership in Bulgarian banking 2000

Country	Number of banks owned
Bulgaria	14
Greece	6
Turkey	2
EBRD	3
Austria	3
France	3
Germany	2
Italy	1
Czech Republic	1
Ireland	1
Holland	1
United Kingdom	1
USA	1

Source: BNB (www.bnb.bg, accessed 4 August 2019).

sector (Stavrova 2005a, 2005b). Their presence had resulted in the transfer of banking technology and expertise from the parent banks and led to a qualitative change in service quality. This stage coincided with a process of mass privatization elsewhere in the former socialist bloc because of which Bulgaria, under Ivan Kostov, attracted substantial capital inflows.

The formation of the EU, the European banking market and the introduction of the euro during this stage shaped Bulgarian banking in a number of ways, including: (1) the transfer of resources through banking channels to establish monetary unions and unify the global regulatory framework; (2) financial innovation which accelerated transfers and linked banks to global financial networks; and (3) concentration in the non-banking sector including in credit and payment institutions, and factoring companies, to offer an enriched range of products.

This period of consolidation was disrupted by the global financial crisis and during 2008–12 there were perceptible shifts in banking sector regulation. This was necessitated by the need for tighter regulation and concerns associated with financial innovation. Revised regulation for banks sought to improve their capital bases, the transparency of their operations and the management of debt-based assets. European banks responded to these changes through the sale of their branches in Bulgaria, which resulted not only in a concentration of ownership but also the exit of capital. By the end of 2014, ownership patterns looked very different compared to a decade previously: ownership in the Bulgarian banking system is depicted

Table 8.4   Foreign ownership changes in Bulgarian banking 2014

Country	Number of owned banks
Bulgaria	10 (–4)
Greece	3 (–3)
Turkey	2
EBRD	0 (–3)
Austria	2 (–1)
France	2 (–1)
Germany	1 (–1)
Italy	1
Czech Republic	0 (–1)
Ireland	1 (–1)
Holland	1
United Kingdom	0 (–1)
USA	0 (–1)

Source: BNB (www.bnb.bg, accessed 4 August 2019).

in Table 8.4, which shows that many countries either reduced their share or left altogether.

Note that while the absence of Russian investment in Bulgarian banking is conspicuous – given the absence of banks there with official Russian state or private ownership (Bechev 2010) – there are a number of large Russian investments elsewhere in the Bulgarian economy. These include Lukoil Neftochim Burgas (a monopoly in the processing of oil), Vivacom mobile operator owned by Vneshtrogbank (one of the largest Russian banks), Overgas Ink (gas distribution, gas trade); EAD 'Sok Kamchia' (sanatorium and health complex); Yukos Petroleum (wholesale of fuels); FairPlay Properties REIT (other financial intermediation, without insurance and insurance through independent funds); Optma KA Ltd. (purchase and sale of own real estate); FRABFAB BULGARIA (issuance of standard software); Interbuild EOOD (construction); Balkani-LK EOOD (construction of other installations); Black Sea Investment Trust EAD (intermediary activity of real estate agencies); and Michaniki Bulgaria (mediation activities of real estate agencies).

Concerns around these Russian investments in Bulgaria – also in other Eastern European nations, including Latvia, Serbia, Hungary and Slovakia – are centered on risks to sovereignty and political stability. According to some estimates, these risks are particularly worrying when Russian ownership approaches or exceeds the critical threshold of 12 percent of GDP (Conley et al. 2016).

Stage 5: Crisis Again

Stage 5 is known for the bank crisis of 2014 which saw the license of the CCB withdrawn. Bank runs ensued and it cost the government BGN4.5 billion in payments to cover the guaranteed deposits of the public (IMF 2017).

3.   CROSS-BORDER RISKS AND THREATS TO THE FINANCIAL SYSTEM DURING THE GLOBAL FINANCIAL AND ECONOMIC CRISIS

Foreign investment has tended to expose Bulgarian banking to a number of risks. For example, Greek banks owned assets amounting to BGN15.78 billion at the beginning of the crisis of 2009. This amount represents 29.25 percent of the assets of the Bulgarian banking system (Table 8.5). The incursion of Greek banking capital into Bulgaria came with its entry into the eurozone, cheap euro-denominated credit, and investment opportunities in Bulgaria in real estate and finance. However, supervision appeared to be lax and allowed heavy lending to inexperienced businesses. Social conflicts, weak state finances owing to the catastrophic increase in Greek government debt and the Greek central bank's policy responses posed a threat to the stability of the banking system in Bulgaria. In particular, the policy of the central bank of Greece to not support the rescue of the overseas branches of Greek banks was disastrous for the banking system in Bulgaria.

The global financial crisis and post-crisis recovery measures have played a key role in shaping the domestic processes of national banking systems. Cerutti and Zhou (2018, p. 1) observe that despite a 'decline in aggregate cross-border banking lending volumes, some parts of the global banking

Table 8.5   *Relative share ownership of Greek banks in the assets of the banking system of the Republic of Bulgaria in 2009*

Bank	Market share	Asset growth
UBB	11.84	12.84
Eurobank	7.82	92.49
Piraeus	5.95	61.29
Emporiki	0.68	–
Alfa	3.08	–

Source: BNB (www.bnb.bg, accessed 4 August 2019).

network are currently more interlinked regionally than before the Global Financial Crisis', but this appears to more accurate for banking systems at the core of the European banking system and less so for those outside, which are seen to be undergoing regionalization. This is borne out by an increase in lender–borrower connections within the same region and associated with increased cross-border lending by foreign banks, especially those banks outside the main global banking systems. This has important implications for foreign direct investment.

The motivation for foreign bank presence in Bulgaria is multidimensional and includes incentives related to business, the legal system, linguistic and cultural factors, and institutional factors related to banking supervision, international regulation and so on. Regionalization is also stimulated by the abolition of constraints on cross-border flows and local funding. Investment flows in the banking sector also include illegal cross-border flows.

A major adjustment that has followed the global financial crisis of 2009–09 is in the predilection of banks to seek entry into countries with tighter regulations. This is a shift from earlier trends in which banks were attracted to relatively lax regulations (Cerutti and Zhou 2018). This trend is associated with commercial banks and may be contrasted with the global trend of regulatory arbitrage for shadow banks where investment portfolios in countries with mild regulation draw in foreign capital (Stavrova 2013).

4.   BULGARIAN BANKING IN GLOBAL VALUE ADDED CHAINS

Of crucial importance for Bulgaria has been the inclusion of its banking system in global chains of value creation. This process has benefited not only multinational banks but also other major participants in the financial markets. Computerization and monitoring technology has meant that any bank branch may provide a better service than its main office. Globalization can bring global banking services to local bank customers. This occurs when logistical and technological differences between local and global banks are a source of competitiveness, particularly given differing costs of resources in the global financial markets. Higher risks are associated with higher returns, and this logic has dictated the appeal of investments in the banking sectors of post-socialist countries

The Bulgarian banking sector has acquired new features through the disclosure of subsidiaries, domestically and in neighboring countries, after its inclusion in global value creation chains. This is shown in Table 8.6.

Table 8.6   Bulgarian banks as a part of global value chains

Holding banks	Banks in the Bulgarian banking system	Bank subsidiaries
Allianz Bulgaria Holding	Allianz Bank Bulgaria	
BNP Paribas S.A., Republic of France	BNP Paribas S.A. – Sofia Branch	
	Bulgarian-American Credit Bank	
	Bulgarian Development Bank	
	Central Cooperative Bank	CCB-Macedonia
EuroBank-Greece	EURO BANK-PostBank	
Citibank Europe Plc., Republic of Ireland	Citibank Europe, Bulgaria Branch	
Fuat Güven	D Commerce Bank	
OTP Bank RT, Hungary	DSK Bank	
	First Investment Bank	Universal Investment Bank-Macedonia
ING Bank N.V., Kingdom of the Netherlands	ING Bank N.V., Sofia Branch	
	International Asset Bank	
	Investbank	
TBIF Financial Services B.V., Kingdom of the Netherlands	TBI Bank	
	Municipal Bank PLC	
Piraeus Bank-Greece	Piraeus Bank Bulgaria	
Procredit Holding AG & CO.KGAA, Federal Republic of Germany	ProCredit Bank, Bulgaria	
Raiffeisen Bank International AG (Raiffeisen SEE Region Holding GmbH), Republic of Austria	Raiffeisenbank, Bulgaria	
Société Générale S.A., Republic of France	Société Générale Expressbank	
KBC BANK N.V., Kingdom of Belgium	UBB	
T.C. Ziraat Bankasi A.Ş., Republic of Turkey	T.C. Ziraat Bank, Sofia Branch	
	Texim Bank	
Tokushukai Incorporated, Japan	Tokuda Bank	
UniCredit S.P.A., Republic of Italy	UniCredit Bulbank	
	Victoria Commercial Bank	

Source: BNB (www.bnb.bg, accessed 4 August 2019).

Table 8.7 Shadow banking goes to West

Financial firms	Firms in Bulgaria	Firms subsidiaries
	Easy Credit	Ukraine, Romania, Macedonia, Kosovo, Poland, Czechs Republic
	Credissimo	Macedonia
ProfiCredit-Czechs Republic	ProfiCredit-Bulgaria	ProfiCredit-Macedonia, Slovakia, Poland
	Alfa Finance Group	Capital Bank-Macedonia

Source: BNB (www.bnb.bg, accessed 4 August 2019).

While cross-border financial sector investments are a potential channel for the export of crises, they also have the potential to export stability; highly interconnected systems can convey economic exuberance and also systemic risk. However, when this risk is dispersed and spread across jurisdictions and economic systems, it is easier to control.

The Bulgarian presidency of the Council of Europe attempted to establish a position on the countries of the western Balkans as a part of the European Common Market and the steps to be taken towards further integration into the European Economic Community. The first steps for cross-border capital movements were taken in the banking industry, including the shadow banking sector (Table 8.7). This arrangement offers additional incentives to build joint ventures, cross-border mergers and foreign direct investment in the real sector (Stavrova 2017). For instance, investments through the shadow banking sector in Serbia were made outside of banking channels with Bulgarian capital operating under license in the Serbian banking market.

5.   COLLABORATIONS WITH INTERNATIONAL FINANCIAL INSTITUTIONS

International financial institutions, particularly the World Bank Group and the IMF, have played a crucial role in Bulgaria's financial transformation. During 1991–94, Bulgaria was practically in international isolation. By imposing a moratorium on foreign debt payments, the country had severed its links with external financial markets. The IMF was thus Bulgaria's only link to global finance.

Under the supervision of the IMF, the country reached an agreement with the London Club to restructure its foreign debt obligations.

As Vucheva (2001) notes, this support was crucial during the years of economic reform, given its complicated nature with risks and political shocks. Since the 1990s, Bulgaria has cooperated with the IMF and the World Bank as part of socio-economic reform, and this relationship is central to the country's ability to service its external debt. From 1991 to 2006, Bulgaria received US$1.8 billion in IMF loans, and much more as aid. Ganchev and Stavrova (2009) note that the IMF's assistance in resolving three major problems for the further development of the country was centered on: (1) solving the problem of excessive money supply and laying the foundations of anti-inflationary policy; (2) overcoming the banking crisis and hyperinflation; and (3) managing the currency board and the relationship between the budget deficit and the current account deficit. The IMF's approach to these issues was successful and resulted in curbing inflation and creating the basis for an economic recovery (Ganchev et al. 2012). Since joining the IMF, Bulgaria has entered three stand-by agreements totaling 1025 billion special drawing rights (SDR)

The World Bank, in accordance with its role as an institution for financing structural projects and with a long-term horizon, has so far granted loans to Bulgaria in a number of areas including energy, rail infrastructure, telecommunications, agriculture, foreign debt management, private business initiative support and social security.

6.   CONCLUDING REMARKS

The transformation of the Bulgarian banking system has been shaped by repeated crises followed by recovery. This process may be seen as typical for when a small open economy seeks entry into a global – in this case, the unified European – financial market. Being connected in this way carries risks that foreign banks could transmit when lending from their host economies, and could influence key mechanisms for transmitting external shocks. The use of domestic capital markets is therefore increasingly important.

The inclusion of the Bulgarian banking sector in global value chains has provided significant advantages for global technology and banking culture, and has also made it possible. The success of the currency board was central to maintain financial stability between 2008 and 2012, particularly given the global financial crisis. Future developments hinge on further European integration through participation in the single currency and the EU banking union.

While globalization offers markets, choices and alternatives, it also strengthens competition and advantages stronger players over weaker ones. It's potential to result in concentrated wealth and power is a concern.

NOTES

1. As mentioned in Domanski (2005), this was a standard approach used to counter volatility in emerging market economies, and was also applied in Latin America and East Asia in the 1990s.
2. https://stats.oecd.org/glossary/detail.asp?ID=6805 (accessed 4 August 2019).
3. http://www.bnb.bg/bnbweb/groups/public/documents/bnb_law/laws_bnb_bg.pdf (accessed 4 August 2019).
4. https://www.euromoney.com/article/b1320fkqv5thv7/finance-minister-of-the-year-1998-le szek-balcerowicz (accessed 4 August 2019).
5. http://www.bnb.bg/bnbweb/groups/public/documents/bnb_law/laws_bnb_bg.pdf (accessed 4 August 2019).

REFERENCES

Bechev, D. (2010), 'Russia's influence in Bulgaria', New Direction, Brussels, accessed 25 July 2019 at https://europeanreform.org/files/ND-report-RussiasInfluence InBulgaria-preview-lo-res_FV.pdf.
Bogetic, Z. and Hillman, A.L. (eds) (1995), *Financing Government in the Transition – Bulgaria: The Political Economy of Tax Policies, Tax Bases, and Tax Evasion*, Washington, DC: World Bank.
Caporale, G., Miller, J., Hristov, K., Nenovsky, N. and Petrov, B. (2002), 'The banking system in Bulgaria', in Z. Sevic, (ed.), *Banking Reforms in South-East Europe*, Cheltenham, UK and Northampton, MA, USA: Edward Elgar, ch. 11.
Ceruttu, E. and Zhou, H. (2018), 'The global banking network: what is behind the increasing regionalization trend', IMF Working Paper No. WP/18/46, International Monetary Fund, Washington, DC.
Conley, H.A., Mina, J., Stefanov, R. and Vladimirov, M. (2016), *The Kremlin Playbook: Understanding Russian Influence in Central and Eastern Europe*, Washington, DC: CSSI and Rowman & Littlefield.
Domanski, D. (2005), 'Foreign banks in emerging market economies: changing players, changing issues', *BIS Quarterly Review*, December, 69–81.
Ganchev, G. (2010), *Finances as a System: Evolution, Theory, Politics*, Blagoevgrad: South-West University Publishing House 'Neofit Rilski', pp. 145–59.
Ganchev, G. and Stavrova, E. (2009), *International Finance and Financial Politics*, Blagoevgrad: South-West University Publishing House 'Neofit Rilski'.
Ganchev, G., Stavrova, E. and Tsenkov, V. (2012), 'Testing the twin deficit hypothesis: the case of Central and Eastern Europe countries', *International Journal of Contemporary Economics and Administrative Sciences*, **23** (4), 1–21.
International Monetary Fund (IMF) (2017), 'Bulgaria – financial sector assessment program', IMF Country Report No. 17/202, International Monetary Fund, Washington, DC.
Minasyan, G. (1999), 'The currency board – the beginning and beyond, Monetary Council in Bulgaria: preconditions and results, prospects national', *Economic Archive*, **LII** (1), 5–9.
Stavrova, E. (2005a), 'Perspective in development to Bulgarian bank system in European globalised financial market', *Journal Economics and Management*, **1** (1), pp. 24–32.

Stavrova, E. (2005b), 'Banking sectors of the Central and Eastern Europe Countries – Proceeding no. 4, The route of change', Proceedings of the International Conference 'Investment in the Future', Varna, 20–22 October, pp. 94–102.

Stavrova, E. (2013), 'Ethics Paradigm of global financial crisis', *Yearbook of St Kliment Ohridski University of Sofia, Faculty of Economics*, **11**, 265–72, https:// www.ceeol.com/search/article-detail?id=412277.

Stavrova, E. (2017), 'Conventional and shadow banking sectors – comparative aspects of the post-crisis period in time on Currency Board – Bulgaria case', *CBU International Conference Proceedings*, **5**, pp. 345–75.

Tanzi, V. (1999), 'Transition and the changing role of government', *Finance & Development*, **38** (2), 1–22.

Tochkov, K. and Nenovsky, N. (2011), 'Institutional reforms, EU accession, and bank efficiency in transition economies: evidence from Bulgaria', *Emerging Markets Finance and Trade*, **47** (1), 113–29.

Vucheva, H. (2001), *Ikonomicheskata politika: 1991–2001 (Economics Policy: 1991–2001)*, Sofia: University Publishing House, pp. 37–49.

Yonkova, A. and Alexandrova, S. (2001), 'Development of banking sector in Bulgaria', IME analytical paper, Institute for Market Economics, Sofia, accessed 4 August 2019 at https://ime.bg/bg/articles/development-of-the-banking-sector-in-bulgaria/.

9. Banking reform in Vietnam: persistence of the state?

Guanie Lim and Thong Tien Nguyen

1. INTRODUCTION

As one of Asia's most recent latecomer economies, Vietnam is often singled out for its boldness in rolling out a series of liberalization policies to rejuvenate its former ailing command and control economy, starting from its famed 1986 *doi moi* (renovation) economic reform. Such reforms have yielded positive outcomes as Vietnamese gross domestic product (GDP) grew by 7.1 percent per year (on average; current US$) from 1986 to 2016, in addition to significant improvements in most socioeconomic indicators (Asian Development Bank 2014). Vietnam's stellar performance has not gone unnoticed in the popular media and scholarly community, drawing plaudits such as the 'next China' (Straszheim 2008) and the 'new Asian dragon' (Schaumburg-Müller and Pham 2010). Some analysts attribute this success to the introduction of market forces and governance reforms modelled on the Washington Consensus, and iterative versions of it (see Vu 2015). Macroeconomic indicators such as the rapid inflow of foreign direct investment (FDI) and the mushrooming of private firms versus the ailing state-owned enterprises (SOEs) are commonly presented as evidence to support the success of these initiatives (for example, Jennings 2017; The Economist 2016). However, the topic is complex and continues to evoke spirited debate. For example, Lim (2018) and Painter (2014) do not regard Vietnam's liberalization story as an a priori process, and question orthodox, Western-centric scholarship rooted in the neoliberal economic logic of the Washington Consensus, which has been resilient despite repeated crises (see, for example, Aalbers 2013; Peck and Tickell 2002; Stiglitz 2016). Using data from two Vietnamese border provinces, Lao Cai in northern Vietnam and Tay Ninh in southern Vietnam, Gainsborough (2007) shows that main-stream arguments about the impact of changes in cross-border flows and the rise of private and transnational actors may need to be qualified when the focus is on developing economies, of which Vietnam is a key member. Gainsborough illustrates that where economies are less integrated into the global financial architecture and where domestic private capital has close and opaque ties with the state, the impact of both changes in flows and the rise of private actors is unlikely to precipitate a diminution of state power.[1]

Against the backdrop described above, in this chapter we shed light on the Vietnamese banking industry; an industry earmarked for economic reform in the aftermath of the 1986 *doi moi*. We account for Vietnam's unique historical context as well as the pressure exerted by international agencies and transnational corporations (TNCs) to coerce the Vietnamese state into adopting neoliberal governance reforms. As are many of the contributions in this edited volume, this chapter is situated within the broader notion of geobanking and finance. It also sheds light on the various public and private aspects of banking that shape geopolitical trends, and vice versa, focusing on the experience of Vietnam, a key transition economy that has been among the world's fastest-growing economies over the past two decades. We thus discuss how global, neoliberal trends interact and mesh with Hanoi's state-led development model. More crucially, it argues that the influence of neoliberalism on the workings of the Vietnamese state has been relatively subdued. In spite of policy muddling through and slow implementation, Vietnam has seemingly struck a balance between welcoming international capital while still maintaining control over the critically important banking industry. That is, Vietnam has retained and exercised a significant degree of policy autonomy in the modernization of industry. The continued relevance of the state in an era of supercharged globalization underlines Vietnam's resistance to surrender control over its banks and to commit to reforms fully. We also examine the reorganization process and outcome of the Vietnamese banking industry, defying conventional binaries of state-owned (domestic) versus private (foreign).

The chapter begins with an overview of the economic situation in Vietnam: the unevenness of reforms in the Southeast Asian nation show that although Vietnam has welcomed international capital and adopted neoliberal ideals in its liberalization drive, it has not entirely ceded control of the economy. Subsequently, we focus on the banking industry, which reveals the gradual, uneven pace of liberalization. This is followed by a discussion of the privatization process of the Joint Stock Commercial Bank for Foreign Trade of Vietnam, also known as Vietcombank, the first majority state-owned bank listed on the Ho Chi Minh Stock Exchange. Vietcombank's lengthy privatization illustrates the contradictions of opening up the banking industry only to a selected group of foreign players. Through a nominal commitment to competition and change, Hanoi's core efforts seek to resist or delay reforms whenever there are misgivings over ceding control over its banks. We conclude with a summary of the main arguments and findings.

2.   AN OVERVIEW OF VIETNAM'S ECONOMIC PROGRESS

The dramatic collapse of multiple centrally planned economies in the years leading up to and after the dissolution of the former Soviet Union and the adoption of the *doi moi* in 1986 revived a moribund economy and cemented the position of the Vietnamese Communist Party (VCP). The reforms required Vietnam to loosen and even discard protectionist policies: they thus created new trade and investment avenues and injected dynamism into the economy. Socioeconomic indicators such as food production, inflation rate and GDP all showed visible improvement in the post-*doi moi* era (Freeman 1996; Vu 2015), and Vietnam's open stance was embraced by international investors keen on setting up production in a relatively populous, low-wage economy. Initially popular among Western and Japanese TNCs, Vietnam has in recent years also been noticed by those TNCs originating from developing economies such as Malaysia and Thailand (Lim 2017). Figure 9.1 shows that, despite some occasional slowing down, FDI flowing into the country since the *doi moi* remains high, especially from 2006 onwards.

While it was predominantly SOEs that drove the economy before 1986, Vietnam has since then been adept at tapping into other sources of growth.

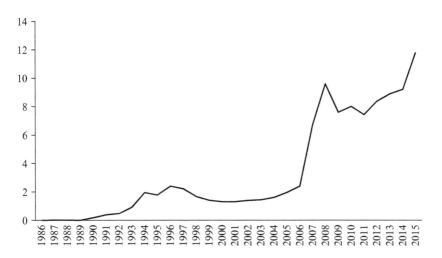

Source: United Nations Conference on Trade and Development online database, accessed 1 May 2018 at https://unctadstat.unctad.org/wds/ReportFolders/reportFolders.aspx?sCS_Ch osenLang=en.

Figure 9.1   Vietnam's inward flow of foreign direct investment, 1986–2015 (current US$ billion)

Foreign direct investment is welcome, but it has contributed in only a small way towards enterprise formation. The contribution of foreign investment is also limited and accounts for not more than 4 percent of all enterprises between 2000 and 2015. Instead, it is the homegrown non-state enterprises that are the backbone of the economy. Figure 9.2 shows that from 2000 to 2015, the share of non-state enterprises in the economy grew from 82.8 percent to 96.7 percent of all enterprises. The number of SOEs in the economy correspondingly shrank steadily from 13.6 percent to 0.6 percent of all enterprises over the same period.

The vibrancy of the non-state sector is expressed in the net turnover breakdown of enterprises. Figure 9.3 shows that the non-state enterprises and FDI enterprises had gradually increased their combined share of net turnover from 45.1 percent in 2000 to 81.8 percent in 2015. The performance of the non-state enterprises during the same period is worth noting, more than doubling its net turnover contribution from 25.1 percent to 54.0 percent. Inversely, the SOEs have contributed an increasingly smaller share of net turnover in the Vietnamese economy, from a high of 54.9 percent in 2000 to only 18.2 percent in 2015.

Notwithstanding the general picture of success and Vietnam's apparent conformance to neoliberal prescriptions, the state's influence, especially through the SOEs, continues to loom large. This paradox is unpacked by providing more context to, and reinterpreting, the data provided previously in this chapter. First, FDI, while large in absolute terms, is not exceptionally significant if it is compared to the overall size of the economy (see Figure 9.1). Figure 9.4 shows that, apart from briefly reaching 12 percent of GDP in 1994, inward FDI to the economy has been kept beneath the 1994 levels. Further solidifying this observation are the levels of inward FDI recorded in 1996 and 2008, both years widely considered to have been good years for Vietnam for attracting FDI. During these two years, inward FDI amounted to merely 10 percent of Vietnamese GDP. More relevant, it can even be argued that Vietnam is not particularly reliant on inward FDI to industrialize itself. Tracking the growth of Asia's major economies in the post-World War II era, Wong and Cheong (2014) argue that South Korea, Taiwan and China have consciously reduced their reliance on FDI for growth and development compared with Malaysia and Singapore which depend considerably more on investment from TNCs.[2] While it is not the intention to compare Vietnam with the more mature Asian economies, we suggest that FDI has not taken up too large a role in its economic structure, implicitly granting Hanoi more autonomy to design and encourage its own industrialization agenda (see also Doner and Schneider 2016).

Secondly, Figure 9.5 shows that the SOEs have generated at least 30 percent of GDP for most of the period from 1990 to 2014. While

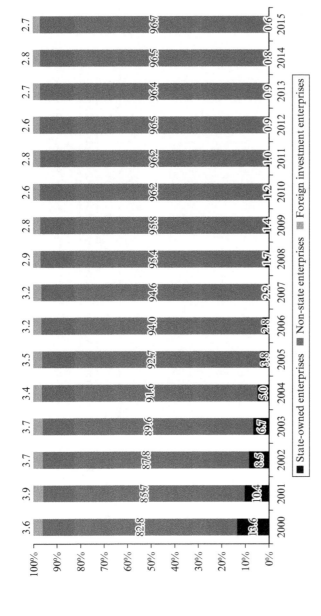

Source: General Statistics Office online database, accessed 1 May 2018 at https://www.gso.gov.vn/default_en.aspx?tabid=776.

Figure 9.2   Classification of enterprises in Vietnam, 2000–2015 (percentage)

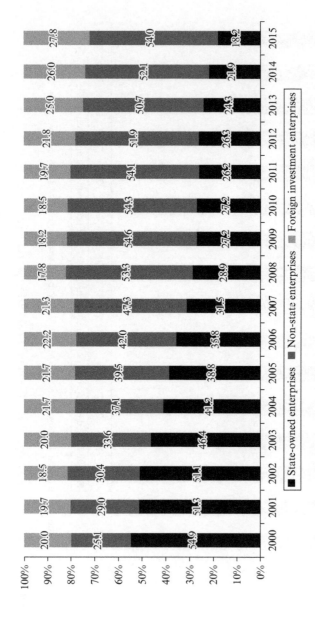

100%

90%

80%

70%

60%

50%

40%

30%

20%

10%

0%

| | 2000 | 2001 | 2002 | 2003 | 2004 | 2005 | 2006 | 2007 | 2008 | 2009 | 2010 | 2011 | 2012 | 2013 | 2014 | 2015 |

State-owned: 20.0 | 19.7 | 18.5 | 20.0 | 21.7 | 21.7 | 22.2 | 21.3 | 17.8 | 18.2 | 18.5 | 19.7 | 21.8 | 25.0 | 26.0 | 27.8

Non-state: 25.1 | 29.0 | 30.4 | 33.6 | 37.1 | 39.5 | 42.0 | 47.3 | 53.3 | 54.6 | 54.3 | 54.1 | 51.9 | 50.7 | 52.1 | 54.0

Foreign: 54.9 | 51.3 | 51.1 | 46.4 | 41.2 | 38.8 | 35.8 | 31.5 | 28.9 | 27.2 | 27.2 | 26.2 | 26.3 | 24.3 | 21.9 | 18.2

■ State-owned enterprises ■ Non-state enterprises ■ Foreign investment enterprises

Source: General Statistics Office online database, accessed 1 May 2018 at https://www.gso.gov.vn/default_en.aspx?tabid=776.

Figure 9.3   Net turnover of enterprises in Vietnam, 2000–2015 (percentage)

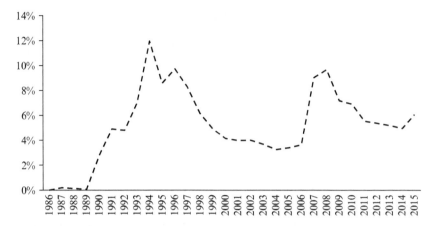

Source: United Nations Conference on Trade and Development online database, accessed 1 May 2018 at https://unctadstat.unctad.org/wds/ReportFolders/reportFolders.aspx?sCS_Ch osenLang=en.

Figure 9.4   *Vietnam's inward flow of foreign direct investment as a percentage of gross domestic product, 1986–2015 (percentage)*

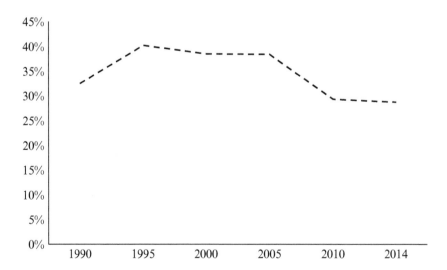

Sources: General Statistics Office (2015, 2016); Pincus (2015) and Sakata (2013).

Figure 9.5   *Contribution of state-owned enterprises to Vietnam's gross domestic product, 1990–2014 (percentage)*

non-state enterprises constitute the largest group of enterprises, amounting to 96.7 percent of all enterprises in 2015, they do not generate as much economic output as the more technology- and capital-intensive SOEs (see Figure 9.2). The disproportionate impact of the SOEs on the GDP is explained by the VCP's desire to let the former, in spite of their generally unsatisfactory performances, play a leading role in building a 'socialist-oriented market economy' (Sakata 2013, p. 7). This role is demonstrated most explicitly in strategic industries such as motorcycle manufacturing, telecommunications and shipbuilding (Fujita 2013; Lim 2016; Ngo 2017; Nguyen and O'Donnell 2017).[3]

Related to the previous issue is the persistently high profit rates captured by the SOEs (see Figure 9.6). Between 2009 and 2015, the SOEs have garnered profits exceeding 40 percent of the entire Vietnamese corporate sector.[4] This trend was broken in 2010, 2014 and 2015: a rupture has thus emerged in the low contribution of SOEs to net turnover (see Figure 9.3). For the non-state enterprises, their profit is disproportionately marginal given their large presence in the economy. More worryingly for them, the profit captured seemed to have been shrinking from 2009 to 2013, although it did rebound above the 20 percent-mark in 2014 and 2015. As for foreign investment enterprises, a similar situation to the SOEs has emerged. Contributing less than 25 percent of turnover for most of the period

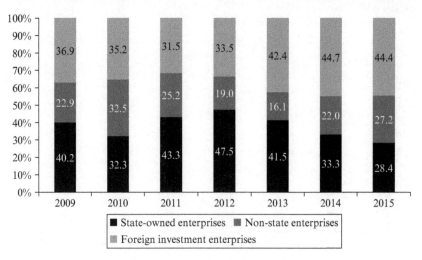

Source: General Statistics Office online database, accessed 1 May 2018 at https://www.gso.gov.vn/default_en.aspx?tabid=776.

Figure 9.6   Structure of profit before taxes by types of enterprise in Vietnam, 2009–15 (percentage)

between 2009 and 2015, they have garnered a disproportionately large share of corporate profit, ranging from 31.5 percent to 44.7 percent of total profit. Their stranglehold on corporate profit has also seemingly tightened from 2013 onwards, garnering annual profit above the 40 percent-mark.

3. REFORMING THE BANKING INDUSTRY

As part of the *doi moi*, Vietnam began to abolish the monobanking system in 1988.[5] Following the enforcement of the Ordinance on the State Bank of Vietnam (SBV) and Ordinance on Banks, Credit Cooperatives and Financial Companies in 1990, the banking industry migrated into the current two-tier system (a system that separated the central bank and commercial banks).[6] Also, the private sector was allowed to take part in commercial banking, although they still had to compete against the four large, capital-intensive state-owned commercial banks (SOCBs) (Ogimoto 2013). Nevertheless, this legislation had the positive effect of promoting the establishment of a cluster of commercial banks, which soon evolved into a huge network of banks and related financial institutions.

Many of these reforms have been motivated by Vietnam's entry into international trade and investment treaties, such as the US–Vietnam Bilateral Trade Agreement in 2001, as well as its accession to the World Trade Organization (WTO) in 2007. Vietnam has thus gradually allowed the entry of foreign banks, granting licenses to wholly foreign-owned banks in 2008. In January 2014, the ownership limit for a single foreign investor was raised from 15 percent to 20 percent, with maximum ownership for all foreign investors capped at 30 percent. Moreover, the state has permitted partial privatization of the SOCBs and promoted efforts to achieve compliance with international capital standards under the Basel capital accords (Tran et al. 2015). These reforms were to achieve two interrelated objectives (see Asian Development Bank 2014; IMF 2017). First, the introduction of foreign-owned banks was to increase the level of competition among all the participants. Secondly, the partial privatization of SOCBs was envisioned to reduce the state's share in the banking industry, moving it towards the banking norms of developed economies.[7]

Given data on three different spheres of the Vietnamese banking industry, namely, the (1) distribution of assets and chartered capital, (2) credit distribution to the economy, and (3) distribution of investment, these two objectives have arguably failed, or at least not achieved, their intended outcomes. For Malesky and Taussig (2009), this has worrying implications. The Vietnamese banking industry is still seen as transitioning towards a healthier system. The rule of law has not kept pace with the growth of the private sector and the financial system: Malesky and Tausig (2009) demonstrate that Vietnamese banks place greater value on connections than on performance, and that the firms with greater access to bank loans are no more profitable than firms without them. By some measures, connected firms are significantly less profitable than the less connected firms. The broader outcome of the reliance on connections means that a disproportionate share of credit is allocated to connected firms (including, but not limited to, the SOEs) in less competitive regions or industries.[8] Inversely, the most profitable investors in Vietnam have forgone the formal banking system, preferring to finance their activities out of reinvested earnings or informal loans.

4. ASSETS AND CHARTERED CAPITAL

The Vietnamese banking industry is diversified, with four SOCBs, 33 joint stock commercial banks (JSCBs), five joint venture banks and five wholly foreign-owned banks. The JSCBs have a more diversified shareholding structure than SOCBs. That is, their main shareholders range from domestic private firms to SOEs and foreign investors. For example, the Military Commercial Joint Bank (MBB), the largest listed JSCB in Vietnam, is 15 percent owned by the state-owned Viettel Group. It was originally established as a JSCB to finance military enterprises, but has since diversified to consumer and commercial banking products and services (Tran et al. 2015). The joint venture banks have a relatively straightforward shareholding structure, usually comprising only two or three shareholders. For example, VinaSiam Bank is 34 percent owned by the state-owned Agribank, with the remaining 66 percent owned jointly by two Thai partners (Siam Commercial Bank and the Charoen Pokphand Group). The five wholly foreign-owned banks are relative newcomers to the industry. The state only permitted them entrance after Vietnam's 2007 accession to the WTO. These five banks have garnered high profits owing to high demand by foreign investors to open bank accounts with them for business-related purposes (for example, trade financing and foreign exchange services) (see Asian Development Bank 2014; Tran et al. 2015).

Despite a large number of participants, the industry remains highly skewed towards the SOCBs. Figure 9.7 displays the distribution of banking industry assets according to type of firm. It is evident that the four SOCBs hold the largest stake in the industry, accounting for 44 percent of all assets. The JSCBs, despite their large numbers, hold only 42 percent of banking assets, while 11 percent of assets are held by joint venture

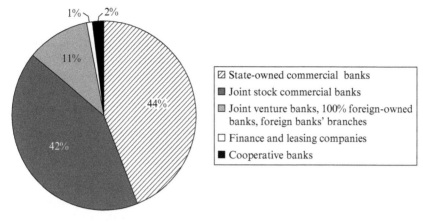

Source: Tran et al. (2015).

Figure 9.7 Banking industry assets by types of banks, 2014 (percentage)

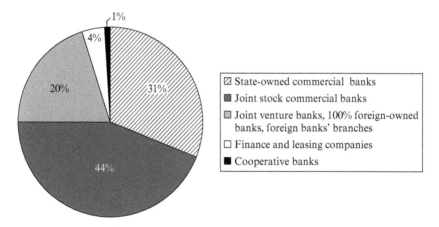

Source: Tran et al. (2015).

Figure 9.8 Banking industry chartered capital by types of banks, 2014 (percentage)

banks, wholly foreign-owned banks and the foreign banks' branches in Vietnam. Dwarfed by the larger banks, finance and leasing companies and cooperative banks take up only a combined 3 percent of banking assets. The situation is only marginally better when it comes to the chartered capital of the banking industry. Figure 9.8 shows that the SOCBs account for 31 percent of total chartered capital, trailing only that owned by the JSCBs (44 percent of total chartered capital). Joint venture banks, wholly foreign-owned banks and the foreign banks' branches in Vietnam account for approximately 20 percent of total chartered capital, while a total of 5 percent of assets is contributed by the finance and leasing companies as well as cooperative banks.

5.   CREDIT DISTRIBUTION TO THE ECONOMY

The lopsided nature of the industry is also evidenced in the credit distribution to the Vietnamese economy. Figure 9.9 shows the four SOCBs dominating the distribution of credit in the economy from 2005 to 2013. While the market share of the SOCBs has reduced from a high of 72 percent in 2005 to 45 percent in 2013, it still overshadows the rest of the industry participants. Perhaps more encouragingly for the industry is the performance of the JSCBs as well as that of the joint venture and foreign banks. The JSCBs have increased their market share from only 8 percent in 2005 to close to one-third in 2013. For the joint venture and foreign banks, they have only made noticeable inroads in 2013, more than doubling their credit market share from the previous year (9 percent).

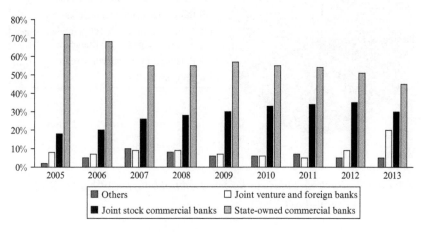

Source: Asian Development Bank (2014) and Tran et al. (2015).

Figure 9.9   Credit market share types of banks, 2005–13 (percentage)

6. DISTRIBUTION OF INVESTMENT

We can observe the stubborn presence of the state in the distribution
of investment. Table 9.1 shows that Hanoi had gradually reduced its
investment in the economy from 2005 to 2008, but intensified its presence
from 2008 onwards, primarily because of the onset of the global financial
crisis. The dominance of the state also means that investment efforts from
the non-state enterprises and foreign enterprises are kept at bay. Table

Table 9.1 *Investment at current prices by types of ownership, 2005–14
(percentage)*

	State sector	Non-state sector	Foreign invested sector
2005	47.1	38.0	14.9
2006	45.7	38.1	16.2
2007	37.2	38.5	24.3
2008	33.9	35.2	30.9
2009	40.5	33.9	25.6
2010	38.1	36.1	25.8
2011	37.0	38.5	24.5
2012	40.3	38.1	21.6
2013	40.4	37.7	21.9
2014	39.9	38.4	21.7

Source: General Statistics Office (2015).

Table 9.2 *State investment at current prices by investment source, 2005–14
(percentage)*

	State budget	Loan	Equity of state-owned enterprises and other sources
2005	54.4	22.3	23.3
2006	54.1	14.5	31.4
2007	54.2	15.4	30.4
2008	61.8	13.5	24.7
2009	64.3	14.1	21.6
2010	44.8	36.6	18.6
2011	52.1	33.4	14.5
2012	50.4	36.8	12.8
2013	46.9	36.8	16.3
2014	42.7	40.7	16.6

Source: General Statistics Office (2015).

9.2 shows that investment from the state has also evolved since 2008. While Hanoi disbursed a heavy portion of its investment (more than 50 percent) through the state budget from 2005 to 2008, it has preferred to rely more on loans from 2008 onwards. The loan component of the state investment more than doubled between 2008 and 2014 as Hanoi opted for monetary easing to revive its economy. The reliance on loans has, in turn, reduced the equity portion of the SOEs, with the latter being increasingly marginalized.

7. EQUITIZATION OF VIETCOMBANK

The long-drawn-out equitization of Vietcombank reflects how the state has managed the liberalization of the industry.[9] Vietcombank is a good proxy of the state's intentions because it is the second largest bank in Vietnam, controlling approximately 5.9 trillion Vietnam dong (VND) in assets. Vietcombank was founded in 1962 as part of the SBV specializing in foreign trade. It became a commercial bank only in 1990 as a result of the enforcement of the Ordinance on the State Bank of Vietnam and Ordinance on Banks, Credit Cooperatives and Financial Companies. According to Huynh and Rosengard (2009), the 2004 equitization of Vietcombank was both an experiment for equitizing big SOEs and for reforming the banking industry. If the process was successful, it would become the catalyst promoting more wholesale equitization of the SOEs and a more streamlined banking system.

The equitization process of Vietcombank can be divided into three periods: preparation, the first phase of the initial public offering (IPO) and the second phase of the IPO (see Huynh and Rosengard 2009). The preparation period lasted for about three years, starting in February 2004 (when the equitization plan was announced) and ending in February 2007 (when the advisory firm was chosen). This period witnessed frequent shifting of plans and incoherence between different stakeholders. To this end, the equitization involved multiple debates related to its timeframe and definitions and methods such as stock valuation and choice of advisory firm. One of the most glaring instances saw Nguyen Tan Dung, the then Deputy Prime Minister who subsequently became Prime Minister from 2006 to 2016, publicly declaring that he expects the equitization to be implemented in 2005 after a high-level meeting with the management of Vietcombank in January of the same year. Dung's stance was also supported by Prime Minister Phan Van Khai (in office from 1997 to 2006), who rebuked the SBV for what was perceived as procrastination. In return, Lee Duc Thuy, the SBV Governor (in office from 1999 to 2007) responded that 'Everyone knows that equitizing banks is touching to (*sic*) a sensitive issue. The party and the state consider banks as the artery of the economy, especially state-owned commercial banks . . . Now touching to (*sic*) this pillar, if carelessly . . . may cause negative effects for economics and politics and society' (Huynh and Rosengard 2009, p. 5).

The first phase of the IPO began on 12 February 2007 when Credit Suisse, the deal advisor, was chosen. It ended on 26 December 2007 when the first phase of the IPO was conducted.[10] As in the previous period, the first phase was marked by inconsistencies from the Vietnamese state. Decision 1289/QD-TTg (dated 26 September 2007), approved by the Prime Minister, outlined that price is not the sole determining criteria for finding a foreign strategic investor. Other criteria include a commitment to technical support and future investment cooperation, especially in holding the shares of Vietcombank for an extended period after the IPO was conducted. The Vietnamese also agreed to select a foreign strategic investor before the IPO, in an attempt to follow global norms. However, this commitment was breached after Hanoi discovered that it failed to get the valuation it expected from international investors. More specifically, the state expected a valuation of VND100000 per share for the IPO, with 97.5 million shares (equivalent to 6.5 percent of the bank's equity) to be auctioned off.

However, it soon emerged that a group of international investors led by the Japanese investment bank, Nomura, had only offered a price of VND43000 to 67000 per share (see Huynh and Rosengard 2009). This pricing mismatch did not go down well with the Vietnamese, who soon changed the equitization process by conducting the IPO before choosing the strategic investors. In the final plan, the price offered to the strategic investors was set as the average price of the IPO. A spokesperson from Vietcombank explained that this move was necessary because too low an IPO price might damage state assets and the interest of individual investors. When the first phase of the IPO was eventually conducted on 26 December 2007, the results were much better. The Vietnamese state succeeded in exceeding its expected IPO price of VDN100000 per share as the average auction priced was VND107860 per share. It also managed to sell all 97.5 million of Vietcombank's shares. Of the 6.5 percent equity sold, 1.9 percent was taken up by foreign investors, with another 2.0 percent and 2.6 percent snapped up by domestic strategic investors and the general public, respectively (Nguyen and Ho 2007).[11]

Nevertheless, the second phase of the IPO was markedly less successful. Vietcombank failed in finding the elusive foreign strategic investor. While it did come close to an agreement with US-based General Electric, the global financial crisis in 2008 sent bank valuations around the world plummeting and made agreement on price impossible (Tudor 2011). Vietcombank's share price dipped as Vietnam's economy contracted, in line with the rest of the world. It was not until March 2011 that business confidence picked up, which allowed Credit Suisse to restart the auction. Even then, it took Vietcombank a further seven months to clinch a deal to sell a 15 percent stake for US$567.3 million to Japan's Mizuho. Although Mizuho would infuse Vietcombank with technical services to improve its business performance, including sending Japanese experts to Vietnam, training Vietcombank staff and offering business opportunities, it took the Vietnamese almost four years from the conclusion of the first phase of the IPO to persuade Mizuho (Hong 2011).

Throughout the Vietcombank's equitization experience, the state has conformed only partially to its promise to the international investors and agencies. In addition to Hanoi's backpedaling on several key issues (for example, a refusal to accept a lower than expected IPO price), there have also been occasional clashes of opinion between key authorities, one of which was the Prime Minister's public show of displeasure with the central bank for a perceived slowing down of equitization. Hanoi has undertaken the process gradually and inconsistently. This observation reinforces the research of Lim (2018) and Painter (2014), who argue that Vietnam's approach to economic liberalization does not fit well into the orthodox, neoliberal economic ideology espoused by the Washington Consensus. Following Gainsborough's (2007) study on cross-border financial flows, in this chapter we also assert that Vietnam's banking industry has evolved in this manner in large part because it is not well integrated into the global financial system and because it continues to be dominated by the SOCBs, often with the tacit support of the state. More broadly, the development of the Vietnamese banking industry mirrors that of the broader economy as well as the strategic industries (for example, motorcycle manufacturing and shipbuilding), with the SOEs still playing a large role, despite some seemingly token moves to liberalize. To this end, Vietnam has forged a fairly creative pathway to incorporate international best practices, while still preserving some of its political philosophy and related institutions (such as the desire to let the SOEs play a leading role in building a socialist-orientated market economy).

8.   CONCLUSION

In this chapter we have demonstrated that Vietnam has maintained its policy independence despite its often declared commitment to economic openness. We have done so by first highlighting the unevenness of reforms in the broader economy, before doing likewise for the banking industry. We have shown that the Vietnamese banking industry is still lopsided, with the state holding on to a large role as seen in state's dominance in the distribution of assets and chartered capital, credit distribution to the economy and distribution of investment. The presence of the state is also revealed in the equitization of Vietcombank. In theory, the equitization of an SOCB such as Vietcombank can increase the level of competition in the industry as it will bring in better managed foreign players and will modernize Vietnam's derelict banking industry. It can also reduce the state's share in the industry, nudging it towards the norms of the developed economies. However, Hanoi has behaved in a relatively guarded manner in Vietcombank's equitization. While the Vietnamese state suffers from inefficient execution and lack of coordination, as well as occasional policy U-turns to suit its objectives – such as changing the rules of the IPO of the Vietcombank by conducting the IPO before choosing the strategic investors, reversing its initial pledge to select a foreign strategic investor before the IPO – it has managed to strike a balance between welcoming international capital while still maintaining control over the critically important banking industry.

Not all of Hanoi's attempts to resist or delay market reforms come across as triumphs: the long-drawn-out search for a strategic investor to uplift the Vietcombank is a case in point. However, what is explicit is that the influence of neoliberalism on the working of the Vietnamese state has been relatively muted. This finding dispels the conventional wisdom that globalization has limited the autonomy of states, particularly small ones such as Vietnam. If anything, Vietnam's handling of its banking industry underlines that the state remains a crucial player in devising and implementing policy measures. This sway has important, wider implications for other developing economies aspiring to craft a modernization pathway compatible with their specific socio-historical circumstances.

NOTES

1. See Ngo (2017) for a more detailed account of how such opaque ties can, in the right circumstances, be molded into a formidable upgrading collation, stimulating Vietnam's industrialization process through the harnessing of developmental rent.
2. Between 1980 and 2010, FDI entering South Korea, Taiwan and China has never exceeded 15 percent of their respective national GDP. This figure is comparably higher for both Malaysia and Singapore, in large part because of their more outward orientated economic strategies, which require more open forms of cooperation with the other economies.
3. Vietnam's track record in these strategic industries is uneven. While it has seemingly groomed fairly strong national champions in the telecommunications industry, such as the Viettel Group and Vietnam Posts and the Telecommunications Group, it has

suffered massive losses in its attempt to cultivate its state-owned shipbuilding firm, Vinashin. Previously regarded as one of the pioneers in industrializing the country, Vinashin got into trouble after a financial scandal, which came to light in 2008. In 2017, Hanoi handed two death penalties and a life sentence to three former executives of the SOE who were judged to have embezzled a total of more than US$11.5 million. The Vinashin scandal remains one of the biggest corruption cases in the corporate history of Vietnam (Viet Nam News 2017).
4. The data prior to 2009 is not available, so we can only analyze the structure and distribution of corporate profit from 2009 onwards.
5. According to Ogimoto (2013), the monobanking system refers to a system in which the central bank, the State Bank of Vietnam, monopolistically carried out the functions of both central banking and commercial banking.
6. By separating its central banking functions from its commercial activities, the SBV effectively hived off the latter to four newly created state-owned commercial banks, each targeting a different segment of the economy. The SBV's industrial and commercial lending department was converted to the Vietnam Industrial and Commercial Bank (formerly Incombank, now Vietinbank), agricultural department to the Vietnam Bank for Agriculture and Rural Development (Agribank), international trade department to the Bank for Foreign Trade of Vietnam (Vietcombank) and infrastructure department to the Bank for Investment and Development of Vietnam (BIDV) (Tran et al. 2015). In 2018, there remained four SOCBS in Vietnam. Technically, SOCBs are 100 percent or majority owned by the state.
7. By developed economies, the implicit understanding of much of the contemporary scholarship takes the Anglo-American banking model as its benchmark, in which commercial banking functions are almost entirely carried out by private firms. This chapter, however, notes that there is a significant variation of this model in other developed economies such as Germany, Sweden, Singapore and Japan (see Carney and Zheng 2016; Hall and Soskice 2001).
8. According to Vu (2015), the rise of a group of politically well-connected private firms in recent years has complicated the situation. Their close ties to the Vietnamese elites have allowed them to tap into domains traditionally reserved for the SOEs, in effect becoming quasi-SOEs in the process.
9. Equitization refers to the process of converting SOEs into joint stock companies. It is a de facto privatization process, although the Vietnamese prefer to use the term equitization.
10. The Vietnamese state divided the IPO into two rounds in a cautious attempt to better manage the equitization process. In the first round, Vietcombank will auction only 6.5 percent of its equity (equivalent to 97.5 million shares). In the second round, progressively more shares will be sold off, with a planned eventual shareholding of SBV (65 percent), foreign strategic investors (20 percent), domestic strategic investors (5 percent) and general public (10 percent).
11. In accordance with the SBV's regulations, foreign investors are not allowed to own more than 30 percent of shares offered. In addition, no single foreign shareholder can own more than a 20 percent stake in a Vietnamese bank.

REFERENCES

Aalbers, M. (2013), 'Neoliberalism is dead . . . long live neoliberalism!', *International Journal of Urban and Regional Research*, **37** (3), 1083–90.
Asian Development Bank (2014), *Viet Nam: Financial Sector Assessment, Strategy, and Road Map*, Manila: Asian Development Bank.
Carney, R. and Zheng, L.Y. (2016), 'Institutional (dis)incentives to innovate: an

explanation for Singapore's innovation gap', *Journal of East Asian Studies*, **9** (2), 291–319.

Doner, R. and Schneider, B. (2016), 'The middle-income trap: more politics than economics', *World Politics*, **68** (4), 608–44.

Freeman, D. (1996), 'Doi moi policy and the small-enterprise boom in Ho Chi Minh City, Vietnam', *Geographical Review*, **86** (2), 178–97.

Fujita, M. (2013), 'The rise of local assemblers in the Vietnamese motorcycle industry: the dynamics and diversity of industrial organization', in S. Sakata (ed.), *Vietnam's Economic Entities in Transition*, Basingstoke: Palgrave Macmillan, pp. 146–66.

Gainsborough, M. (2007), 'Globalisation and the state revisited: a view from provincial Vietnam', *Journal of Contemporary Asia*, **37** (1), 1–18.

General Statistics Office (2015), *Statistical Handbook of Vietnam 2014*, Hanoi: Statistical Publishing House.

General Statistics Office (2016), *Efficiency of Business of Domestic Enterprises in the Period 2005–2014*, Hanoi: Statistical Publishing House.

Hall, P. and Soskice, D. (2001), *Varieties of Capitalism: The Institutional Foundations of Comparative Advantage*, Oxford: Oxford University Press.

Hong, P. (2011), 'Japan's Mizuho invests US$567 mil. in Vietcombank', *Saigon Times*, 3 October, accessed 30 March 2018 at http://english.thesaigontimes.vn/19566/Japan's-Mizuho-invests-US$567-mil-in-Vietcombank.html.

Huynh, T.D. and Rosengard, J. (2009), *Vietcombank Equitization*, Ho Chi Minh City: Fulbright Economics Teaching Program.

International Monetary Fund (IMF) (2017), *IMF Country Report No. 17/191: Vietnam: Selected Issues*, Washington, DC: International Monetary Fund.

Jennings, R. (2017), 'Vietnam's economic growth will accelerate in 2018 as investors flood the country', *Forbes*, 27 December, accessed 26 July 2019 at https://www.forbes.com/sites/ralphjennings/2017/12/27/vietnams-economy-will-soar-again-in-2018-because-investors-just-love-it/#3390556a55df.

Lim, G. (2016). 'Managing technological development: a study of Vietnam's telecommunication goods industry', *Journal of Comparative Asian Development*, **15** (2), 276–99.

Lim, G. (2017), 'What do Malaysian firms seek in Vietnam?', *Journal of Asia-Pacific Business*, **18** (2), 131–50.

Lim, G. (2018), 'Public policy with Vietnamese characteristics: the case of the motorcycle industry', *Journal of Asian Public Policy*, **11** (2), 226–44.

Malesky, E. and Taussig, M. (2009), 'Where is credit due? Legal institutions, connections, and the efficiency of bank lending in Vietnam', *Journal of Law, Economics, and Organization*, **25** (2), 535–78.

Ngo, C.N. (2017), 'Local value chain development in Vietnam: motorcycles, technical learning and rents management', *Journal of Contemporary Asia*, **47** (1), 1–26.

Nguyen, M.H. and O'Donnell, M. (2017), 'Reforming state-owned enterprises in Vietnam: the contrasting cases of Vinashin and Viettel', *Asian Perspective*, **41** (2), 215–37.

Nguyen, N.L. and Ho, B.M. (2007), 'Update 2: Vietcombank IPO raises $652 mln, market cautious', *Reuters*, 27 December, accessed 5 May 2018 at https://www.reuters.com/article/asia-271328-vietnam-vietcombank-ipo/update-2-vietcombank-ipo-raises-652-mln-market-cautious-idUSHAN2103920071227.

Ogimoto, Y. (2013), 'Development and prospects for the Vietnamese banking sector: before and after accession to the WTO', in S. Sakata (ed.), *Vietnam's Economic Entities in Transition*, Basingstoke: Palgrave Macmillan, pp. 167–203.

Painter, M. (2014), 'Governance reforms in China and Vietnam: marketisation, leapfrogging and retro-fitting', *Journal of Contemporary Asia*, **44** (2), 204–20.

Peck, J. and Tickell, A. (2002), 'Neoliberalizing space', *Antipode*, **34** (3), 380–404.

Pincus, J. (2015), 'Why doesn't Vietnam grow faster? State fragmentation and the limits of vent for surplus growth', *Journal of Southeast Asian Economies*, **32** (1), 26–51.

Sakata, S. (2013), 'Introduction: the changing status of economic entities in Vietnam', in S. Sakata (ed.), *Vietnam's Economic Entities in Transition*, Basingstoke: Palgrave Macmillan, pp. 1–22.

Schaumburg-Müller H. and Pham, H.C. (eds) (2010), *The New Asian Dragon: Internationalization of Firms in Vietnam*, Copenhagen: Copenhagen Business School Press.

Stiglitz, J. (2016), 'Globalization and its new discontents', *Project Syndicate*, 5 August, accessed 5 August 2016 at https://www.project-syndicate.org/commentary/globalization-new-discontents-by-joseph-e--stiglitz-2016-08.

Straszheim, D. (2008), 'Is Vietnam the next China?', *Forbes*, 6 December, accessed 6 December 2008 at http://www.forbes.com/2008/06/12/vietnam-china-inflation-oped-cx_dhs_0612viet.html.

The Economist (2016), 'Vietnam's economy: the other Asian Tiger, *The Economist*, 4 August, accessed 5 May 2018 at https://www.economist.com/leaders/2016/08/04/the-other-asian-tiger.

Tran, B.T., Ong, B. and Weldon, S. (2015), *Vietnam Banking Industry Report*, Singapore: Duxton Asset Management.

Tudor, A. (2011), 'Mizuho to buy 15% of Vietnamese bank', *Wall Street Journal*, 30 September, accessed 1 May 2018 at https://www.wsj.com/articles/SB10001424052970204138204576602261666129684.

Viet Nam News (2017), 'Two executions, one life sentence in Vinashin case', *Viet Nam News*, 23 February, accessed 26 July 2019 at http://vietnamnews.vn/politics-laws/351702/two-executions-one-life-sentence-in-vinashin-case.html#i0HIZioTib9FjyVl.97.

Vu, M.K. (2015), 'Can Vietnam achieve more robust economic growth? Insights from a comparative analysis of economic reforms in Vietnam and China', *Journal of Southeast Asian Economies*, **32** (1), 52–83.

Wong, C.-Y. and Cheong, K.-C. (2014), 'Diffusion of catching-up industrialization strategies: the dynamics of East Asia's policy learning process', *Journal of Comparative Asian Development*, **13** (3), 369–404.

PART III

Micro-Level Action and Reaction of People and Firms

10. Cross-currency swaps and local credit money creation in the Turkish banking system

Engin Yılmaz

1. INTRODUCTION

This chapter studies the Turkish banking system's experience with local loan expansion, which comes across as excessively large given the relatively small base of local deposits. The analysis of the financial sector carried out here shows how local loan growth, which surpasses and is disproportionate in relation to local deposit growth, has been enabled by the cross-currency swap mechanism. The liabilities of the Turkish banking system have come to be dollarized[1] as they move away from local deposit bases. This debt-fuelled growth model has been a salient feature of economic strategy over the past two decades and has created what may be described as fictitious wealth. Cross-currency swaps are of particular relevance to a discussion about debt-driven consumption, presented here using the example of the Turkish economy for which cross-currency swaps are a necessary component of loan creation based on foreign currency.

Policy-makers in Turkey have come to rely on these derivatives to maintain high economic growth rates. Banks support this approach to create local loans and drive consumption. Particularly since the global financial crises of 2008–09, local loan creation has been spurred by the quantitative easing policies of core – Anglo-American and European – economies, owing to which, in 2012, loans in Turkey surpassed deposits. The disparity between loans and deposits may be seen as the outcome of (1) a chronic savings deficit and (2) the low interest rate implemented by the Turkish central bank. An easy monetary policy from the central bank has pushed down the rate of return available to deposits and driven many away from the banking system.

The remainder of this chapter addresses the following questions: (1) why and when do local loans surpass local deposits? (2) How have banks managed their balance sheets? (3) What is the government role in debt fuelled growth strategies? Section 2 presents an overview of derivatives with basic definitions and explanations. Section 3 surveys the empirical literature on how banking systems and economies are shaped by cross-currency swaps. Section 4 is a discussion on how local currency in the banking system is created through the use of cross-currency swaps. Section 5 examines the balance sheets of the Turkish banking sector and draws attention to the role of foreign currency liabilities. Section 6 examines the off-balance sheet structure of Turkish banks to show how money swaps are the main instrument for cross-currency swaps. Concluding remarks, which link the analysis to the geopolitical context of Turkish banking, are offered in section 7.

2. DERIVATIVES IN TURKEY: A CONCISE OVERVIEW

A derivative is a financial instrument with a value that depends on, or is derived from, the value(s) of other, more basic, underlying variables (Hull 2014).[2] Derivatives may also be seen as an agreement between a future buyer and future seller, or counterparties (Durbin 2010). Derivative markets focus on future prices: the participants in these markets are either sellers or buyers in the exchange process. In the past three decades, derivatives have become increasingly important in the global economy and a huge variety of different derivative products are either traded on organized markets or agreed directly with counterparties in what is known as the over-the-counter market (Chisholm 2010; Mihalek and Packer 2010). Organized markets run on standardized regulations for every operation and transaction, but over-the-counter markets stretch these regulations and the contract is made directly between two parties; there are no standardized regulations or standardized contracts and everything is dictated by the preferences of the parties involved.

A swap is an agreement between two counterparties that agree to exchange the principals or interest payments from two different financial instruments. Usually the principals do not change hands and one cash flow is generally fixed, while the other is variable and based on a benchmark interest rate, floating currency exchange rate or index price. A number of derivative financial instruments are based on swap agreements. These include interest rate swaps, currency swaps, cross-currency swaps, commodity swaps, debt-equity swaps and credit default swaps; for the purpose of analysing loan creation in the Turkish economy, we discuss the first three.

For an interest rate swap, the principals are in the same currency and only interest payments are exchanged. This is the most common form

Table 10.1   The conceptualization of cross-currency swap, currency swap and interest rate swap

	Exchanged		Currency
	Principal	Interest payment	
Interest rate swap	–	+	Same
Currency swap	+	–	Different
Cross-currency swap	+	+	Different

Source: Author's conceptualization.

of swap, and contracts are executed primarily between businesses or financial institutions and customized for the needs of both parties. For a currency swap, principals are in different currencies and only principals are exchanged. For a cross-currency swap, principals are in different currencies and exchanged as well as interest payments.[3]

Cross-currency swaps are typically used for comparative advantage, hedging, speculation and the specific purposes of national and international banks. There has been limited academic engagement with the wider effects of cross-currency swaps on the economy and on the banking system, particularly given the mystique that is often associated with the balance sheet accounting and reporting policies of banks.

An alternative conceptualization of the three different swaps is available in Table 10.1. Here it is shown that for interest rate swaps, two counterparties exchange interest payments on floating rates or fixed rates: one counterparty can pay a floating rate and the other counterparty can pay a fixed rate. In the cross-currency swap, counterparties exchange interest payments in the three different ways: fixed-fixed, floating-floating or floating-fixed rates. These definitions may be enlarged and different definitions may be added to the table.

A summary of a basic cross-currency swap transaction between two banks is depicted in Figure 10.1. At the start of the cross-currency swap, the two banks exchange principals denominated in two different currencies which are equivalent in value at the spot exchange rate.[4] At the start of the contract, bank A lends 100 euros to bank B and borrows 150 dollars from bank B. During the term, bank A pays US$ Libor and bank B pays euro Libor quarterly. At maturity, bank A gives back 150 dollars to bank B and bank B returns 100 euros to bank A. The exchange rate is fixed in the principal amounts during the process. An exchange rate revaluation at maturity, regardless of the final spot rate, does not change notional amounts which are paid at the start of the contract. The counterparties

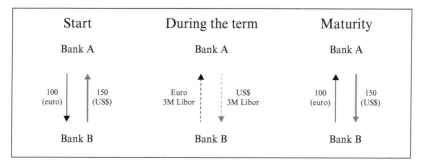

Note: 1 euro = 1.5 dollars.

Source: BIS (2008).

Figure 10.1   *The conceptualization of cross-currency swap transaction*

select the form of interest rate payments: floating-floating, fixed-fixed or floating-fixed rates.

Why do financial markets use cross-currency swap agreements? Three sets of motivations have drawn attention over recent decades. The first is the comparative advantage argument. One counterparty has a relative advantage borrowing on, say, a fixed rate basis and another has a relative advantage borrowing on a floating rate basis (Corb 2012). The second set of motivations is based on the hedging argument. A hedge is an investment to minimize the risk of adverse price movements in an asset. The third set of motivations is the speculation argument, which claims that swaps are used to capture gains from price movements in an asset. The Turkish banking system uses cross-currency swaps for creating local loans while controlling currency risk in its balance sheet.

It is difficult to arrive at a precise quantitative measure of the use of cross-currency swaps because accounting practices apply both on and off the balance sheets of banks. Whereas access to and the analysis of bank balance sheets is generally uncomplicated, the situation is different for off-balance sheet items. These are assets or liabilities that do not appear on a bank's balance sheet but are nonetheless effectively assets or liabilities of the banks. These items differ significantly from country to country; in Turkey they are categorized as guarantees, commitments and derivatives. Derivatives are further classified as forwards, money swaps, interest swaps and other derivatives. Turkish derivatives contained in the off-balance sheet exposures of Turkish banks are investigated later in this chapter.

3. SURVEY OF LITERATURE

The swap spread boom associated with the 2008–09 global financial crises, and related shifts in dollar borrowing in the international markets, has been the subject of economic literature centred on currency derivatives in emerging markets (Chang and Schlögl 2012; Du et al. 2017; Shim and Baba 2011; Zurawski and Ossolinski 2010). In addition, there are specific works on the cross-currency swaps and their effects on the economy. In Sweden, the central bank has taken a special interest in this issue and published various working papers and reports. Ryden et al. (2012) indicate that Swedish banks fund some of their long-term lending – mostly mortgage loans – in Swedish kronor by issuing bonds and certificates in foreign currency. Swedish banks do not directly exchange foreign currency debt for Swedish kronor on the spot market because it results in an open foreign currency position in their balance sheets. Instead, Swedish banks use a cross-currency swap mechanism to hedge themselves against currency risk (Eklund et al. 2012). The volume of Swedish bank foreign currency financing for this purpose is substantial (Blåvarg 2013). For banks, surplus funding in dollars serves two purposes: (1) pension and insurance companies may borrow dollars without taking on currency risk, and (2) Swedish banks may access kronor to lend or invest in Swedish assets (Riksbank 2013). The counterparties of Swedish banks in such cross-currency swaps appear to be the pension and insurance companies: interestingly, as noted by Hilander (2014), data on cross-currency swap transactions in Sweden shows that foreign banks participate in these swaps as intermediaries between Swedish banks and Swedish non-bank financial companies. For instance, a foreign bank may execute a short-term swap (three months) with a Swedish pension company to obtain domestic currency, and exchange this domestic currency with a Swedish bank in a long-term swap (five years). Figure 10.2 depicts such an arrangement.

The case of Norwegian banking demonstrates the relationship between a loans–deposits gap and non-deposit liabilities for banks (Molland 2014; Syed 2011). As shown by Syed (2011), Norwegian banks issue bonds in foreign currency and swap this foreign currency for Norwegian kroner through a combination of currency and interest rate swap contracts. Banking groups exchange foreign currency for Norwegian kroner, and this foreign currency is returned before the loan matures. Foreign exchange derivatives, especially various forms of currency swap, have characteristics that are particularly suited to this purpose (Molland, 2014). The International Monetary Fund (IMF) has issued warnings for the Norwegian banking system about the term inconsistency of foreign cur-

Note: The transaction commences with the Swedish bank issuing a covered bond in euros with a maturity of five years. To exchange euros to kronor, the Swedish bank subsequently concludes a long-term swap with a five-year maturity with a foreign bank. In turn, the foreign bank funds this transaction by concluding a currency swap with a three month maturity with a pension company.

Source: Hilander (2014).

Figure 10.2 Swedish bank's cross-currency swap transaction

rency debts which are used in swap transactions: the maturities of currency swaps can be different from the foreign funding maturities and expose banks to maturity mismatches and rollover risks (IMF 2015).

Hungary is another country proficient with cross-currency swaps: these have tended to be used for hedging foreign currency lending in Hungary. As Mák and Páles (2009) note, Hungarian banks finance much of their foreign currency lending through local currency in swaps markets.

Arsov et al. (2013) describe the role of cross-currency swaps in the Australian financial system in the context of reforming the management of over-the-counter (OTC) derivatives markets. In the Australian financial system, a large chunk of bank funding relies on the issuance of foreign currency bonds in offshore markets and the use of cross-currency swaps to hedge the associated foreign exchange (Arsov et al. 2013).

The Turkish academic literature on the use of cross-currency swaps is sparse. Existing studies include Duran and Küçüksaraç's (2012) work on investigating the long-run equilibrium relationship between the cross-currency swap and Treasury bond markets. Şimşek (2015) explores the determinants of currency swaps in the Turkish banking system. Also, Keleş (2016) analyses the fundamentals that drive a wedge between the local currency government bond yield curve and the swap curve to understand price setting for an emerging country fixed income market. These studies contain limited, if any, engagement with the implications of cross-currency swaps for the Turkish economy and banking system.

4.   SIMULATING CROSS-CURRENCY SWAPS

The simulations presented in this section demonstrate how banks can create money in the form of local currency (1) without a cross-currency swap, and (2) with a cross-currency swap. The former leads to an open foreign currency position on the bank's balance sheet. The hazards of this materialized in the Turkish economy when the financial crisis hit in 2001. However, when banks create local currency with a cross-currency swap, dollarization occurs. The effects of cross-currency swaps on the bank balance sheet may be viewed through a double-entry accounting lens and conceptualized as in Table 10.2.

Table 10.2 depicts a hypothetical open foreign currency position in a bank balance sheet. The initial position (T) is when the bank is in equilibrium because the amount of local (foreign currency) assets is equal to the amount of the local (foreign currency) liabilities (Table 10.3).

The bank takes the hypothetical foreign currency debt and this increases its assets and liabilities in foreign currency in the T + 1 time period

Table 10.2   Creating local money without the cross-currency swap (1 FX =
1 TRY)

Balance sheet		
T		
Assets	Liabilities	
100 TRY	100 TRY	
100 FX	100 FX	
T + 1		
(+ 100 FX debt)		
Assets	Liabilities	
100 TRY	100 TRY	
200 **FX** ⬆	200 **FX** ⬆	
T + 2		
(+ 100 FX turns to new 100 TRY in the assets)		
Assets	Liabilities	
200 **TRY** ⬆	100 TRY	
100 **FX** ⬇	200 FX	

Note: FX = foreign currency; TRY = Turkish lira.

Source: Author's conceptualization.

Table 10.3   Creating local money without cross-currency swap (1 FX = 1 TRY) in the T time

T	
Assets	Liabilities
100 TRY	100 TRY
100 FX	100 FX

Note: FX = foreign currency; TRY = Turkish lira.

Source: Author's conceptualization.

Table 10.4   Creating local money without cross-currency swap (1 FX = 1 TRY) in the T + 1 time

T + 1 (+ 100 FX debt)			
Assets		Liabilities	
100 TRY		100 TRY	
200 **FX**	↑	200 **FX**	↑

Note: FX = foreign currency; TRY = Turkish lira.

Source: Author's conceptualization.

(Table 10.4). There is no open position on the balance sheet in the T + 1 time period.

The bank uses this foreign currency to create local currency on its balance sheet using 100 FX to create 100 TRY in the T + 2 time period. This process creates more local currency assets but it also creates an open foreign currency position in the balance sheet in the T + 2 time period: 200 FX in liabilities relative to 100 FX in assets (Table 10.5).

There are several risks in this method of financing. Perhaps the most obvious is from the assumption that one unit of FX is equal to one unit of TRY throughout the entire process. In a situation when this parity does not hold – for instance, if 1 FX becomes equivalent to 1.50 TRY – Turkish banks will pay more for foreign currency debt. A second risk is the possibility that a substantial part of overall gross loan portfolios could become classified as non-performing loans. This form of vulnerability has been faced by Turkish banks in the past: for instance, Bredenkamp et al. (2009) observe that many banks were overleveraged and had large

Table 10.5   Creating local money without cross-currency swap (1 FX = 1 TRY) in the T + 2 time

T + 2		
(+ 100 FX turns to new 100 TRY in the assets)		
Assets		Liabilities
200 **TRY**	↑	100 TRY
100 **FX**	↓	200 FX

Note: FX = foreign currency; TRY = Turkish lira.

Source: Author's conceptualization.

open positions in foreign exchange in the 2001 crisis in Turkey. Data for the period preceding the crisis indicates that these open foreign currency positions exceeded US$22 billion in October 2000 (Akyüz and Boratav 2003). Given this history, it is no surprise that Turkish banks embraced an alternative financing method, which allowed them to create local currency denominated loans without currency risk. This was achieved through the strategic tool of cross-currency swaps.

Table 10.6 depicts a cross-currency swap simulation for both the balance sheet and the off-balance sheet of a hypothetical bank in the accounting of cross-currency swap transaction. A key distinction between Table 10.2 and Table 10.6 is that there is no open foreign currency position in the latter's balance sheet for the T + 2 time period.

Here, the hypothetical bank does not exchange foreign currency with local currency in the spot market and thus does not bring currency risk to its balance sheet. Instead, local currency is obtained from the swap market in exchange for foreign currency: in this process money is created from foreign currency. This swap is revealed on both the balance sheet and off-balance sheet of the hypothetical bank in the T + 2 time period (Table 10.7).

At maturity – the conclusion of the swap transaction – the bank returns the local currency and takes foreign currency from the counterparty (Table 10.8). This cross-currency swap arrangement thus overcomes the problem of the open foreign currency position.

5.   BALANCE SHEETS AND NON-CORE LIABILITIES

The assets and liabilities structure of the Turkish banking system captures the chronic problems of this sector, including a loans–deposits gap and an

Table 10.6   Creating local money with cross-currency swap (1 FX = 1 TRY)

Balance sheet		Off-balance sheet	
T (=)		T (=)	
Assets	Liabilities	Assets	Liabilities
100 TRY 100 FX	100 TRY 100 FX	0 TRY 0 FX	0 TRY 0 FX
T + 1 (+ 100 FX debt)		T + 1 (=)	
Assets	Liabilities	Assets	Liabilities
100 TRY 200 **FX** ↑	100 TRY 200 **FX** ↑	0 TRY 0 FX	0 TRY 0 FX
T + 2 (Start of swap)		T + 2 (Start of swap)	
Assets	Liabilities	Assets	Liabilities
200 **TRY** ↑ 100 **FX** ↓	100 TRY 200 FX	0 TRY 100 FX ↑	100 TRY ↑ 0 FX
T + 3 (End of swap)		T + 3 (End of swap)	
Assets	Liabilities	Assets	Liabilities
100 TRY 200 FX	100 TRY 200 FX	0 TRY 0 FX	0 TRY 0 FX

Note: FX = foreign currency; TRY = Turkish lira.

Source: Author's conceptualization.

Table 10.7   Creating local money with cross-currency swap (1$ = 1 TRY) in the T + 2 time

T + 2 (Start of swap)		T + 2 (Start of swap)	
Assets	Liabilities	Assets	Liabilities
200 **TRY** ↑ 100 **FX** ↓	100 TRY 200 FX	0 TRY 100 FX ↑	100 TRY ↑ 0 FX

Note: FX = foreign currency; TRY = Turkish lira.

Source: Author's conceptualization.

Table 10.8   Creating local money with cross-currency swap (1 $ = 1 TRY) in the T + 3 time

T + 3 (End of swap)		T + 3 (End of swap)	
Assets	Liabilities	Assets	Liabilities
100 TRY	100 TRY	0 TRY	0 TRY
200 FX	200 FX	0 FX	0 FX

Note: FX = foreign currency; TRY = Turkish lira.

Source: Author's conceptualization.

Table 10.9   Structure of the Turkish banking sector liabilities, December 2017 (percentage)

Liabilities	%
Deposits	52.5
Payables to banks	14.5
Securities issued	4.4
Other liabilities	3.5
Payables to money market	3.4
Funds from repo transactions	3.0
Payables to the central bank	1.7

Source: BRSA (2017).

assets–liabilities gap, both relating to local money. The Turkish banking system has sought to address these gaps through foreign currency liabilities – generally non-core liabilities – using cross-currency swaps. An analysis of balance sheets and off-balance sheets in the Turkish banking system reveals how this is done.

Banking dominates the Turkish financial sector. Banking is responsible for 87 per cent[5] of domestic financial sector liabilities and, as shown in Table 10.9, the main source of loanable funds in the Turkish banking sector is deposits. As per Shin and Shin (2010), liabilities due to an ultimate domestic creditor – mainly households – are classified as core liabilities and liabilities due to an intermediary and a foreign creditor are classified as non-core liabilities. As observed by Yılmaz and Süslü (2016), the reliance of the Turkish banking system on non-core liabilities has deepened since the beginning of 2012.

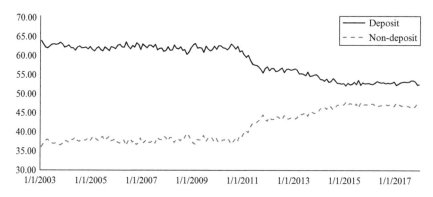

Source: BRSA (2017).

Figure 10.3 Non-deposits and deposits in the Turkish banking system, monthly, 2003–17 (percentage)

Table 10.10 Structure of the Turkish banking sector assets December 2017 (percentage)

Assets	%
Loans	64.4
Securities available for sale (net)	8.2
Required reserves	6.9
Securities held to maturity (net)	3.6
Receivables from central bank	3.4
Receivables from banks	3.2

Source: BRSA (2017).

Figure 10.3 highlights how the Turkish banking system transitioned from an emphasis on deposits to an emphasis on non-deposits (hereafter, non-core liabilities) following the global financial crisis of 2008–09. Yılmaz and Süslü (2016) points out that most of the non-core liabilities of the Turkish banking system are denominated in foreign exchange with a medium-term structure on average.

The heterogeneous composition of Turkish bank assets is presented in Table 10.10. The ascendancy of loans indicates that Turkish banks have shifted their focus from financing government debt – given that before 2001 Turkish banks had extensively financed government debt – to market-based intermediation. The hallmark of a sound banking system is in the capacity of loans to be funded through deposits, but

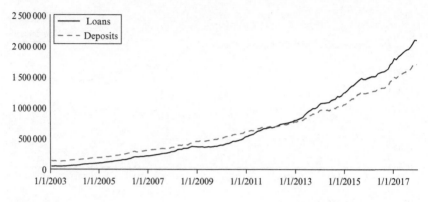

Source: BRSA (2017).

Figure 10.4   Loans and deposits (million liras) in the Turkish banking system, monthly, 2003–17

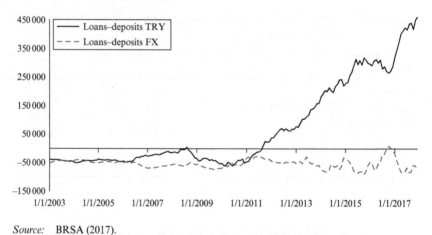

Source: BRSA (2017).

Figure 10.5   Loans–deposits gap in TRY and FX (million liras) in the Turkish banking system, monthly, 2003–17

the situation in the Turkish banking system is different, with loans exceeding deposits by a large margin. Loans first surpassed deposits in the Turkish banking sector in the first quarter of 2012 (Figure 10.4). This imbalance continues to date and has been enabled primarily by non-core liabilities.

The gap between loans and deposits is presented in Figure 10.5 in two different currencies: TRY represents Turkish lira and FX represents

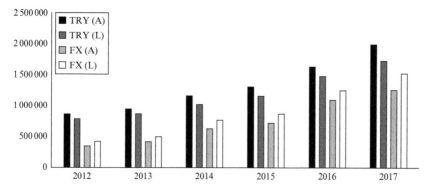

Source: BRSA (2017).

Figure 10.6   TRY and FX structures of Turkish banking balance sheet (million liras) system, yearly, 2012–17

foreign currency. Historical data shows that there is no loans–deposits gap in foreign currency terms during the 2003–17 period: foreign currency deposits consistently exceed foreign currency loans during the period under consideration. However, after the first quarter of 2012 a loans–deposits gap appears in local currency. This gap increased until the final period under consideration, December 2017, when local currency loans amounted to 1.414 billion Turkish lira and local currency deposits 954 billion Turkish lira. In the global banking system, the Turkish local currency loans–deposits gap is the most acute. An investigation of the currency structure of the assets and liabilities in the balance sheets offers a more detailed analysis of this disparity.

Figure 10.6 shows the position of Turkish lira relative to foreign currency in Turkish bank balance sheets. TRY (A) represents local currency denominated 'assets'; TRY (L) represents local currency denominated 'liabilities'; FX (A) represents foreign currency denominated 'assets'; and FX (L) represents foreign currency denominated 'liabilities'. The growth of bank assets results from the growth of local currency denominated assets. However, the growth of the local currency denominated assets cannot be financed only by local currency denominated liabilities and requires funding in the form of foreign currency denominated liabilities.

Foreign currency deposits and non-core liabilities in the Turkish banking system are depicted in Figure 10.7. Consistent with the previous analysis, non-core liabilities – denominated in foreign currency – began to increase in the first quarter of 2012, eventually hovering

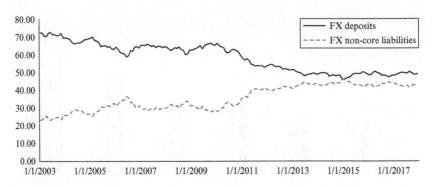

Source: BRSA (2017).

*Figure 10.7   FX deposits and FX non-core liabilities in Turkish banking
balance sheet system, yearly, 2003–17 (percentage)*

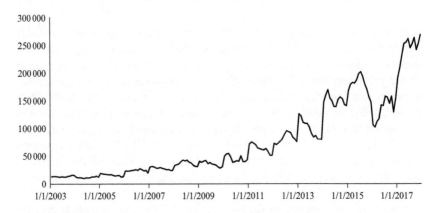

Source: BRSA (2017).

*Figure 10.8   The difference between local money assets and local money
liabilities (million liras) in Turkish banking balance sheet
system, monthly, 2003–17*

at levels close to foreign currency deposits. Non-core liabilities cover
payables to banks, securities issued, payables to the money market,
funds from repo transactions and payables to the central bank. This
arrangement highlights how foreign currency liabilities, particularly
non-core foreign currency liabilities, are crucial for plugging the local
currency assets–liabilities gap.

The Turkish lira gap between local currency assets and local currency liabilities in the Turkish banking system is shown in Figure 10.8. While amounting to only 14 billion Turkish lira in 2003, it widened noticeably in 2012 and reached a peak – of 270 billion Turkish lira – in the last quarter of 2017.[6] This gap is filled by a foreign currency liability surplus in the balance sheet. The surplus[7] is overwhelmingly in the form of non-core liabilities.

6. THE OFF-BALANCE SHEET OF TURKISH BANKS AND THE CROSS-CURRENCY SWAPS

Turkish banks use cross-currency swaps to finance the local currency assets–liabilities gap in the domestic banking system. The mechanisms that underlie this process can be extrapolated from the off-balance sheet of banks. Given double-entry accounting practices, the foreign currency asset surplus in the off-balance sheet should be equal to the foreign currency liability surplus in the balance sheet.

Table 10.11 highlights that derivative financial instruments are dominated by money and interest swaps. Money and interest swaps are responsible for nearly 76 per cent of total derivative financial instruments. The accounting treatment for cross-currency swap transactions is realized under the head of money swaps, which are approximately 52.2 per cent of total derivative financial instruments. The importance of derivatives in the Turkish banking system emanates from their capacity to create domestic money through foreign currency. The net foreign currency amounts associated with these instruments are shown in Table 10.12.

The local money assets–liabilities gap is financed by the foreign currency liabilities' surplus in the balance sheet of Turkish banking system. It is known that the foreign currency liabilities' surplus is 270 billion Turkish lira (December 2017) in the balance sheet and this gap is largely compensated by the foreign currency assets' surplus in off-balance sheet.

Table 10.11   Derivative financial instruments in off-balance sheet in Turkish banking system, December 2017

Derivative financial instruments	(Million TRY)	%
Forward FX transactions	231 817	9.3
Money swaps	1 327 763	52.2
Interest rate swaps	619 611	24.3
Other derivatives	363 072	14.2

Source: BRSA (2017).

*Table 10.12   Net foreign currency amounts of derivative financial
              instruments in off-balance sheet in Turkish banking system,
              December 2017*

Derivative financial instruments	(Million TL)
Forward FX transactions	14 711
Money swaps	236 737
Interest rate swaps	32
Other derivatives	−39 456

Source: BRSA (2017).

7.   CONCLUSION

Turkish banks became adept at using cross-currency swaps after the 2001 financial crisis since this particular derivative instrument allowed for the creation of local loans in the absence of an otherwise necessary deposit base, without resulting in an open foreign currency position. The Turkish experience demonstrates how the use of this financial tool extends beyond the textbook arguments of comparative advantage, hedging and speculation as a basis for cross-currency swaps.

Turkish banks have seen immense asset growth on the back of foreign currency liabilities through swap transactions. The ruling party (2002–17), which currently has governed Turkey for nearly two decades, has not intervened in this situation because policies of debt-fuelled growth have driven their electoral success. Although local loan expansion has raised household debt burdens, it has also led to a consumption boom in the Turkish economy. This boom has provided temporary and fictitious growth for households as well as in the broader macroeconomy. Debt-fuelled growth policies thus reveal a tacit agreement between the sitting government and the banking system.

This arrangement has compromised financial stability and prompted a reliance on non-core liabilities, including those denominated in foreign currency. As banks have created a distance between local loans and local deposits, the banking system has become increasingly dollarized and less sound; a sound banking system being a system in which local loans are financed by core liabilities and local currency liabilities, since the supply of non-core liabilities and the foreign currency liabilities can be erratic and changeable.

NOTES

1. Dollarization occurs when a foreign currency is used together with or instead of the domestic currency in the banking liabilities. The composition of Turkish banks' liabilities is changed in favour of foreign currency.
2. Very often the variables underlying derivatives are the prices of traded assets.
3. Currency swaps are sometimes described as FX swaps to make the distinction between currency and cross-currency swaps: in the former the principal is exchanged with a counterparty at a particular point in the future, and in the latter there is an exchange of interest and principal.
4. In the example used here 1 euro = 1.5 dollar.
5. See www.turkstat.gov.tr.
6. This is shown in Figure 10.6.
7. Foreign currency liabilities are greater than foreign currency assets.

REFERENCES

Akyüz, Y. and Boratav, K. (2003), 'The making of the Turkish financial crisis', *World Development*, **31** (9), 1549–66.

Arsov, I., Moran, G., Shanahan, B. and Stacey, K. (2013), 'OTC derivatives reforms and the Australian cross-currency swap market', *RBA Bulletin*, June, 55–64.

Bank for International Settlements (BIS) (2008), 'The basic mechanics of FX swaps and cross-currency basis swaps', *BIS Quarterly Review*, March, 73–86.

Banking Regulation and Supervision Agency (BRSA) (2017), 'Banking Regulation and Supervision Agency statistics', December, Istanbul.

Blåvarg, M. (2013), 'Funding the Swedish banking system', Handelsbanken's Series of Small Publications No. 29, Handelsbanken, Stockholm.

Bredenkamp, H., Josefsson, M., Lindgren, C.J. and Serdengeçti, S. (2009), 'Turkey's renaissance: from banking crisis to economic revival', in E. Brau and I. McDonald (eds), *Successes of the International Monetary Fund*, London: Palgrave Macmillan, pp. 64–84.

Chang, Y. and Schlögl, E. (2012), 'Carry trade and liquidity risk: evidence from forward and cross-currency swap markets', QFR Center Research Paper No. 310, Quantitative Finance Research Centre, University of Technology, Sydney.

Chisholm, M. (2010), *Derivatives Demystified: A Step-by-Step Guide to Forwards, Futures, Swaps and Options*, New York: Wiley.

Corb, H. (2012), *Interest Rate Swaps and Other Derivatives*, New York: Columbia Business School.

Du, W., Tepper, A. and Verdelhan, A. (2017), 'Deviations from covered interest rate parity', NBER Working Paper No. 23170, National Bureau of Economic Research, Cambridge, MA.

Duran, M. and Küçüksaraç, D. (2012), 'Are swap and bond markets alternatives to each other in Turkey?', TCMB Çalışma Tebliği (CBRT Working Paper) No.12/23, August, Central Bank of the Republic of Turkey, Ankara.

Durbin, M. (2010), *All about Derivatives*, New York: McGraw-Hill.

Eklund, J., Milton, J. and Rydén, A. (2012), 'Swedish banks' use of the currency swap market to convert funding in foreign currencies to Swedish kronor', *Sveriges Riksbank Economic Review*, **2**, 18–43.

Hilander, I. (2014), 'Short-term funding in foreign currency by major Swedish banks and their use of the short-term currency swap market', *Sveriges Riksbank Economic Review*, **1**, 1–23.

Hull, J. (2014), *Options, Futures and Other Derivatives*, Harlow: Pearson Education.

International Monetary Fund (IMF) (2015), 'Norway Financial sector assessment program Technical note – stress testing the banking sector', September, IMF, Washington, DC.

Keleş, G. (2016), 'Analysis of fixed income securities in an emerging market', PhD thesis, Bilkent University, accessed 13 April 2018 at http://repository.bilkent.edu.tr/handle/11693/29153.

Mák, I. and Páles, J. (2009), 'The role of the FX swap market in the Hungarian financial system', *MNB Bulletin*, May, 24–34.

Mihaljek, D. and Packer, F. (2010), 'Derivatives in emerging markets', *BIS Quarterly Review*, December, 67–80.

Molland, J. (2014), 'Norwegian banks' foreign currency funding of NOK assets', Norges Bank Staff Memo No 2, Norges Bank, Oslo.

Riksbank (2013), 'The major Swedish banks' funding in US dollar', Financial Stability Report No. 1, pp. 53–6.

Shim, I. and Baba, N. (2011), 'Dislocations in the won-dollar swap markets during the crisis of 2007–09', BIS Working Papers No. 344, Bank for International Settlements, Basel.

Shin, H.S. and Shin, K. (2010), 'Procyclicality and monetary aggregates', NBER Working Paper No. 16836, National Bureau of Economic Research, Cambridge, MA.

Şimşek, Ç. (2015), 'Türk Bankacilik Sektörü Kur Riski Yönetiminde Türev Ürünler: Döviz Swap İşlemleri ile Makroekonomik Faktörler Arasindaki İlişki' ('Derivatives in the Turkish banking sector's currency risk management: the relationship between foreign currency swap transactions and macroeconomic factors'), *Üçüncü Sektör Sosyal Ekonomi*, **50** (2): 72–101.

Syed, H. (2011), 'Markets for Norwegian banks' long-term funding – implications of changes in market conditions and the regulatory framework', *Norges Bank Economic Bulletin*, **82**, 51–63.

Yılmaz, E. and Süslü, B. (2016), 'Turkish non-core bank liabilities', *South-Eastern Europe Journal of Economics*, **14** (1), 75–92.

Zurawski, A. and Ossolinski, C. (2010), 'The financial crisis through the lens of foreign exchange swap markets', *RBA Bulletin*, June, 47–54.

11. Geographical aspects of recent banking crises in Italy

Marco Percoco

1. INTRODUCTION

Recent international financial and banking crises demonstrate the role of geography in the spatial propagation of shocks. The international diversification of portfolios was a major driver of the contagion spreading across economies. This chapter, however, considers a different case: that of the crisis that affected four major local banks in Italy. These banks are (1) Cassa di Risparmio di Ferrara, (2) Banca delle Marche, (3) Cassa di Risparmio della Provincia di Chieti and (4) Banca Popolare dell'Etruria e del Lazio. In particular, this chapter reveals that the high spatial concentration of activities of those institutions was a clear threat to their stability, given the spatial concentration of branches and loans and that the loss of international competitiveness of export-oriented local economies has resulted in financial imbalances leading to bail-outs. The following geographical analysis of the banking crisis in Italy indicates the perils of a low spatial diversification of banking operations.

The world is interconnected, and its interconnectivity has grown steadily over the years as both a cause and a consequence of globalization. The 2008–09 financial crisis has shown, in an empirical though dramatic way, that the international contagion of the crisis that originated in domestic environments spread relatively quickly and worked through a real economic channel (namely, trade) as well as through financial markets.

When addressing the causes and consequences of the 2008–2009 financial crisis, analysts typically cite the bankruptcy of the Lehmann Brothers and the financial difficulties of global or international banks, yet they often give limited attention to the destiny of small banks and the local geography of the propagation of international crises.

In the global network of financial institutions – connected by flows of investments, loans and guarantees, as well as by institutional setups and governance structures – local banks seem to play a marginal role, given the geography of deposits and lending. However, their role for local economies is important, especially for systems of limited economic size (Usai and Vannini 2005).

In recent years, a growing body of literature has considered the link between economic growth and financial development. Economists have debated the impact of finance on economic growth since Joseph Schumpeter's *Theory of Economic Development* (1911 [1934]) argued that banks play an important role in the development process because they choose which firms get to use society's savings. As stated by Deidda (2006), the industrial economics literature emphasizes two sets of considerations: (1) financial institutions have a strong impact on funds allocation by providing insurance against productivity and liquidity shocks, and (2) the banking industry's predilection for scale economies is a key factor that shapes economic development.

As argued by Fry (1989, p. 16):

> for many years, practising development economists made pronouncements on the importance of developing the financial sector to accelerate economic growth based on slender theoretical grounds. Indeed, the vast bulk of theoretical work relating financial conditions to economic development published before 1973 detected possibilities for negative, at best, neutral effects of financial development on income levels.

The Shaw (1973)–McKinnon (1973) framework provides strong arguments that financial repression can (1) reduce the flow of loanable funds through the banking sector, (2) arbitrarily vary the interest rate among borrowers and (3) undermine the self-financing of firms and households.

Following this approach, Dreese (1974) considered a cross-section of 40 US counties and found that unemployment is a negative function of the availability of loans. Using a cross-section of countries over the period 1960–85, Jappelli and Pagano (1994) found that liquidity constrains the effect of the saving rate, and that imperfections in the credit market can foster productivity growth.

Evidence concerning Italy shows that (1) growth pattern of the southern regions is strongly affected by financial incentives, (2) a link exists between cooperative credit conditions and economic performance, and (3) results from the market dimensions of banks and their impact on regional growth are ambiguous (Bongini and Ferri 2005; De Gregorio and Guidotti 1995). Usai and Vannini (2005) found that the overall size of the banking sector has no significant effect on regional growth in Italy; however, they also found that small banks in the form of cooperative banks are important for local economies because of their lending activities to small and medium enterprises.

As noted by Dixon (2018), power asymmetries are at the heart of the relationship between the financial sector and the real economy. In the global economy, this power is exerted by financial centres:

the acquisition of this power is in part a function of geography and the emergence of the financial centre, or rather the spatial structure of the asset management industry . . .. Put simply, financial centers (which occur at various spatial scales along a hierarchy from the regional to the global) exist to pool economic resources and transfer those resources across space and time. (Dixon 2018, p. 130)

At the local level, or for local financial institutions, such as the banks considered in this chapter, power relationships are exacerbated by the intrusion of politics into the management of banks and by the soft information leveraging the governing credit allocation (Flögel 2018).[1]

The geographical dimension calls for a focus on local economies that are specialized in export-orientated industries and are accompanied by a corporate governance structure; in that directors have strong ties with local economies. This type of arrangement has generated an ideal environment for the international crisis to spread to local banks; not through the usual financial channels but through a real economic channel. This chapter offers a framework to analyse how the crisis of the four banks under consideration was generated through the loss of competitiveness of local export-orientated industries coupled with the spatial strategy of banks. In particular, the framework proposes that the crisis of local banks may occur not only through the classical financial channel of transmission, but also through shocks to trade and the spatial strategies adopted by the banks. To support this argument, this chapter first states its hypotheses (section 2) and then provides evidence of the spatial concentration of branches, loans and non-performing loans (NPLs) for the banks under consideration (section 3). It concludes with some ideas for future research (section 4).

2.   SPATIAL STRATEGIES AND BANK CRISES

The geographical aspects of banking crises generated by recent economic downturns have not been fully explored by academic research in financial geography. Martin (2011) argued that the spatial diversification of bank activities was a major driver of the spatial propagation of the 2007–08 financial crisis, as low interest rates pushed banks to invest in more risky markets in search of higher yields. A similar argument was proposed by Marshall et al. (2012), who suggested investigating the contagion of the international crisis at local levels.[2]

The argument that the spatial diversification of investment propagated the crisis is convincing, as it clearly and directly identifies the links of the global network of banks and financial institutions as well as their international investment strategies. However, this view is incomplete for at least two reasons. First, it assumes that the only channel of spatial transmission of the shock is financial. Second, it implies that only banks with a considerable international diversification of activities are directly affected by the crisis.

This chapter complements this argument with the trade channel of transmission and the impact of the spatial concentration of activities. To this end, this chapter proposes a framework in which banks do not diversify internationally; deposits are local, and loans are provided to local firms. In such a scheme, these banks are immune to the effects of international financial crisis, as they may not be exposed to shocks in risky markets.

In the context of the economic turmoil of the past decade, this situation would imply the existence of banks with limited financial activities abroad and strong ties with local firms. Ideally, these firms are relatively isolated because they mainly serve the local market, which results in a type of economic island; that is, a small closed economy with limited interaction with other economic systems. However, this case is of limited empirical relevance, given the improbability of it occurring in a contemporary neoliberal economy. The case of a small open economy, with export-orientated firms and banks concentrating loans locally, is more interesting. Under these circumstances, banks may be affected by an international shock through a trade channel, which, as this chapter argues, was the case of four local banks in Italy: Cassa di Risparmio di Ferrara, Banca delle Marche, Cassa di Risparmio della Provincia di Chieti and Banca Popolare dell'Etruria e del Lazio.

The proposed framework documents two separate domains: the (implicit) incentives for banks to spatially concentrate their activities, and the genuine exposure of local economies to fluctuations of international trade.

As regards the incentives for local banks to invest locally, this strategy may be implemented to leverage local social networks to control loans through systems of social pressure. Furthermore, for banks of limited size, the acquisition of knowledge to evaluate firms' creditworthiness may be costly; thus, the focus on some specific areas may serve to reduce these information costs.[3]

Barbagallo (2017), however, argued that social networks were also used to channel credit toward firms with low credit scores and, hence, a low probability of repayment of the loan. This narrative – also espoused by the Bank of Italy as in the testimony of Barbagallo (2017) – is that the disproportionate amount of credit provided locally was the outcome of managerial practices influenced by local connections. In particular, it is argued in public discourse that credit was channelled to some extent toward risky firms based on social or even friendship networks (Rizzo 2018).

Compelling evidence of such a hypothesis is not yet available. Currently, we cannot exclude a priori that the provision of credit to local firms was the outcome of a strategy addressing the need to increase the return on investment by taking more risks. Furthermore, if the hypothesis that the spatial concentration of loans was intended to exploit local social ties and leverage informal channels of transmission of information is accepted, then it should not be surprising to observe a spatial concentration of NPLs in the same spatial context. In principle, whether the occurrence of NPLs is disproportionately higher in the areas where banks under scrutiny have focused their activities should be investigated. However, in such a case, the strategy of spatial concentration may still be rational. It should be noted that the proposed argument is similar in spirit to that proposed by Flögel (2018), although this chapter highlights the adverse effects of social ties when dealing with soft information to channel credit.

The four banks under examination in this chapter are located in areas with a high density of export-orientated, small and medium-sized enterprises, which are linked to local industrial clusters. The 2007–08 crisis resulted in a significant contraction in international trade, possibly produced by a reduction in US demand. Windfalls in international trade have, in turn, generated a significant drop in the profitability of local firms – a situation further exacerbated by the competitive pressure of Chinese firms (Bugamelli et al. 2018). As a consequence, firms may have become problematic debtors for local banks.

In summary, this chapter does not investigate the fundamental reasons for the spatial concentration of loans, but it shows that this deliberate strategy, which was also probably influenced by social ties, was detrimental to the stability of these banks. Section 3 explores the geographies of local bank strategy.

3. THE ANATOMY OF THE LOCAL BANKS' CRISIS IN ITALY

Local banks have a long history in Italy; they date back to the fifteenth and sixteenth centuries and the period of the early financialization of economies. These banks have always been tools to exert power at the local level through credit channelling, governed by political or economic elites. This chapter shows that this strategy leads to a considerable spatial concentration of credit with considerable risk borne by banks, and this, in turn, proved to be unsustainable during the recent economic crisis.

Cassa di Risparmio di Ferrara was founded in 1838. Between 1994 and 2005, the bank went through the acquisition of several financial institutions, such as Banca di Credito Agrario di Ferrara (1994), Commercio e Finanza e Banca di Treviso (2002), Banca Popolare di Roma and Credito Veronese (2003), Finproget (2004), and Banca Modenese and Banca Farnese (2005). Mergers with Banca di Credito e Risparmio di Romagna, Banca Popolare di Roma, Banca Modenese, Banca di Credito e Risparmio and Finproget were also undertaken between 2008 and 2012.

Since 2013, Cassa di Risparmio di Ferrar has been managed by administrators appointed by the Ministry of the Economy and Finance because of a tier 1 capital ratio of 6.41 per cent in December 2012. In November 2015, the bank, together with the other banks considered in this chapter, was the first to be bailed out in Italy after the approval of the Bank Recovery and Resolution Directive.

Banca delle Marche was established in 1994 as the result of a merger between Cassa di Risparmio della Provincia di Macerata and Cassa di Risparmio di Pesaro. After the merger with the Cassa di Risparmio di Jesi and the acquisition of Cassa di Risparmio di Loreto and Mediocredito Fondiario Centroitalia, the bank controlled 26.7 per cent of total loans in the Marche region, with peaks in the province of Macerata (55 per cent) and Ancona (32.3 per cent). However, in December 2012, the tier 1 capital ratio was 5.62 per cent and, as a result, in 2013m the bank went through special administration and was eventually bailed out.

After the merger between Cassa di Risparmio di Marrucina and Cassa di Risparmio di Guardiagrele, Cassa di Risparmio della Provincia di Chieti was established in 1938 and, as in previous cases, special administrators were appointed in 2013 and a bail-out was set up in 2015.

Banca Popolare dell'Etruria started in 1971 from the merger of three local banks in Tuscany: Banca Mutua Popolare Aretina, Banca Popolare Senese and Banca Popolare della Provincia di Livorno. Between 1972 and 2008 the bank acquired several local banks in the centre-north of Italy, such as Banca Popolare di Montepulciano (1972), Banca Popolare di Pontevalleceppi (1982), Banca Popolare di Cagli (1985), Banca Popolare di Gualdo Tadino (1987), Banca Cooperativa di Capraia Montelupo e Vitolini (1990), Banca Federico Del Vecchio (2006) and Banca Popolare Lecchese (2008).

In 1988, after the merger with Banca Popolare dell'Alto Lazio, the bank's name was changed to Banca Popolare dell'Etruria e del Lazio. Owing to having a tier 1 capital ratio of 6.6 per cent in 2012, the bank went through special administration and a bail-out.

From the histories of the four banks considered in this chapter, it emerges that these banks implemented strategies for expanding this market share into local markets through mergers and acquisitions with other local banks. In section 2 it was proposed that the spatial strategies adopted by the four banks are a substantial part of the reasons for the crisis. Figures 11.1a–d show the geography of local branches for the four banks

Figure 11.1a   The geography of local branches of Cassa di Risparmio di Chieti

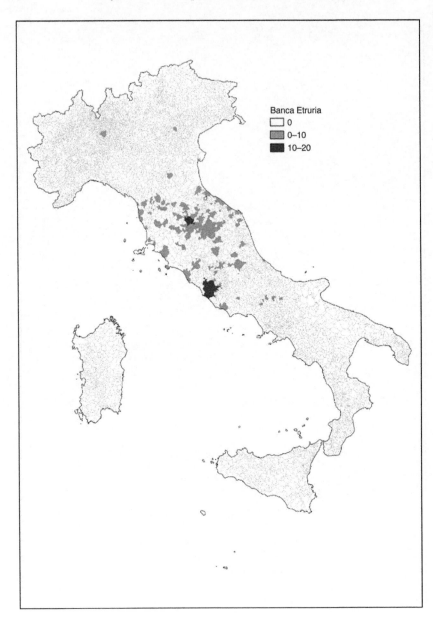

Figure 11.1b   The geography of local branches of Banca Etruria

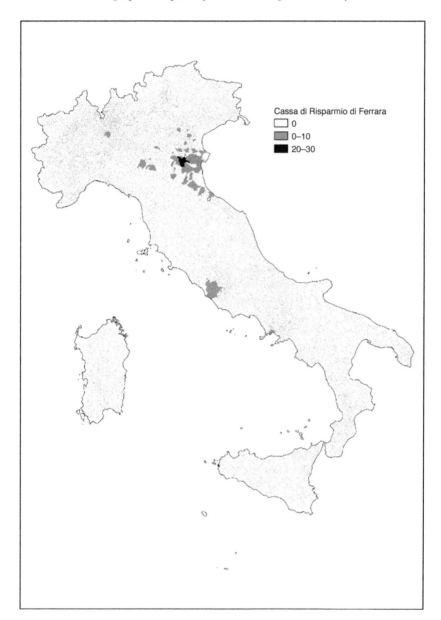

Figure 11.1c   *The geography of local branches of Cassa di Risparmio di Ferrara*

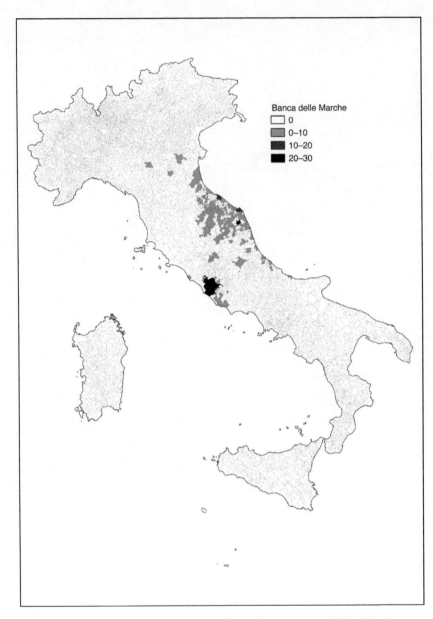

Figure 11.1d   The geography of local branches of Banca delle Marche

under investigation. The highest concentration of branches is in the head-quarters cities, namely, Chieti, Ferrara, Ancona, Arezzo and Rome. The spatial concentration of branches is also confirmed in Figure 11.2, where the total amount of branches across banks is plotted. Taken together, these maps show a high concentration of savings taken by these banks.

Figure 11.3 shows the spatial concentration of loans of the four banks in the macro area of the location of the headquarters; in particular, the south for Cassa di Risparmio della Provincia di Chieti, the centre for Banca Popolare dell'Etruria e del Lazio, the northeast for Cassa di Risparmio di Ferrara and the centre for Banca delle Marche. All four exhibit a high spatial concentration of loans, ranging between 70 per cent for Cassa di Risparmio di Ferrara in the northeast and 81.3 per cent of Banca delle Marche in the centre of Italy.

Figure 11.4 shows the share of NPLs in the total amount of loans provided by the banks. The Italian average in 2013 was 16 per cent, whereas the same ratio ranges from 25.4 per cent for Banca delle Marche to 32.8 per cent for Banca Popolare dell'Etruria e del Lazio – almost double the national average. A similar figure emerges for Cassa di Risparmio di Ferrara, whereas in the case of Cassa di Risparmio della Provincia di Chieti the ratio is slightly lower than 30 per cent.

The concentration of loans in areas with a considerable export orienta-tion and specialization in industrial districts might have been a risky strategy. The contraction in international trade could result in economic troubles for local firms. Figure 11.5 shows the ratio of NPLs and total loans provided in the macro area of the location of the headquarters and the spatial concentration of NPLs in the macro area. Interestingly, the local NPL ratio of all banks is lower than the average NPL ratio for each bank. In the case of Cassa di Risparmio di Ferrara, the local NPL ratio amounts to 24 per cent, whereas the average is 33 per cent. In the case of Banca dell'Etruria e del Lazio, the average NPL ratio was 32.8 per cent, whereas it is only 18 per cent in the centre. A similar figure emerges for the cases of Cassa di Riparmio della Provincia di Chieti and Banca Popolare dell'Etruria e del Lazio. Though relatively high, local NPL ratios of the four banks under review are almost in line with the average NPL ratio of the whole banking system. Nevertheless, Figure 11.3 also shows a disproportionate concentration of NPLs in the macro area of the location of the headquarters.

The data appears to confirm the hypothesis that the strategy of providing loans locally was not irrational, as *ex post* it proved to be safer. However, a disproportionate amount of credit was concentrated locally, perhaps above an optimal level. This was the major driver of the bank-ing crisis, together with higher exposure to the corporate loans market

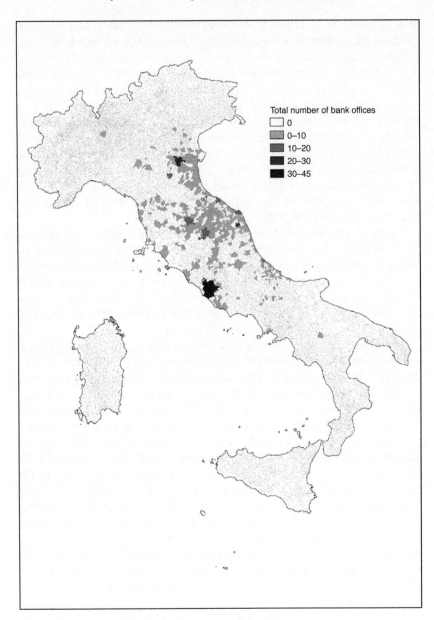

Figure 11.2   Geography of local branches of the four local banks

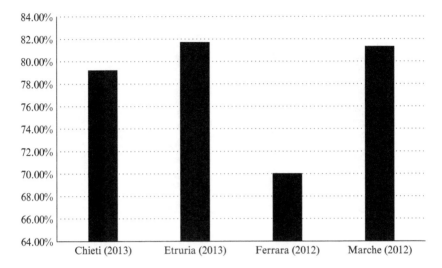

Notes: Chieti is the Cassa di Risparmio della Provincia di Chieti and refers to the share of loans in the south in 2013. Etruria is the Banca Popolare dell'Etruria e del Lazio and refers to the share of loans in the centre in 2013. Ferrara is the the Cassa di Risparmio di Ferrara and refers to the share of loans in the northeast in 2012. Marche is the Banca delle Marche and refers to the share of loans in the centre in 2012.

Source: Author's elaboration on data from Barbagallo (2017).

Figure 11.3   Share of loans in the macro area of location of the headquarters

(Figure 11.6), which was particularly problematic in the areas of the banks' specialization.

The precise economic reasons for the adoption of such a strategy and whether or not they were made explicit are unknown. There may be an institutional reason why banks might decide to provide credit locally for statutory purposes. Such circumstances might also have had implications for the governance of the bank with managers with strong local ties. From an economic perspective, the belief might have been that social ties and knowledge of the local economy could have proved useful to manage even a large amount of credit. Despite the lack of information on the causes of the spatial concentration of loans, the sketched framework described in this chapter identifies the crucial role of the interaction between spatial strategies of credit allocation and exogenous shocks.

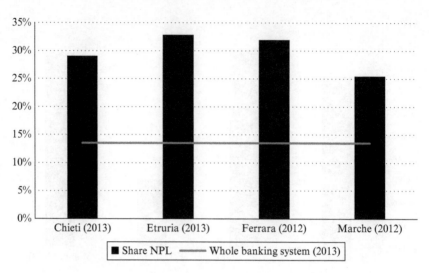

Notes: Chieti is the Cassa di Risparmio della Provincia di Chieti in 2013; Etruria is the
Banca Popolare dell'Etruria e del Lazio in 2013; Ferrara is the Cassa di Risparmio di
Ferrara in 2012; Marche is the Banca delle Marche in 2012.

Source: Author's elaboration on data from Barbagallo (2017).

Figure 11.4   Share of NPL on the total amount of loans

4.   CONCLUDING REMARKS

The chapter has provided a preliminary analysis of the geographical
aspects of the crisis that affected four local banks in Italy: Cassa di
Risparmio di Ferrara, Banca delle Marche, Cassa di Risparmio della
Provincia di Chieti and Banca Popolare dell'Etruria e del Lazio. The
fundamental reasons for such crises can be found not only in the context
of the financial investments made by banks in risky markets, but also in the
explicit spatial strategy adopted by the banks under scrutiny.

This chapter has offered some evidence showing that the banks
concentrated their loans locally on firms and households as the outcome
of a corporate strategy that provided credit to local economies. This
strategy was detrimental for the financial stability of those banks, as
the local productive systems specialized in export-orientated industries,
which were profoundly affected by the loss of competitiveness in
international markets as well as by the contraction in international
trade. Also, descriptive evidence shows that loans provided to the local
economies were no riskier than other loans. The spatial concentration of

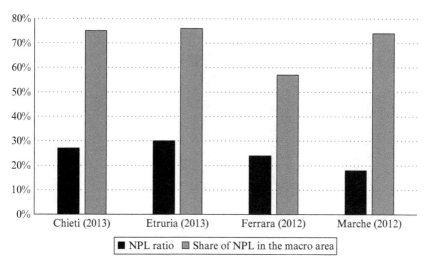

Figure 11.5   The NPL ratio and share of NPL in the macro area of the location

NPLs was driven by the spatial concentration of loans and not by riskier allocations of credit. That is, it seems that banks did not fail in evaluating firms' and households' creditworthiness owing to a type of local bias. Instead, this figure is compatible with the view that those banks provided loans locally to minimize asymmetric information, eventually through social ties.

The chapter is only a very preliminary attempt to disentangle the geographies of crises to local banks, and further research is needed in several different areas. First, the geographical analysis of corporate strategies of banks is a promising field of research, especially when studying optimal asset allocations. Often, geography is considered implicitly and *ex post* through the location of firms and households to which credit is channelled, whereas no explicit role is attributed to local factors.

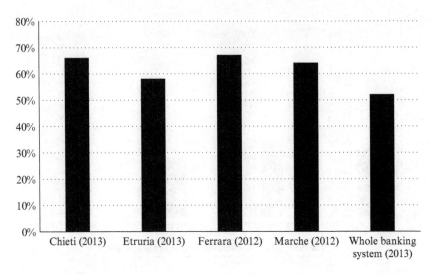

Notes: Chieti is the Cassa di Risparmio della Provincia di Chieti in 2013; Etruria is the Banca Popolare dell'Etruria e del Lazio in 2013; Ferrara is the Cassa di Risparmio di Ferrara in 2012; Marche is the Banca delle Marche in 2012.

Source: Author's elaboration on data from Barbagallo (2017).

Figure 11.6   Share of loans provided to firms

Second, at the time of writing, the literature has focused on the positive relationship between bank activities and the local economies. However, the histories of the local banks considered in this chapter as well as the narratives accompanying these stories note a darker side of the relationship between banks and territories. The study of such financial cronyism and how it is supported by local social networks might prove to be useful.

Finally, on a more macroeconomic scale, it would be interesting to analyse the interplay between globalization and spatial strategies of local banks. This interaction may increase the likelihood of local banking crises. However, further research on the mechanisms governing the anatomy of crises is needed to verify such a hypothesis.

NOTES

1. A complete statistical analysis of the network of Italian banks can be found in Papi et al. (2017).
2. On a related note, Dupuy et al. (2010) supported the view that the analysis of the

diversification of the portfolio of investment of institutional investors must consider the global and geographical view.

3. On a similar issue, see also Petersen and Rajan (2002).

REFERENCES

Barbagallo, C. (2017), 'Cassa di Risparmio di Ferrara, Banca delle Marche, Cassa di Risparmio della Provincia di Chieti, Banca Popolare dell'Etruria e del Lazio' ('Cassa di Risparmio di Ferrara, Banca delle Marche, Cassa di Risparmio in the province of Chieti, Banca Popolare dell'Etruria e del Lazio'), testimony before the Committee on the banking and financial systems, Senate of the Republic and Chamber of the Representatives, Rome.

Bongini, P. and Ferri, G. (2005), *Il Sistema bancario meridionale (The Banking System of Southern Italy)*, Bari: Editori Laterza.

Bugamelli, M., Fabiani, S., Federico, S., Felettigh, A., Giordano, C. and Linarello, A. (2018), 'Back on track? A micro-macro narrative of Italian export', Working Paper No. 1, Dipartimento del Tesoro, Ministero dell'Economia e delle Finanze, Rome.

De Gregorio, J. and Guidotti, P.E. (1995), 'Financial development and economic growth', *World Development*, **23** (3), 433–48.

Deidda, L. (2006), 'Interaction between economic and financial development', *Journal of Monetary Economics*, **53** (2), 233–48.

Dixon, A. (2018), 'Reflections on the power in and the power of financial markets', in M. Coleman and H. Agnew (eds), *Handbook on the Geographies of Power*, Cheltenham, UK and Northampton, MA, USA: Edward Elgar, pp. 123–36.

Dreese, G.R. (1974), 'Banks and regional economic development', *Southern Economic Journal*, **40** (4) 647–56.

Dupuy, C., Lavigne, S. and Nicet-Chenaf, D. (2010), 'Does geography still matter? Evidence on the portfolio turnover of large equity investors and varieties of capitalism', *Economic Geography*, **86** (1), 75–98.

Flögel, F. (2018), 'Distance and modern banks' lending to SMEs: ethnographic insights from a comparison of regional and large banks in Germany', *Journal of Economic Geography*, **18** (1), 35–57.

Fry, M.J. (1989), 'Financial development: theories and recent evidence', *Oxford Review of Economic Policy*, **4** (5), 13–28.

Jappelli, T. and Pagano, M. (1994), 'Saving, growth and liquidity constraints', *Quarterly Journal of Economics*, **109** (1), 83–109.

Marshall, J.N., Pike, A., Pollard, J.S., Tomaney, J., Dawley, S. and Gray, J. (2012), 'Placing the run on Northern Rock', *Journal of Economic Geography*, **12** (1), 157–81.

Martin, R. (2011), 'The local geographies of the financial crisis: from the housing bubble to economic recession and beyond', *Journal of Economic Geography*, **11** (4), 587–618.

McKinnon, R.I. (1973), *Money and Capital in Economic Development*, Washington, DC: Brookings Institution.

Papi, L., Sarno, E. and Zazzaro, A. (2017), 'The geographical network of bank organizations: issues and evidence from Italy', in R. Martin and J. Pollard (eds), *Handbook on the Geographies of Money and Finance*, Cheltenham, UK and Northampton, MA, USA: Edward Elgar, pp. 156–96.

Petersen, M.A. and Rajan, R.J. (2002), 'Does distance still matter? The information revolution in small business lending', *Journal of Finance*, **57** (6), 2533–70.
Rizzo, S. (2018), *Il pacco: Indagine sul grande imbroglio delle banche italiane*, Milan: Feltrinelli.
Schumpeter, J.A. (1911), *The Theory of Economic Development: An Inquiry into Profits, Capital, Credit, Interest, and the Business Cycle*, English trans 1934, New Brunswick, NJ: Transaction Books.
Shaw, E.S. (1973), *Financial Deepening in Economic Development*, New York: Oxford University Press.
Usai, S. and Vannini, M. (2005), 'Banking structure and regional economic growth: lessons from Italy', *Annals of Regional Science*, **39** (4), 691–714.

12. Shadow financial citizenship and the contradictions of financial inclusion in Pakistan

Juvaria Jafri

1. INTRODUCTION

Financial inclusion is presented as a remedy for financial exclusion. However, this relationship – in which financial inclusion and exclusion are opposites and also mutually exclusive – is dubious given the notion of financial citizenship which 'confers a right and ability on individuals and households to participate fully in the economy and to accumulate wealth' (Leyshon 2009, p. 153). Despite the growing recognition that financial inclusion is not the same as financial citizenship, the former is still used as a development intervention in the form of tools such as microloans and mobile money. These forms of inclusive finance are thus inextricably, and increasingly, tied to what is known as 'the financialization of development' (Roy 2010, p. 47) and underlie a fundamental contradiction of inclusive finance: the tendency to promote economic dualism by bifurcating the financial sector. The contribution of this chapter is to highlight the connection between these two notions, through the concept of shadow financial citizenship. Because strategies that financialize development also bifurcate finance, they execute an inferior form of inclusion and of access to finance. The phenomenon of shadow financial citizenship is thus a feature of finance geared to economies that some scholars describe as dualistic (Lewis 1954) and where the lines between informal and formal financial markets have hardened (Dymski 2005) due to banking strategies that target the poor, working and earning in informal markets (Karnani 2009; Prahalad 2005).

The notion that inclusive finance is a form of shadow banking is not novel: Ghosh et al. (2012) note that shadow banking in developing countries is exemplified by finance companies and microcredit lenders who provide credit and investment to underbanked communities, subprime customers and low-rated firms. Lyman et al. (2015) focus on the destabilizing role of shadow banks. They note that despite similarities, inclusive finance tends to be closely regulated and is therefore far removed from the shadow banks responsible for the financial crisis of the past decade. However, as argued here, concerns about the intrusion of shadow banking into inclusive finance transcend the risks of instability and of potential crises, and pertain to uneven development akin to what Andrew Leyshon and Nigel Thrift attribute to transformations in American and British banking and finance in the 1990s (Leyshon and Thrift 1993, 1995).

It is observations such as these that inform the notion of geobanking; the various public and private aspects of banking that shape geopolitical trends. The geographical variation in access to finance that resulted from changing models of banking, in the Anglo American economies, is identified by Leyshon and Thrift (1995) as underlying the geography of wealth and income. Such disparities came to seen as a problem of financial exclusion; a phenomenon which geographers attach to the structure of the financial system and the attitude of the state to finance (Dymski 2005; Leyshon and Thrift 1993, 1995). This chapter applies a similar approach to examine financial inclusion in the Global South, the poor-country counterpart of the same problem. The nature of financial inclusion is shaped by the shadow banking industry, demonstrating how finance, both public and private, shapes geopolitical trends.

The outcome of this is an institutional form of shadow financial citizenship whereby the poor – those previously described as unbanked or financial excluded – are offered higher costs and limited access for the same services used by their relatively wealthier counterparts. These issues of inequality and its reproduction (Bateman and Chang 2012; Taylor 2012) have been aggravated by the rise of financial technology (fintech) and what Gabor and Brooks (2017) call 'the digital revolution in financial inclusion', that is, the quest to generate surpluses from the mapping, expansion, and monetization of digital footprints. There are two components to this discussion of shadow financial citizenship. The first is the process whereby inclusive finance becomes shadow finance, and the second is the nature of financial citizenship offered by such shadow financial institutions.

2.   BIFURCATED BANKING: DUALISTIC FINANCE IN PAKISTAN

An empirical setting for this discussion is the financial sector of Pakistan. The bifurcation of banking here, and in other poor countries, is the outcome of a separation of mainstream and inclusive finance. The role of the regulators offers a context for examining two key trends that have occurred in Pakistan's microfinance market: the transition from informal finance to formal finance, and the commercialization of microfinance under the umbrella of financial inclusion. Nevertheless, even in a formal, commercial iteration, inclusive finance tends to be closer, both in terms of clientele and lending strategy, to informal finance than to formal finance. This is unsurprising given that the origins of the financial inclusion are in the Grameen Bank model which was designed with the explicit purpose of providing an alternative to existing systems of finance, both formal and informal.

> Founded by Muhammad Yunus in 1983, the Grameen Bank pioneered a simple model of credit whereby small groups of poor women are able to secure small loans at reasonable rates of interest. The model is meant to serve as an alternative to both formal systems of banking that demand collateral and exclude the poor and informal systems of finance that prey on the poor. (Roy 2010, p. 3)

2.1 Colonial Legacies and the Regulation of Informality

Unregulated and often described as usurious, informal finance[1] is in many studies on poor countries presented as a temporary phenomenon, eventually to be replaced by formal finance. The concepts of informal and formal finance are analogous to those of the informal and formal economy. These are frequently associated with the work of the Nobel Laureate, Sir Arthur Lewis, whose two-sector model of a capitalist and a subsistence sector highlighted the wage gap between the two sectors (Lewis 1954). The differential was attributed to the exclusivity of reproducible capital, which was available only to the capitalist sector. Analysing informal finance in the Global South, Fischer (1994) expresses scepticism over the use of this dualist lens, which underestimates the substance of contemporary informality, because empirical evidence shows informality to persistent and resilient. The transient nature of informal finance has been the subject of studies by numerous economic anthropologists, including Geertz (1962), Drake (1980), Kurtz (1973) and Chandavarkar (1985). The logic of such scholarship is that informal finance is a residual category, created from the marginalization that occurs owing to formal finance's penchant for mainstream economic activity. As Andrew Fischer (1994, p. 6) notes:

> In the 1950s, when theories of growth were popular and colonialism was still kicking, informal finance was considered by most academics and policy makers to be a manifestation of traditional (indigenous) economic attitudes. The attention towards basic needs in the 1970s led many to interpret informal finance as an adaptation by the third world poor to their marginalisation from formal economic activities. And of course, the drift towards neoclassicism in the late 1970s and 1980s generated a focus on informal finance as a mutant yet liberal response to overly interventionist governments.

The formal–informal divide in finance may also be seen as an artefact of colonialism. This perspective is attributed by Roy (2016, p. 327) to the 'new institutional economic history' approach; the same lens used by Acemoglu and Robinson (2012) in their *Why Nations Fail* hypothesis. A key feature of colonial financial development was a duplicitous stance by imperial governments on monopolies. Restricted at home but not in the colonies, where they were propped up for extractive reasons, they benefited from local production and trade (Fischer 1994). The outcomes of this were, first, a heavy concentration in colonial finance that was anomalous relative to the banking system at home and, second, an overt preference for the formal which allowed informal financial institutions and practices to thrive as colonial finance was absent in the local economy (Fischer 1994).

Roy (2016) observes how policy-makers' unease, in the late-colonial period, around informal finance and related local phenomena obliged them to conduct a large-scale banking enquiry in 1929–30. However, following independence from British rule in 1947, the state took steps to outlaw indigenous banking in India (Roy 2016). In Pakistan, simultaneously and newly independent, the situation appears to have been different. Indian policy makers had managed to bring down the share of informal financiers – who tended to be professional moneylenders – in rural credit to less than 36 per cent, from 80 per cent over the 1951 to 1971 period (Binswanger and Khandker 1995). For Pakistan, Manig (1996) shows that in 1972, 89 per cent of credit was drawn from informal sources, who were principally friends and family. This divergence in informal credit use was probably the outcome of multiple factors, including the shape of government policy. A comparative analysis is outside the scope of this chapter but the rate at which interest tended to be charged for such informal transactions in South Asian economies is probably of relevance. Manig (1996) noted that most informal credit in Pakistan, owing to Islamic practices combined with the embedding of credit relations in other economic and social interactions, was being offered without interest. This is corroborated by survey data (Irfan et al. 1999) which indicates that formal lenders charge an interest rate of 19 per cent while informal lenders charge 23 per cent. It is telling that money lenders, which are included in the calculation for informal rates, drag up the average considerably as they charge interest ranging from 48 per cent to 120 per cent. Relatively low informal rates in Pakistan could explain why a supply-lead approach, in which the state actively promotes formal finance to replace informal finance, was more likely to be efficacious in India than in Pakistan.

In Pakistan, the stance of the government is also reflected in its involvement in key initiatives such as the Orangi Pilot Project (OPP) and the Aga Khan Rural Support Programme (AKRSP), which pioneered the microfinance movement in the urban and rural context, respectively. The OPP and the AKRSP share commonalities with the original Grameen vision of Dr Muhammad Yunus. This is owing to their mutual roots in the Comilla model, associated with the Dhaka-based – and subsequently Karachi-based[2] – social scientist, Dr Akhtar Hameed Khan. Originally developed at the Bangladesh (formerly East Pakistan) Academy of Rural Development, the Comilla model sought to integrate several public and private resources to build an institutional base for various development programmes. The OPP was thus initiated as a grassroots development project, emphasizing self-help as the primary means of developing the 'katchi abadis' (informal sector) of urban Karachi (Zaidi 2001). Similarly, the AKRSP was established in 1982 by the Aga Khan Foundation with a specific geographical focus: development interventions in the Northern Areas of Pakistan (Khan 2010). For both of these initiatives, microcredit was one component of the development interventions the organization sought to deliver; other components included health, education, and sanitation. Interestingly, the microcredit component was eventually absorbed by the financial sector, on the pretext of financial liberalization.

2.2 Phases of Development and the Regulation of Liberalization

The banking sector in Pakistan, which became independent from British colonial rule in 1947, has passed through several distinct phases. The current phase is the continuation of a financial liberalization process – initially pushed by the International Monetary Fund (IMF) and the World Bank – that began in the 1990s and installed the feature of central bank autonomy.

When colonial rule ceased in the sub-continent, the Reserve Bank of India was the de facto central bank for both newly independent countries. The Pakistan banking industry felt disadvantaged by this arrangement so a separate central bank, the State Bank of Pakistan (SBP), was formed in 1948 (SBP 2016). Shortly after that, in 1949, a nationalized commercial bank, the National Bank of Pakistan, was formed. The State Bank of Pakistan Act was introduced in 1956 and the Banking Companies Ordinance in 1962. These would undergo amendments decades later to facilitate the liberalization of the banking industry, following rounds of nationalization in the 1970s and then privatization in the 1990s (Burki and Ahmad 2010).

The Bank Nationalisation Act 1974 allowed the government to merge all domestic banks into five state-owned commercial banks. Under this arrangement, the banking sector was instrumental to a state-led development policy based on channelling credit to specific economic sectors (Burki and Ahmad 2010). At the time, this direct lending approach was immensely popular in the developing world – including across the border, in India – given the accomplishments of the East Asian economies, particularly South Korea, Japan and Taiwan (Kohli 1997). However, in the 1980s, widespread corruption in staffing and loan disbursements led to the nationalized banks becoming bloated and inefficient with poor asset quality (Burki and Ahmad 2010). Reports of this, combined with growing disdain in policy circles for interventionist state models, set the tone for market-based approaches to financial development.

> The clearest policy statement on the future of these programmes, which is to be found in the World Bank (1989), dismisses directed credit programmes as an ineffective policy measure for achieving growth and redistributive objectives. It argues instead for financial reform by moving towards a market-based alloca- tion of resources so that investments with high rates of return are financed, leading to an increase in the average productivity of investment and rate of economic growth. (Kohli 1997, p. 2667)

Financial liberalization commenced in 1991 with amendments to the Bank Nationalisation Act. The Privatisation Commission was also estab- lished in the same year. Several domestic and foreign banks were permitted to operate and preparations made for the government to divest ownership in the nationalized banks. In 1997, backed by a US$300 million World Bank loan, these institutions launched voluntary golden handshake schemes to eventually release 21 966 employees over a two-year period (Burki and Ahmad 2010). Other important features of the reforms included the removal of interest rate ceilings and efforts to create a mechanism for determining a market rate of interest (Hanif 2002) as well as the closure of over 2000 bank branches over a six-year period (Burki and Ahmad 2010).

2.3   Financialized Development and the Regulation of Microfinance

It was in this environment of reform that microfinance was incorporated into the financial landscape. The government, with a loan from the ADB (Asian Development Bank), undertook the initiative to offer regulated microfinance services and requested established commercial banks in Pakistan to become shareholders in a newly created microfinance institu- tion. The Khushhali Bank Ordinance was specially passed in 2000 to support the creation of Khushhali Bank under the ADB's Microfinance Sector Development Program and also the Government of Pakistan's Poverty Reduction Strategy (ADB 2008). The Microfinance Institutions Ordinance 2001 and prudential regulations for microfinance banks were subsequently introduced to specifically deal with the incorporation, regula- tion and supervision of microfinance banks in Pakistan (ADB 2008).

Table 12.1   Share of gross loan portfolio by institution type (percentage)

	2012	2013	2014	2015	2016
MFB	57	60	58	61	68
MFI	23	22	24	23	20
RSP	20	18	18	16	12

Source: PMN (2016).

Since then, teething issues aside, microfinance in Pakistan has strengthened its hold as a noticeable feature of banking in Pakistan. Currently there are three categories of microfinance lenders – microfinance banks (MFBs), microfinance institutions (MFIs) and rural support programmes (RSPs) – and two regulators. The central bank, the SBP, is the regulator for MFBs. The Securities and Exchange Commission is the regulator for MFIs and RSPs.

Microfinance banks are licensed and regulated by the SBP for the purpose of providing microfinance services. More specific details are available in the prudential regulations which describe 'microfinance services' as 'mobilizing deposits from the public and providing credit to poor persons[3] and microenterprises' (SBP 2014, p.3). Microfinance institutions and RSPs are not permitted to take deposits. Since 2016 these non-deposit taking institutions have been regulated by the Securities and Exchange Commission of Pakistan (SECP), which is an autonomous body. The current mandate of the SECP includes the regulation of the corporate sector and capital market, as well as the supervision and regulation of insurance companies, non-banking financial companies and private pension schemes. In addition, it is responsible for overseeing various external service providers to the corporate and financial sectors, including chartered accountants, credit rating agencies, corporate secretaries, brokers and surveyors. Of note in this structure is that the dominant form of microfinance in Pakistan is commercial in nature; most of it offered by MFBs (see Table 12.1) – deposit-taking institutions regulated by the central bank – and the nature of wholesale funding through apex funds emphasizes sustainability even within the non-deposit taking institutions that operated on a non-profit basis in the past.

2.4   The Commercialization of Inclusion

The ascendancy of commercial microfinance may be heavily attributed to the support of two key institutions: the SBP and the World Bank.

The backing of the central bank for microfinance, and subsequently the financial inclusion movement, has been unwavering since the early 2000s when the first licences for MFBs were issued. In 2006, the SBP took measures to encourage commercial banks to offer microfinance services, which could otherwise be offered by microfinance banks operating under a separate legal and regulatory framework. At the time Pakistan was one of only a handful of countries to have special prudential regulations for microfinance (SBP 2006).

In 2007–08, the SBP was able to enlist the support of the UK Department for International Development (DfID), together with the Government of Pakistan, to launch the Financial Inclusion Programme (FIP) to 'provide equitable and efficient market-based financial services to the otherwise excluded poor and marginalized population including women and young people' (SBP 2008, p. 1). The salient features of the FIP include (1) a strategy that sought to engage the wider banking sector, particularly commercial banks, in enhancing access to financial services, and (2) a planned shift from 'reliance on subsidies to market based, sustainable and inclusive financial services' through the use of commercial bank debt, syndication arrangements, and term finance certificates, and also government-backed credit guarantee schemes (SBP 2008, p. 3). The SBP Microfinance Credit Guarantee Facility (MCGF) has been particularly successful[4] in this regard by channelling wholesale funds from the commercial banks to the microfinance sector (SBP 2017a). The overall strategy appears to have been fruitful based on the standard measures for sustainability: the industry's operational self-sufficiency (OSS) and financial self-sufficiency (FSS) have both been consistently above 100 per cent since 2012, and have also been widening relative to each other since 2014 (PMN 2017). This widening captures the role, primarily, of cheap credit, indicating that despite success in commercializing microfinance, financial expenses for the sector are often at rates below the market cost of funds. This observation is a basis for drawing the role of apex funds – and the World Bank – into this discussion.

Apex funds are an example of 'blended finance' strategies: these are 'financing mechanisms that link a grant element, provided by ODA, with loans from publicly owned institutions or commercial lenders', representing a major shift which not only moves Official Development Assistance (ODA) from the public to the private sector but also replaces it with private finance (Bonizzi et al. 2015; Van Waeyenberge 2016). Apex funds altered Pakistan's microfinance landscape in 2000 when the Pakistan Poverty Alleviation Fund (PPAF) commenced operations as an autonomous not-for-profit company. This organization had been in existence since 1997 but underwent regulatory changes following official approval in 1999 for a five-year World Bank project.

The World Bank funded Pakistan Poverty Alleviation Fund Project was designed to reduce poverty and empower the rural and urban poor in Pakistan. The project provides access to much-needed microcredit loans and grants for infrastructure and capacity building. As such, the PPAF project aims to help the rural poor in Pakistan get out of a cycle of misery, and get into a virtuous cycle of opportunities. (World Bank 2005)

The total project cost was US$107 million; the Government of Pakistan committed to US$10 million as equity; the World Bank credit of US$90 million was provided through the International Development Association – the bank's concessionary lending arm – as a single-currency loan repayable in 35 years with a 10-year grace period; and the remainder was to be in the form of community contributions. This project came to be known as PPAF 1 and concluded in 2005. It was followed by PPAF 2 which began in 2006 and concluded in 2011. Pakistan Poverty Alleviation Fund 3 began in 2009 and concluded in 2016. The respective tranches for these subsequent programmes from the World Bank were US$238 million and US$250 million.[5]

The next major advance in the commercialization of microfinance was the launch of the Pakistan Microfinance Investment Corporation (PMIC) in 2016. The PMIC has the sole purpose of providing wholesale funding for microfinance by allowing the PPAF to spin off its microfinance operation and establish a new company in partnership with the Karandaaz Foundation: the Kreditanstalt für Wiederaufbau (KfW). The Karandaaz Foundation is a non-profit organization backed by the UK's DFID and the Bill and Melinda Gates Foundation, whereas the KfW, based in Frankfurt, is a German government-owned development bank. The objective of the PMIC is to attract funding from 'development agencies, financiers, commercial banks and capital markets' using a commercial – that is, profit-focused – structure (PMIC 2018, p. 4). Despite being a private sector investment company, the PMIC plays a central role in official government policy for financial inclusion. This is evident from the emphasis on micro and small and medium enterprise (SME) lending in the National Financial Inclusion Strategy (NFIS) which was launched in 2015 and which explicitly mentions the creation of the PMIC for the objective of enhancing commercial funding for both MFBs and MFIs.

The NFIS 2015 is the cornerstone for a number of policies that emphasize alternatives to traditional banking – for example, bank agents, automated teller machines (ATMs), mobile money agents and remote access through mobile phones and the Internet – for countering the issue of financial exclusion. Backed by the Ministry of Finance, the SBP and the Securities and Exchange Commission, this initiative calls for enhancing access to credit for SMEs as well as financial inclusion and deepening (SBP 2015a).

Most financial institutions have focused on the upper end of the business and retail markets and have not developed the skills, techniques and products required to serve other market segments profitably. While microfinance banks have developed this knowledge for microfinance clients, there is a large 'missing middle' which is currently not being served. (SBP 2015a, p. viii)

2.5   Branchless, Digital and Mobile: The Evolution of Transactions

The strategy also notes that universal access to formal accounts need not be limited to traditional savings and transaction accounts but can also include digital transactional accounts (DTAs), primarily branchless banking accounts, for which Pakistan is a rapidly growing market (SBP 2015a). This advance was catalysed by the introduction, in 2008, of the Branchless Banking Regulation which permitted banks to leverage rapidly expanding mobile phone networks for financial services: nearly 80 per cent of Pakistanis aged 15 years and over have access to a mobile phone (Rashid 2015).

The focus on digitization is an extension of wider, international trends reflected in the multilateral institutions shaping finance in the Global South, and consequently endorsing the expansion of this geobanking structure. Three organizations are of particular relevance here: the Alliance for Financial Inclusion (AFI), the Better Than Cash Alliance (BTCA) and the Financial Action Task Force (FATF). The influence of these institutions ensures that the nature of financial transformation in Pakistan is circumscribed within the directives that they issue, reflected in the NFIS.[6]

Much of the NFIS is influenced by the AFI which was founded in 2008 as a project of the Bill and Melinda Gates Foundation and also supported by the Australian Agency for International Development (AusAid). The AFI bases its practices on a South–South peer learning approach and truly member-driven governance (Alliance for Financial Inclusion 2017). The Maya Declaration is arguably the AFI's most widely known initiative. Launched in 2011 at the Global Policy Forum (GPF) in Riviera Maya, Mexico, it is known as the first global and measurable set of commitments to financial inclusion (Alliance for Financial Inclusion 2017) and counts over 80 countries, including the SBP, among its signatories.

When a country commits to the Maya Declaration, they make measurable commitments in four financial inclusion areas: create an enabling environment to harness new technology that increases access and lowers costs of financial services; implement a proportional framework that advances synergies in financial inclusion, integrity, and stability; integrate consumer protection and empowerment as a key pillar of financial inclusion; utilize data for informed policymaking and tracking results. (Center for Financial Inclusion 2013, p. 2)

Also emphasized in the NFIS are government-to-person (G2P) transactions: this reveals the influence of the BTCA, which was launched in 2012 and jointly funded by the Bill and Melinda Gates Foundation, Citi Foundation, MasterCard, Omidyar Network, United States Agency for International Development, and Visa Inc., and housed within the United Nations Capital Development Fund. The overriding objective of this organization is to shift from cash to digital payments: this is ostensibly a tool to promote financial inclusion and thus reduce poverty.

> The harsh reality is that the only way to make or receive payments for many poor people across the world is by using paper money in the informal sector – which is a barrier to the use of formal financial services. Cash-based transactions are also typically unsafe, expensive, inconvenient, inefficient, and lack transparency for governments, companies, and citizens alike. (Better Than Cash Alliance 2017, p. 2)

One focal point here is the issue of corruption; another is the perception that G2P arrangements allow for the attainment of scale through bulk payments (SBP 2015a) and may thus function as an 'on-ramp to financial inclusion' (Stuart 2015). Pakistan's membership of the BTCA makes it eligible for technical assistance and funding to support the transition from cash to digital for G2P payments.

2.6 Systemic Vulnerability and the Regulation of Security

Issues of terror funding and money laundering are of particular relevance in a Global South context, a point noted by the FATF which was established in 1989 as a Paris-based, intergovernmental policy-making body that 'works to identify national-level vulnerabilities with the aim of protecting the international financial system from misuse' (FATF 2018). The FATF's incursion into the inclusive finance movement began in 2011, when the organization issued a guidance paper to ensure that countries 'meet the national goal of financial inclusion, without compromising the measures for combating crime': this paper was updated in 2013 and subsequently in 2017 (FATF 2018). Central to FATFs position is the notion of 'a proportionate approach to risk', which mirrors the principles adopted by the Bank for International Settlements (BIS) and the World Bank (Aron 2017). This is reflected in the policy of the SBP on branchless banking (BB). Branchless banking accounts are categorized by three levels with level 0 and level 1 BB accounts for individuals and level 2 accounts for individuals as well as firms, entities, trusts, not-for-profit organizations, corporations, and so on. Know-your-customer (KYC) requirements and daily and monthly transaction limits vary depending on account type (SBP 2015a).

A core feature of inclusive finance via the BB approach in Pakistan is the role of biometric technology. The National Database and Registration Authority (NADRA) of Pakistan is recognized as a global leader in the 'application of identification systems and technology to a range of development issues' (Gelb, cited in Malik 2014, p. 1). The main objective of this institution, since its inception in 2000, is to issue computerized national identity cards (CNICs) with a unique 13-digit number to Pakistanis aged 18 years and over. The CNIC is a requirement for conducting transactions of various types with the government as well as in the private sector; for instance: voting in elections; applying for a passport or driving licence; purchasing vehicles, land and other assets; purchasing a plane or train ticket; obtaining a mobile phone SIM card; opening and maintaining a bank account; and conducting financial transactions.

Following an anti-terror drive in early 2015, the Pakistan Telecommunication Authority proceeded to block all mobile phone SIM cards that had not been biometrically verified (Craig and Hussain 2015). As a consequence, every mobile phone number in Pakistan is now associated not only with a CNIC number but also with a set of fingerprints. This has facilitated Pakistan's commitment to FATF standards as biometric verification eases customer due diligence (CDD) requirements. It is estimated that as much as 98 per cent of Pakistan's adult population is registered with NADRA (Malik 2014).

Owing to the regulatory environment described above, financial inclusion in Pakistan has come to be associated with inclusive finance products that emphasize a form of banking that is commercially orientated, digitally distributed and heavily regulated by national as well as international institutions. Section 3 describes how these practices make it easy for the purveyors of microfinance to resist a banking model based on intermediation, and to position themselves, as shadow banks do, to attract global capital in various forms.

3. SHADOW BANKING AND SHADOW FINANCIAL CITIZENSHIP

The fixation with commercial viability underlies the absorption of inclusive finance by the shadow banking industry, which is distinct from traditional banking because it does not operate 'under one roof' (Ghosh et al. 2012, p. 6). It is therefore different from traditional commercial banks – which are financial intermediaries for depositors and lenders – because it relies on a more complex set of transactions. According to the Financial Stability Board (FSB 2011), a distinguishing feature of shadow banking is that it decomposes the process of credit intermediation into a sequence of discrete operations. This creates a situation which is akin to 'banking upside down', a phrase Helgadóttir (2016, p. 915) uses to refer to the shadow banking system in which: 'As opposed to traditional banking, which carries out the maturity transformation within one institution, shadow banking breaks the process down into several discrete steps that are carried out by different entities' (Helgadóttir 2016, p. 920).

Helgadóttir's (2016) political science frameworks – rent-seeking, institutional adaptation and inequality – used to draw on the shadow banking concept outside of the purely financial literature, are relevant here. Rent-seeking is related to the changes in development policy that have occurred together with transitions in the structure of finance; for instance, the Washington consensus policies, of the World Bank and the IMF, that drove financial liberalization, thus transforming the role of the financial sector. This competitive, investor-orientated setting facilitated a shift in focus for development aid policy: Greenhill et al. (2016) note the increasing share of non-traditional development assistance (NTDA) in finance for development. Apex funds and investment companies entered this space to compete for finance and play the role of credit intermediation; a process that drove the commercialization of inclusive finance.

In addition to credit intermediation, commercial iterations of inclusive finance present an opportunity for private finance to take on the guise and role of development finance. This has been described by Van Waeyenberge (2016, p. 2) as the 'private turn in development finance'. These approaches allow for a leveraged approach to development cooperation in order to attract private flows, including equity stakes, through reduced exposure to risk (Van Waeyenberge 2016). Table 12.2 presents a typology to highlight how sources of debt and equity funds for microfinance in Pakistan are associated with various entities.

In addition to private finance and its capability to extract rents, the second framework, which is that of institutional adaption, presents a useful basis to theorize the responses to regulations. These include those driven by the Basel Accords; although seeking stability, they also engender an antipathy to lending outside the corporate and government sector, especially when the latter is such a heavy borrower. An inequality studies framework is also a central concern of shadow financial citizenship, since it relates to the reproduction of disparity and to uneven development. Inequality occurs, first, when poorer clients face higher borrowing costs, and second, when inclusion is offered in exchange for surveillance.

A main issue relating to financial exclusion in Pakistan is the role of the traditional banking sector. A conspicuous feature of the NFIS is the scant mention of traditional or commercial banks. This can be attributed to an

Table 12.2   Typology of debt and equity funders for microfinance

	Sub-type	Further sub-type	Definition	Example in Pakistan
Development finance institution/ international financial institution	Bilateral	None	Owned by a government to raise private capital to finance projects with development objectives	KfW (Germany), CDC Group (UK), PROPARCO (France)
	Multilateral	None	Owned by two or more governments to finance development projects through private capital	IFC (International Finance Corporation), ADB (Asian Development Bank)
Government	Development programme	None	Government or other public programme with development objectives.	Prime Minister's Interest Free Loans Scheme (Pakistan)
	Government agency	None	Administration, departments, or agencies of any sovereign entity	Luxembourg Ministry of Foreign and European Affairs (Luxembourg)
	Multi/bilateral development agency	None	Bilateral or multilateral aid agencies, owned by governments	Japan International Cooperation Agency (Japan), DFID (UK)
	Regulator	None	Domestic central banks	State Bank of Pakistan
Financial institution	Commercial bank	None	Bank or other regulated financial institution where private entities are majority shareholders	United Bank Limited, HBL
	Public bank	None	Bank or other regulated financial institution where the government is a majority shareholder	National Bank of Pakistan, Bank of Punjab
	Microfinance investment intermediaries (MIIs)	Holding company	Provide financing and technical assistance to MFIs	FINCA, AKAM
		MIV	Microfinance investment companies are independent investment entities open to multiple investors	Triple Jump

Table 12.2   (continued)

	Sub-type	Further sub-type	Definition	Example in Pakistan
		Other MII	Various investment entities with a large microfinance component to investment strategy	ResponsAbility, Triodos, Acumen
Other	Private corporation	None	Registered legal entities except government and financial institutions, often technology companies seeking synergies	VEON
	Individual	None	A person or persons	United International Group (Pvt) Ltd.
	Foundation	None	Non-profit corporation or other non-profit entity	Bill and Melinda Gates Foundation, Aga Khan Foundation
	NGO	None	Non-governmental organization	National Rural Support Programme

Source: Adapted from Sapundzhieva (2011).

emphasis within the NFIS and, to a considerable extent, within the global inclusive finance movement on transactions and payments. This highlights the shifts that have occurred to make financial inclusion the most prominent development paradigm and the successor to the related movements of microfinance and microcredit (Mader and Sabrow 2019). These transitions have shaped the current nature of financial citizenship.

3.1   The Issue of Penetration

Aside from transactions and payments, the other aspects of inclusive finance are access to savings and loans. Savings were seen as a key pillar of the microfinance movement for two reasons; they had the potential to reduce dependence on subsidies and donors by mobilizing funds for on-lending, and they allowed households to smooth consumption and build assets as collateral for future borrowing (Khandker 1998). In his seminal article, Jonathan Morduch notes that the subsidization of credit skewed the incentives for microfinance providers to promote savings:

Moreover, because banks were losing money so steadily on the lending-side but were amply capitalized by governments, they had little incentive to mobilize savings: deposit mobilization is costly and re-lending the deposits would just lead to greater losses. Instead, saving accounts were weighed down with restrictions and downward pressure was put on interest rates on deposits, generally to keep interest rates paid to depositors below the rates charged to borrowers. The result was that real rates on deposits fell to zero or below and savers had little incentive to build up accounts. Ultimately, little saving was generated, and money stayed under mattresses or was moved into nonfinancial assets. (Morduch 2000, p. 620)

Subsidies need not necessarily preclude saving. The successes of forced or involuntary savings programmes in Bangladesh (Khandker 2000) and Indonesia (Morduch 2000) exemplify how savings can reduce the social cost of subsidization. In cases where commercial models are ascendant – as in Pakistan, where subsidies are seen as undermining sustainability – savings may be discussed in the context of deposit mobilization. Owing to the legislative structure permitting deposit-taking, only one-third or so of Pakistani microfinance providers offer savings products; MFBs are allowed to take deposits but MFIs are only permitted to mobilize deposits by requiring that their client place them in commercial banks (PMN 2017).

From the perspective of data, it is difficult to get an overall view of the extent to which microfinance providers – MFBs and MFIs – are responsible for mobilizing deposits, as it is not possible to identify which commercial bank deposit holders are clients of microfinance institutions. However, the newest data for MFBs illustrates success in deposit mobilization, with 2015–16 experiencing a jump of 88 per cent in the number of depositors, rising to 15.9 million from 10.7 million in 2015. In value terms, this amounted to 41 per cent, taking the deposit base to Rs118 billion from Rs60 billion a year earlier (PMN 2017).

This surge may be attributed to the recent moves by MFBs to compete with commercial banks for deposit mobilization, by offering double-digit rates on deposits; up to 13 per cent, compared with 7 per cent offered by commercial banks. This strategy has been facilitated by the directive, issued in late 2015 by the SBP, permitting MFBs to use the same clearing system as that used by commercial banks (SBP 2015b). The outcome of this, for those banks that have opted for this tactical approach, is a decrease in cost of funds and an increase in the ratio of deposits to gross loan portfolio (PMN 2017). Through this, many MFBs have not only enhanced their efficiency but also their liquidity.

For some analysts of the missing-middle phenomenon, this improved liquidity offers perceptible opportunities. The standard approach to the missing middle is that it is an issue of access to and lack of finance (World Bank 2017). The NFIS (2015) takes a more measured stance, noting that, according to survey data, access to finance is a less important issue for SMEs than lack of electricity and corruption. Within the perspective that finance is a crucial issue for enterprises, the SBP has been encouraging MFBs to lend to microenterprises. The objective of this policy, as with that of promoting deposit mobilization, is to promote competition between MFBs and commercial banks. In practice, the approach has encouraged a bifurcated banking structure.

3.2 Expensive Lending

From a regulatory standpoint, microfinance banking differs from commercial banking in two ways: licensing requirements and lending requirements. The lending limit imposed on microfinance banks has been contentious – it was revised upwards in 2012 from Rs150000 to Rs500000 in order to promote enterprise lending – and there is support for either raising further or issuing separate licences with higher lending limits to increase coverage (Aslam 2013). Lending rates in Pakistan are not regulated by the central bank. Within the global financial inclusion industry, this is regarded as a best practice; notwithstanding concerns about exploitative and predatory lending practices, capping rates is seen as counter-productive.

> Unfortunately, this often hurts rather than protects the most vulnerable by shrinking poor people's access to financial services. Interest rate ceilings make it difficult or impossible for formal and semi-formal microlenders to cover their costs, driving them out of the market (or keeping them from entering in the first place). (CGAP 2004, p. 3)

In Pakistan, high lending rates are particularly concerning in the current interest-rate environment where the benchmark policy rate is hovering at a 42-year low of 5.75 per cent (PMN 2017). Microfinance practitioners reiterate that it is misleading to draw causal connections between benchmark interest rates and lending rates as it is operating costs, not funding costs, that determine loan terms. These rates are primarily due to expenses such as personnel compensation, supplies, travel and depreciation of fixed assets. It is thus argued that the very practice of making small loans – what the poor require – entails high-interest rates because smaller loans have a higher administrative cost per dollar than do larger loans (Rosenberg et al. 2013).

Given this, and that the alternative to microfinance is very often the unregulated money-lender, Sandberg (2015) argues that it is governments, commercial banks and the international political community that should be held responsible for high interest rates caused by credit rationing. Governments may be held responsible for a lack of direct involvement through rate subsidies and for a lack indirect involvement 'through creating background institutions and/or making infrastructural improvements which could reduce some of the costs for MFIs'; the international political community may also be asked to share the burden for alleviating exorbitant borrowing costs (Sandberg 2015, p. 143).

Despite commercialization, which has entailed a strong nexus with the mainstream banking sector, the financial inclusion agenda has not made convergence between the micro and mainstream finance sectors a priority. Although in many countries microfinance and other services offered under financial inclusion initiatives are regulated, they are nevertheless distinct from, and presented as an alternative to, the formal financial sector. This is clear from the CGAP emphasis on the unbanked, who are excluded from the formal financial sector but offered an alternative in the form of microfinance and information technology (IT) based payments systems (CGAP 2018).

What is the potential for an easing of this separation? Recent efforts in Pakistan and elsewhere in South Asia to focus on the needs of graduates (Shankar 2016) are a step in this direction as they offer a shift away from lending to low-income individuals; a model that relies on small loan sizes and high lending rates. Efforts in Pakistan to earmark the category described as medium small enterprise lending (MSEL) (Aslam 2013) reflect the realization that larger loan sizes are essential for bridging the gap between microfinance and commercial banking. 'This is too low to make a difference to the growth and expansion of MSEs. Average loan size has remained low because the mission of microfinance was believed to consist in provision of finance to low income persons rather than MSEs' (Aslam 2013, p. 6).

Initiatives to draw microfinance banks into MSEL highlight the sense of urgency undoubtedly felt by a central bank confronted with declining – in real terms, relative to previous decades – private sector credit offtake (SBP 2015a).

> While the total assets and deposits of Pakistan's banking sector have doubled since 2008, private sector credit to GDP [gross domestic product] has declined from 22 per cent in 2009 to just 14.7 per cent in June 2014. The decline in credit provided to SMEs has been particularly pronounced, falling from 16 per cent of bank lending in 2008 to just 7 per cent in June 2014. (SBP 2015a, p. vi)

Fresher data indicates that improvements have been small, with private sector credit at 16.2 per cent in June 2017 (SBP 2017b). This weakening and its persistence are ascribed to a number of factors. Khalid and Nadeem (2017) attribute the initial decline to knock-on effects from the global crisis of 2008, which coincided with security concerns, political instability and energy shortages in Pakistan. Five years of double-digit interest rates followed, with counter-cyclical monetary policy vetoed because of parched FDI inflows and a balance of payments crisis from a feeble external sector. The outcome is the familiar scenario of an unfavourable balance of payments – necessitating IMF-led demand compression and stabilization policies – eventually compromising deregulation and liberalization by quashing market mechanisms for interest rate determination (Khalid and Nadeem 2017).

However, it was not simply exogenous factors that placed lenders, and the macroeconomy, in this austere position. Within the broader context it may be argued that it was the liberal reform process of the 1990s, fixated with buttressing regulatory frameworks and enhancing institutional stability, which compromised financial inclusion, primarily by cost-cutting strategies that led to downsizing and branch closures (Khalid and Nadeem 2017). Although the SBP was conscious of the need to keep the banking sector accessible and took regulatory steps such as preventing banks from refusing to open accounts for prospective clients, provision of free services by banks for the opening and maintenance of regular savings accounts, and some exemptions on minimum balances, between 2004 and 2015, the total number of small accounts fell by 3.1 million (Zaidi 2015, p. 406). This is depicted by Pakistan's position in the IMF's 2015 rankings of financial development: for efficiency the country is ranked 52 but for access to institutions it is ranked 130 (Svirydzenka 2016).

The issue of limited private sector credit offtake is brought into sharp focus when regional comparisons are made; Pakistan not only has one of the lowest proportions of adult population with access to a transaction account, but also has one of the highest ratios of currency to deposits (Khalid and Nadeem 2017). Financial inclusion takes on particular relevance in this context, given the strong association between access to finance and credit penetration.

A key feature of liberal reforms in Pakistan has been the rollback of the state, as evidenced by sharp reductions in government ownership of the banking sector and the abandonment of direct or priority lending strategies. The absence of an official push factor has made it possible for lenders to dodge the comparatively riskier prospect of SME lending. The state in Pakistan controls only 20 per cent of banking assets. This is low compared with other emerging economies – including China, India, Egypt, Sri Lanka, Vietnam, Bhutan, Brazil, Argentina, Indonesia, Bangladesh, Russia and Turkey – where the public share ranges from 30 per cent to 50 per cent (World Bank 2012). The policy of mandatory lending to sectors identified by the state is still practised in a number of countries: India's priority sectors receive over 40 per cent of bank loan portfolios; Brazil's directed lending amounts to over 50 per cent of total credit; and in both Thailand and Indonesia, 20 per cent of lending is allocated to SMEs (Khalid and Nadeem 2017).

Why else have commercial banks been so lax in widening their customer base? This can be at least partially attributed to fiscal patterns: the low tax base, at less than 11 per cent of GDP, compels the government to rely on borrowing for deficit funding (Ministry of Finance 2017). Private businesses account for 40 per cent of bank credit and only 0.4 per cent of all borrowers are responsible for 65 per cent of all bank loans (SBP, 2015a). In the absence of effective measures to widen and also deepen the tax base it is unlikely that commercial banks – which are currently earning heavy spreads by investing in risk-free treasury bills – will shift their focus to the private sector – but away from the corporate sector – particularly for those in lower income segments.

This 'dominant borrower syndrome' is interrogated by Choudhary et al. (2016), who find that persistent government borrowing from commercial banks has limited the sector. The widening of interest rate spreads, lower private sector credit – despite a policy rate that has fallen by over 550 basis points over four years – and a weak transmission of monetary policy have been created by a lack of impetus for credit intermediation, given an ample supply of zero-risk weighted assets in the form of government bonds. This explanation, which rests on the macroeconomic assumption of crowding-out, is simplistic. It is reasonable to infer that stringent capital requirements – as necessitated by the Basel framework – deterred banks from lending to the private sector, especially where high default risk was a feature of incomplete collateral and/or uncertain cash flows. This is an empirically documented tendency discussed in a shadow banking concept by Toporowski (2017). Also, the relationship between government borrowing and banking spreads. In developing economies, the state tends to be insensitive to the cost of borrowing to finance its budget deficit when it has no recourse to other sources; an outcome of a shallow secondary market for lending, suggesting the need for policies to enhance domestic debt markets together with liberal reforms (Choudhary et al. 2016).

The issue of limited penetration in Pakistan cannot be described in the relatively simplistic terms of either excessive government involvement, through crowding-out, or the lack of it, through the absence of direct lending strategies. If inclusive finance is seen as the response to limited penetration, it may be associated with two phenomena: (1) the effect of regulations to enhance financial stability which have made commercial banks eschew lending outside the corporate and public sector, and (2) lack of depth in domestic debt markets which has created an interest inelastic demand from the state for bank borrowing.

The shadow banking concept may be invoked here; not only has crowding-out shaped the need for regulatory fragmentation, but the shortcomings of market depth have positioned inclusive finance as a component of 'a vital infrastructure of the financial system that sustains debt-based funding mechanisms' (Nesvetailova 2017, p. 241).

3.3 Digital Dualism

While the SBP is aware of the structural issues that impede penetration, its response has been to focus on promoting financial inclusion through MSME lending to stimulate credit offtake, and branchless banking to enhance access. The latter refers to the expansion of DTAs, based primarily on 'basic electronic payment services and stored electronic value' (SBP 2015a, p. 18). This is a shift away from more traditional forms of branchless banking which rely on over-the-counter (OTC) transactions based on cash being placed in, and eventually withdrawn from, the system.

This DTA strategy for financial inclusion has been formulated based on the presence of a robust national infrastructure, which includes a regulatory framework, widespread mobile phone ownership and an extensive official biometric databank. There are two drivers behind the DTA strategy. The first is distribution. The existing infrastructure facilitates expansion of DTAs by addressing the issue of national distribution through the proximity and interconnectivity of ATM and point-of-sale (POS) machines linked to mobile phone networks. Account-opening procedures in this type of arrangement are eased by relatively lighter regulatory requirements on KYC procedures using biometric technology. Currently, the branchless banking network is thin, particularly in rural areas; the SBP observes that this problem may be overcome through the participation of third-party service providers (SBP 2015a).

Third party involvement relates to the other driver of the DTA strategy. Within the approach described above, recruiting more third-party service providers is solely an operational matter. Extension of the agent network is dependent on the capability to select, recruit, train and supervise agents, and to establish alliances with existing retail networks to manage the logistical demands of cash availability and interconnectivity. However, this approach does not acknowledge the intrinsic value of data and of the digital footprints created through a combination of biometric verification and algorithmic technology. This is discussed in Gabor and Brooks (2017) as the finance–philanthropy–development (FPD) nexus which uses data technology to interact with the subjects of inclusive finance so that financial institutions may de-risk potential clients (Kaminska 2015).

> In this case, the role of the state is recast to provide 'an enabling environment' for financial capital to flow freely, while allowing the consequences of systemic risks to be transferred to consumers precariously positioned at the 'bankable frontier', while their 'digital footprints' are captured and quantified as evidence of potential income streams against which securitised loans can be made that form the basis for tomorrow's financial 'innovations'. (Kaminska 2015, cited in Gabor and Brooks 2017, p. 433)

Although this application of data technology is not yet commonplace in Pakistan, this situation is changing rapidly with a small number of microfinance banks already using digital transaction data as well as mobile phone/Global System for Mobile Communications (GSMA) activity for credit scoring; a practice tacitly endorsed by the relatively lighter KYC requirement for branchless banking. There is considerable space here for third-party involvement, a pattern which has been facilitated by the development of a venture capital ecosystem in Pakistan. For instance, Finja, which is described as the technology partner and super-agent for Finca Microfinance Bank's branchless banking operations, has received US$1.5 million in series A from Vostok, a Swedish investment company headquartered in Bermuda and specializing in emerging-market fintech (Chakraberty 2017). Another example is Tez Financial Services. Headed by former Citi banker, Nadeem Hussain, Tez – English translation, 'fast' – is a part of PlanetN, a holding group which makes investments in existing companies and houses an accelerator based loosely on the principles of Y Combinator (Husain 2016).

> If you allow me to access your smartphone and carry out a risk assessment, there are 12,000 data points I can take. Let me give you the easiest one. If your contact list consists of 10 people and your friend's list consist of 1,000 people, your friend has a better credit risk profile, because, he or she is more networked than you are. The same goes for travel; credit risk improves with people who have a regular, as opposed to an erratic pattern, or if your phone is on 24 hours a day versus 12 hours a day, then you are a better risk. These are all data points that have been established by machine learning and algorithms. Once we launch this service and defaults happen, the machine will learn and correct the weightages we give; the algorithm learns as it goes along. The idea is to offer customers Rs 5,000 to 10,000 loans, repayable after a month and eventually after three months. All they have to do is download our app and with their consent we will be able to tell within 10 minutes whether they are eligible for a loan. (Hussain, cited in Baig 2017, p. 8)

There is more to this than what is described as 'financial intrusion' (Kaminska 2015). This may be likened to a suspension of rights to privacy associated with the absence of full financial citizenship, a feature of belonging to a class of poor borrowers who are removed, that is, excluded, from the workings of a closed system (Gabor and Brooks 2017). Inclusive finance thus, while countering exclusion, proffers shadow financial citizenship to this class of borrowers.

4. CONCLUSION

This chapter has discussed how the inclusive finance movement relates to the framework of shadow banking. Within this discussion, attention is drawn to a fundamental contradiction of inclusive finance, that is, the tendency to promote economic dualism by bifurcating the financial sector. This bifurcation is attributed to the tendency of inclusive finance to be closer to informal finance than to mainstream finance. So while financial inclusion strategies seek to unseat the hold of informal finance, they replace informal finance with inclusive instead of mainstream finance. As a result, dualism in finance prevails.

In the Pakistan context, this separation has much to do with the relationship of financial inclusion to the agenda of privatization, liberalization and deregulation. Financial inclusion in Pakistan has, with the support of the World Bank, became predominantly commercial and driven by private as well as public sources of funding, including from donor agencies in the form of blended finance. In addition, by positioning itself to benefit from initiatives pushed by international organizations such as the AFI and the BTCA, as well as to comply with FATF regulations, inclusive finance in Pakistan has become increasingly commercially orientated, digitally distributed and heavily regulated. This has led to the industry of inclusive finance becoming an attractive destination for global capital whether in the form of development assistance or private equity investment.

An outcome of this dynamic is that the model of inclusive finance, reliant on wholesale funding particularly via apex funds, is very different from the model of mainstream banking via intermediation. This distinction underlies the separation of inclusive and mainstream finance in a manner similar to how, nearly three decades ago, a changing Anglo-American model of banking and finance drove financial exclusion in the US and the UK.

The notion of shadow banking is invoked to examine this separation of banking models and to identify two contexts in which inclusive finance is proffered by institutions that behave like shadow banks. In one context, inclusive finance may be seen as the 'institutional outcome of regulatory fragmentation and arbitrage'; in another context, inclusive finance is a feature of a core infrastructure that 'converts debt-based funding into income, capital, and wealth' (Nesvetailova 2017, p. 241). These are the contexts that connect inclusive finance to the political economy of shadow banking, a nexus that underlies shadow financial citizenship; since inclusive finance is incapable of offering financial citizenship to extent that mainstream, traditional banks do.

Shadow financial citizenship is thus a tool to critique financial inclusion and a departure from past critiques that focus on developmental outcomes, particularly poverty (Cull and Morduch 2017; Duvendack et al. 2011) when inclusive finance is portrayed as a bespoke solution to tackle one particular, but extraordinarily onerous, developmental gap of the Global South. Shadow financial citizenship casts aspersions both on the novelty and efficacy of such approaches as it highlights the role of geobanking in uneven development.

NOTES

1. 'The popular view of informal finance is of powerful moneylenders who exploit the poor through usurious interest and unfair seizure of collateral' (World Bank 1989, p. 112).
2. This followed the emergence of Bangladesh as an independent country in 1971.
3. The definition of a poor person is 'an individual who has meager means of subsistence but is involved in a livelihood activity and has an ability to repay debt from an annual income (net of business expenses) up to Rs. 500,000/' (SBP 2014, p. 1).
4. The need for the MCGF appears to have been lessened by the launch of the PMIC apex fund, as mentioned in SBP (2017a) which notes that the guarantee scheme successfully demonstrated the viability of microfinance for commercial lenders.
5. Specific details of the implementation and results of the various PPAF funded projects are available at http://projects.worldbank.org/ (accessed 12 April 2018).
6. A list of acronyms containing several of the acronyms used here is available at http://www.sbp.org.pk/ACMFD/National-Financial-Inclusion-Strategy-Pakistan.pdf (accessed 12 April 2018).

REFERENCES

Acemoglu, D. and Robinson, J. (2008), *Why Nations Fail: The Origins of Power, Prosperity, and Poverty*, New York: Crown.
Alliance for Financial Inclusion (2017), '2017 Maya Declaration progress report', Alliance for Financial Inclusion, Kuala Lumpur, accessed 12 April 2018 at https://www.afi-global.org/sites/default/files/publications/2017-09/2017_MAYA_progress%20report_digital.pdf.
Aron, J. (2017), '"Leapfrogging": a survey of the nature and economic implications of mobile money', Working Paper No. 2017/02, Centre for the Study of African Economies, University of Oxford.
Asian Development Bank (ADB) (2008), 'Pakistan: Microfinance Sector Development Program', Project Completion Report 29229, ADB, Manilla.
Aslam, A. (2013), 'Moving towards micro and small enterprise lending opportunities and challenges', Pakistan Microfinace Network, Islamabad, accessed 12 April 2018 at http://www.microfinanceconnect.info.

Baig, M.A. (2017), 'Riding the digital wave', *Aurora*, July–Aug, accessed 12 April 2018 at https://aurora.dawn.com/news/1142150.

Bateman, M. and Chang, H.J. (2012), 'Microfinance and the illusion of development: from hubris to nemesis in thirty years', *World Economic Review*, **1**, 13–36.

Binswanger, H.P. and Khandker, S.R. (1995), 'The impact of formal finance on the rural economy of India', *Journal of Development Studies*, **32** (2), 234–62.

Bonizzi, B., Laskaridis, C. and Toporowski, J. (2015), 'EU development policy and the promotion of the financial sector', Working Paper No. 120, Financialisation, Economy, Society and Sustainable Development (FESSUD) Project, London.

Burki, A.A. and Ahmad, S., (2010), 'Bank governance changes in Pakistan: is there a performance effect?', *Journal of Economics and Business*, **62** (2), 129–46.

Center for Financial Inclusion (2013), 'Forty countries (and counting) committed to the Maya Declaration', 29 August, accessed 12 April 2018 at https://cfi-blog.org/2013/08/29/forty-countries-and-counting-committed-to-the-maya-declaration/.

Chakraberty S. (2017), 'Fintech startup Finja breaks new ground in Pakistan with $1.5m series A funding', *Tech in Asia*, 18 October, accessed 18 March 2018 at https://www.techinasia.com/finja.

Chandavarkar, A. (1985), 'The financial pull of urban areas in LDCs', *Finance and Development*, **22** (2), 24.

Choudhary, M.A., Khan, S., Pasha, F. and Rehman, M. (2016), 'The dominant borrower syndrome', *Applied Economics*, **48** (49), 4773–82.

Consultative Group to Assist the Poor (CGAP) (2018), 'Who are the 2 billion unbanked adults globally?', accessed 18 March 2018 at http://www.cgap.org/about/faq/who-are-2-billion-unbanked-adults-globally.

Craig, T. and Hussain, S. (2015), 'Pakistan's mobile phone owners told: be fingerprinted or lose your sim card', *Guardian*, 3 March, accessed 18 March 2018 at https://www.theguardian.com/world/2015/mar/03/pakistan-fingerprint-mobile-phone-users.

Cull, R. and Morduch, J. (2017), 'Microfinance and economic development', Policy Research Working Paper No. 8252, November, World Bank, accessed 18 March at https://responsiblefinanceforum.org/wp-content/uploads/2017/12/microfinance.pdf.

Drake, P.J. (1980), *Money, Finance, and Development*, New York: Wiley.

Duvendack, M., Palmer-Jones, R., Copestake, J.G., Hooper, L., Loke, Y. and Rao, N. (2011), 'What is the evidence of the impact of microfinance on the well-being of poor people?', EPPI-Centre, Social Science Research Unit, Institute of Education, University of London.

Dymski, G.A. (2005), 'Financial globalization, social exclusion and financial crisis', *International Review of Applied Economics*, **19** (4), 439–57.

Financial Action Task Force (FATF) (2018), 'Who we are', accessed 12 April 2018 at http://www.fatf-gafi.org/about/.

Financial Stability Board (FSB) (2011), 'Shadow banking: scoping the issues', Background Note, 12 April, Basel, accessed 12 April 2018 at http://www.fsb.org/wp-content/uploads/r_110412a.pdf.

Fischer, A. (1994), 'Banking on the edge: towards an open ended interpretation of informal finance in the third world', MA thesis, Economics Department McGill University, Montreal.

Gabor, D. and Brooks, S. (2017), 'The digital revolution in financial inclusion: international development in the fintech era', *New Political Economy*, **22** (4), 423–36.

Geertz, C. (1962), 'The rotating credit association: a "middle rung" in development', *Economic Development and Cultural Change*, **10** (3), 241–63.

Ghosh, S., Gonzalez del Mazo, I. and Ötker-Robe, İ. (2012), 'Chasing the shadows: How significant is shadow banking in emerging markets?', Economic Premise No. 88, World Bank, accessed 12 April 2018 at https://openknowledge.worldbank.org/handle/10986/17088.

Greenhill, R., Prizzon, A. and Rogerson, A. (2016), 'The age of choice: developing countries in the new aid landscape', in S. Klingebiel, T. Mahn and M. Negre (eds), *The Fragmentation of Aid*, London: Palgrave Macmillan, pp. 137–51.

Hanif, M.N. (2002), 'Restructuring of financial sector in Pakistan', accessed 12 April 2018 at http://unpan1.un.org/intradoc/groups/public/documents/APCITY/UNPAN026320.pdf.

Helgadóttir, O. (2016), 'Banking upside down: the implicit politics of shadow banking expertise', *Review of International Political Economy*, **23** (6), 915–40.

Husain, O. (2016), 'He started up at 49 and soon made millions. Now he's investing it all into startups', *Tech in Asia*, 28 September, accessed 12 April 2018 at https://www.techinasia.com/nadeem-hussain-investor-entrepreneur-pakistan.

Irfan, M., Arif, G., Ali, S. and Nazli, H. (1999), 'The structure of informal credit market in Pakistan', Working Paper No. 1999:168, Pakistan Institute of Development Economics, Islamabad.

Kaminska, I. (2015), 'When financial inclusion stands for financial intrusion', *Financial Times Alphaville*, 31 July, accessed 12 April 2018 at http://ftalphaville.ft.com/2015/07/31/2135943/when-financial-inclusion-stands-for-financial-intrusion/.

Karnani, A. (2009), 'Romanticising the poor harms the poor', *Journal of International Development*, **21** (1), 76–86.

Khalid, A. and Nadeem, T. (2017), 'Bank credit to private sector: a critical review in the context of financial sector', SBP Staff Notes 03/17, State Bank of Pakistan, accessed 12 April 2018 at http://www.sbp.org.pk/publications/staff-notes/BankingReforms.pdf.

Khan, F. (2010), 'The limits of success? NGOs, microfinance and economic development in Pakistan's Northern Areas', *Journal of Asian Public Policy*, **3** (1), 53–70.

Khandker, S.R. (1998), *Fighting Poverty with Microcredit: Experience in Bangladesh*, New York: Oxford University Press.

Khandker, S.R. (2000), 'Savings, informal borrowing, and microfinance', *Bangladesh Development Studies*, **26** (2–3), 49–78.

Kohli, R. (1997), 'Directed credit and financial reform', *Economic and Political Weekly*, **32** (42), 2667–76.

Kurtz, D. (1973), 'The rotating credit association: an adaptation to poverty', *Human Organization*, **32** (1), 49–58.

Lewis, W.A. (1954). 'Economic development with unlimited supplies of labour', *The Manchester School*, **22** (2), 139–91.

Leyshon, A. (2009), 'Financial exclusion', in R. Kitchen and N. Thrift (eds), *International Encyclopaedia of Human Geography*, Oxford: Elsevier, pp. 153–8.

Leyshon, A. and Thrift, N. (1993), 'The restructuring of the UK financial services industry in the 1990s: a reversal of fortune?', *Journal of Rural Studies*, **9** (3), 223–41.

Leyshon, A. and Thrift, N. (1995), 'Geographies of financial exclusion: financial abandonment in Britain and the United States', *Transactions of the Institute of British Geographers*, **20** (3), 312–41.

Lyman, T., Scharder, L. and Tomilova, O. (2015), 'Inclusive finance and shadow banking: worlds apart or worlds converging?', CGAP Brief, Consultative Group to Assist the Poor, accessed 12 April 2018 at https://www.cgap.org/sites/default/files/Brief-Inclusive-Finance-and-Shadow-Banking-Sept-2015.pdf.

Mader, P. and Sabrow, S. (2019), 'All myth and ceremony? Examining the causes and logic of the mission shift in microfinance from microenterprise credit to financial inclusion', *Forum for Social Economics*, **48** (1), 22–48.

Malik, T. (2014), 'Technology in the service of development: the NADRA story', essay, Center for Global Development, Washington, DC, accessed 12 April 2018 at https://www.cgdev.org/sites/default/files/CGD-Essay-Malik_NADRA-Story_0.pdf.

Manig, W. (1996), 'The importance of the informal financial market for rural development financing in developing countries: the example of Pakistan', *Pakistan Development Review*, **35** (3), 229–39.

Ministry of Finance (2017), 'Pakistan economic survey 2016–17', Ministry of Finance, Islamabad, accessed 12 April 2018 at http://www.finance.gov.pk/survey_1617.html.

Morduch, J. (2000), 'The microfinance schism', *World Development*, **28** (4), 617–29.

National Financial Inclusion Strategy (NFIS) (2015), 'National Financial Inclusion Strategy: Pakistan', State Bank of Pakistan, accessed 12 October 2018 at http://www.sbp.org.pk/ACMFD/National-Financial-Inclusion-Strategy-Pakistan.pdf.

Nesvetailova, A. (2017), 'Conclusion: shadow banking into the limelight', in A. Nesvetailova (ed.), *Shadow Banking: Scope, Origins and Theories*, Abingdon: Routledge, pp. 238–44.

Pakistan Microfinance Investment Company (PMIC) (2018), 'About us', accessed 12 April 2018 at http://www.pmic.pk/about.html.

Pakistan Microfinance Network (PMN) (2016), 'Annual Report – 2015–16', Pakistan Microfinance Network, Islamabad, accessed 22 February 2019 at http://www.microfinanceconnect.info/.

Pakistan Microfinance Network (PMN) (2017), 'Annual Report – 2016–17', Pakistan Microfinance Network, Islamabad, accessed 12 April 2018 at http://www.microfinanceconnect.info/.

Prahalad, C.K. (2005), *The Fortune at the Bottom of the Pyramid: Eradicating Poverty Through Profits*, New Delhi: Wharton School.

Rashid, N. (2015), 'The promise of mobile money in Pakistan', blog, 22 September, accessed 12 April 2018 at http://www.cgap.org/blog/promise-mobile-money-pakistan.

Rosenberg, R., Gaul, S., Ford, W. and Tomilova, O. (2013), 'Microcredit interest rates and their determinants: 2004–2011', in D. Kohn (ed.), *Microfinance 3.0*, Berlin Heidelberg: Springer-Verlag, pp. 69–104.

Roy, A. (2010), *Poverty Capital: Microfinance and the Making of Development*, New York: Routledge.

Roy, T. (2016), 'The monsoon and the market for money in late-colonial India', *Enterprise & Society*, **17** (2), 324–57.

Sandberg, J. (2015), 'What's wrong with exorbitant interest rates on microloans', in T. Sorell and L. Cabrera (eds), *Microfinance, Rights and Global Justice*, Cambridge: Cambridge University Press, pp. 129–44.

Sapuhdhieva, P. (2011), 'Funding microfinance – a focus on debt financing', *MicroBanking Bulletin*, 1 November, accessed 12 April 2018 at https://www.themix.org/.

Shankar, S. (2016), 'Bridging the "missing middle" between microfinance and small and medium-sized enterprise finance in South Asia', ADBI Working Paper No. 587, Asian Development Bank Institute, Tokyo.

State Bank of Pakistan (SBP) (2006), 'Financial stability review 2006', State Bank of Pakistan, Karachi, accessed 12 April 2018 at http://www.sbp.org.pk/fsr/2006/English/Microfinance.pdf.

State Bank of Pakistan (SBP) (2008), 'About financial inclusion', State Bank of Pakistan, Karachi, accessed 12 April 2018 at http://www.sbp.org.pk/MFD/FIP/inclusion.htm.

State Bank of Pakistan (SBP) (2014), 'Prudential regulations for microfinance banks', State Bank of Pakistan, Karachi, accessed 12 April 2018 at http://www.sbp.org.pk/acd/2014/C3-Annex.pdf.

State Bank of Pakistan (SBP) (2015a), 'National financial inclusion strategy 2015', State Bank of Pakistan, Karachi, accessed 12 April 2018 at http://www.sbp.org.pk/ACMFD/National-Financial-Inclusion-Strategy-Pakistan.pdf.

State Bank of Pakistan (SBP) (2015b), 'Membership of microfinance banks (MFBs) for clearing house', State Bank of Pakistan, Karachi, accessed 12 April 2018 at http://sbp.org.pk/psd/2015/C2.htm.

State Bank of Pakistan (SBP) (2016), 'Origins', State Bank of Pakistan, Karachi, accessed 12 April 2018 at http://www.sbp.org.pk/about/history/Origins.pdf.

State Bank of Pakistan (SBP) (2017a), 'AC&MFD Circular No. 01/2017', State Bank of Pakistan, Karachi, accessed 12 April 2018 at http://www.sbp.org.pk/acd/2017/C1.htm.

State Bank of Pakistan (SBP) (2017b), 'Quarterly performance review of the banking sector (April–June, 2017)', State Bank of Pakistan, Karachi, accessed 12 April 2018 at http://www.sbp.org.pk/publications/q_reviews/2017/Apr-Jun.pdf.

Stuart, G. (2015), 'Government to person transfers: on-ramp to financial inclusion?', Centre for Financial Inclusion, Washington, DC, accessed 12 April 2018 at http://www.centerforfinancialinclusion.org/storage/documents/Government_to_Person_Transfers.pdf.

Svirydzenka, K. (2016), 'Introducing a new broad-based index of financial development', IMF Working Paper No. 16/5, International Monetary Fund, Washington, DC, accessed on 12 April 2018 from https://www.imf.org/en/Publications/WP/Issues/2016/12/31/Introducing-a-New-Broad-based-Index-of-Financial-Development-43621.

Taylor, M. (2012), 'The antinomies of "financial inclusion": debt, distress and the workings of Indian microfinance', *Journal of Agrarian Change*, **12** (4), 601–10.

Toporowski, J. (2017), 'Why overcapitalisation drives banks into the shadows', in A. Nesvetailova (ed.), *Shadow Banking: Scope, Origins and Theories*, Abingdon: Routledge, pp. 181–90.

Van Waeyenberge, E. (2016), 'The private turn in development finance', Working Paper No. 140, Financialisation, Economy, Society and Sustainable Development (FESSUD) Project, London.

World Bank (1989), *World Development Report*, Washington, DC: World Bank Publications.

World Bank (2005), 'Pakistan Poverty Alleviation Fund', August, World Bank, Washington, DC, accessed 12 April 2018 at http://siteresources.worldbank.org/INTPAKISTAN/Resources/PPAF1.pdf.

World Bank (2012), 'Global financial development report 2013: rethinking the role of the state in finance', World Bank, Washington, DC, accessed 12 April 2018 at https://openknowledge.worldbank.org/handle/10986/11848.

World Bank (2017), 'Maximizing finance for development', World Bank Group, accessed 12 October 2018 at http://siteresources.worldbank.org/DEVCOMMINT/Documentation/23758671/DC2017-0009_Maximizing_8-19.pdf.

Zaidi, S.A. (2015), *Issues in Pakistan's Economy: A Political Economy Perspective*, Karachi: Oxford University Press.

Zaidi, A. (2001), 'From the lane to the city: the impact of the Orangi Pilot Project's low cost sanitation model', WaterAid, London, accessed 12 April 2018 at http://washtest.wateraid.org/publications/from-the-lane-to-the-city-the-impact-of-the-orangi-pilot-projects-low-cost-sanitation.

Index

global financial system 1, 33, 54–5,
    65
informal financial system 12, 215–16
local financial system 9, 65, 76
national financial system 79, 145
official financial system 58
urban financial system 79
financial system stabilization 145
financialization 47
    financialization of development 12,
        213
    financialization of economies 15,
        50–51, 55
FinGeo 3, 15
Finland 59
fintech 15, 16, 23–4, 82
fiscal expertise 75
flight-to-quality effects 131
Flögel, F. 121, 134, 197, 199
foreign banks (role of) 139, 141–2, 166
foreign capitals 139, 149, 169, 171
foreign currency 11, 125, 176, 177,
    180–92
foreign investors, *see* foreign capitals
France 35, 145
Frankfurt 37
free zone 69
Freeman, C. 95
Freeman, D. 157
FSB (Financial Stability Board) 48,
    57–9
FSF (Financial Stability Forum) 34
functionalist approach 51

G7 34, 39
G10 34, 39
G20 34, 39
G77 39
Geneva 35
geobanking (and geofinance/
    geobanking or geofinance/
    banking) 7, 11, 15, 20–23, 25, 31,
    214, 236
geofinance (and geography of finance;
    geography of financial systems;
    financial geography) 1, 7, 33, 34,
    66, 76, 79, 120, 138
geofinance/geobanking diamond
    model 7–8, 19–23, 25
geographical factors 32

geography of (banking, powers,
    financial centers, wealth and
    income, offshore) 6, 25, 32, 38, 44,
    66, 70, 72, 79, 120, 139, 214
geohistorical perspective 44, 139
geopolitics 1, 3, 7, 19, 24, 32, 33, 34,
    35, 75
Germany 35, 55, 79, 121, 131, 144, 145
Glass–Steagall Act 55
global financial architecture 32, 34, 38
Global North 33
Global South 12, 33, 214, 215, 222,
    223, 236
global value chain 10, 139, 150
Goldfinger, C. 79
governance of the institutions 32, 37
governing boards 32
government and finance 19, 24, 69,
    135, 171, 231
Grandi, Silvia 1, 15, 17, 20, 22, 31, 32,
    33, 44
grant 16, 31
Great Britain, *see* UK
Greece 94, 141, 145, 148
Grote, M. 3, 33
guarantees 18, 31, 35, 54, 107, 127,
    148, 179, 195, 220

Hanoi 156, 158, 167, 168, 169, 170,
    171
Harvey, D. 18
headquarter (and location) 7, 32, 35,
    36, 40, 44, 81–2, 122, 205–7
Hong Kong 38, 58, 75
Hungary 138, 145
hypercapillarity of finance 82

IADB (InterAmerican Development
    Bank) 35, 39
IAIS (International Association of
    Insurance Supervisors) 34
IASB (International Accounting
    Standards Board) 34
IBRD (International Bank for
    Reconstruction and Development)
    35, 44
IC & Partners 93, 107–8
ICSID (International Centre for
    Settlement of Investment
    Disputes) 35